Literature as Witness

Literature as Witness

Five Masterworks ad Dei Gloriam

Aaron Streiter

WIPF & STOCK · Eugene, Oregon

LITERATURE AS WITNESS
Five Masterworks ad Dei Gloriam

Copyright © 2018 Aaron Streiter. All rights reserved. Except for brief quotations in critical publications or reviews, no part of this book may be reproduced in any manner without prior written permission from the publisher. Write: Permissions, Wipf and Stock Publishers, 199 W. 8th Ave., Suite 3, Eugene, OR 97401.

Wipf & Stock
An Imprint of Wipf and Stock Publishers
199 W. 8th Ave., Suite 3
Eugene, OR 97401

www.wipfandstock.com

PAPERBACK ISBN: 978-1-5326-5175-5
HARDCOVER ISBN: 978-1-5326-5176-2
EBOOK ISBN: 978-1-5326-5177-9

Manufactured in the U.S.A.   12/20/18

To my beloved wife

Contents

Chapter One
Introduction | 1

Chapter Two
The Faerie Queene **(Book One)** | 27

Chapter Three
Macbeth | 63

Chapter Four
Paradise Lost | 89

Chapter Five
The Scarlet Letter | 139

Chapter Six
Crime and Punishment | 174

Chapter One

Introduction

THIS BOOK IS GROUNDED in two assertions regarded as axioms: that every important work of literature is centrally concerned with teaching human beings how to live; and that every such work is carefully structured.

Each of the works discussed in the book presumes that an immutable code of conduct exists, imposed upon human beings by transcendence; that human behavior must conform strictly to the code; and that the consequences of conforming to it, or of failing to do so, are unavoidable.

In every case, the immutable code is Christianity.

Because the God of Christianity is beyond comprehension full of love, and as He has sacrificed, in His incarnation, His very self for human beings, the essential mandate of Christian life is to draw as close as possible to Him, in one of two ways, or by an amalgam of both: by clinging to Him, passionately, intuitively, in response to a salvational impulse venerated by the Christian Bible; or by fidelity to the golden mean, appropriated from Aristotle by Thomistic ethics.

In the works discussed (in chronological order), the force that obstructs intimacy with God is evil, in the universe itself, and in human beings. In neither habitation can it be subdued without the assistance of God. In the universe it will be subdued by Him when time ceases to exist. In human beings it will be subdued by His Grace in time in measure as they govern an inborn, perverse and ineradicable attraction to chaos and self-destruction over which reason has no command, and against which, in the absence of His Grace, they are powerless against evil.

To the extent that human beings contend against evil, within themselves and in the universe, cultivating reason, sacred intuition, or both, and incline towards good, they are commended in the works discussed, and in consequence rewarded. To the extent that they do not contend against evil, or actively embrace it, they are censured, and in consequence punished. Those who contend in an especially impressive fashion are heroes; those adamantly devoted to evil are villains. The sole measure of all of the characters, human and metaphysical, in the works discussed is the relation of their actions and thoughts to good and evil.

Because, for the reason noted, the God of the Christian Bible encourages emulation, and because emulation requires that the balance of good and evil in the soul be improved, in all of the works discussed at least one character strives, or is exhorted to strive, for such improvement; that is to say, for spiritual growth.

The struggle between good and evil is rendered in the works discussed in coherent structures. Each work is divided into a number of clearly defined parts. Each part is divided into clearly defined sections. Each part, and each section of each part, performs a clearly defined function. No part or section can be repositioned without detriment to the total structure, and nothing can be removed from, or added to, the structure without detriment.

In every case, the work discussed is thus an artifact constructed of the appropriate number of parts, each part in working order, and positioned with intelligent intent, the total structure crafted to perform a specific task: to teach human beings how to live as Christians.

Because the God of the Christian Bible is incomprehensibly filled with compassion and with love, as solicitous of human beings as the most tender-hearted shepherd is of his flock, prepared to suffer without complaint even ignominy and death on their behalf, He solicits from them the fear and awe that surpassing virtue warrants. They must fear him. But they must also love him. And through fear at least, but through love if possible, they must aspire to shape their lives in conformity with His will, and even, in their most exalted moments, with His consent and encouragement, easily gained, to encounter Him, through ecstatic vision, or directly. He welcomes human beings, and they must strive for completion only in Him.

In three of the works discussed, whether directly or indirectly God is present throughout. In the other two, evil predominates for a long time, because He enters to contend with it only gradually.

In the first of the three, Spenser's *The Faerie Queene*, (Book One), He does not appear, and His emissaries are not celestial. Two of them, however, almost are, and the third is a paragon of human virtue. In Milton's *Paradise Lost*, He commissions celestial emissaries to instruct human beings. And

INTRODUCTION

in Dostoevsky's *Crime and Punishment*, His work is done by an emissary almost celestial in nature.

In the first of the two, in Shakespeare's *Macbeth*, an inexplicable satanic force itself impervious to defeat and intent on tormenting Macbeth, one of its devotees, for a long time almost completely unopposed wreaks havoc in him and in society. Then a Christian force is mustered against him, and destroys him (though not the satanic force). And in the second of the two, almost to the end of Hawthorne's *The Scarlet Letter* Satan actively corrupts, without effective opposition, almost every human soul at risk. Then God himself intervenes to save two sinners from destruction, and an innocent child from a task that torments her.

In *The Faerie Queene*, (Book One), the God of the Christian Bible does not appear, nor is conversation with Him imaginable. Nonetheless, His presence is felt throughout, in three of His emissaries, two virtually celestial in character, the other His unwaveringly faithful servant. The essential task of human life is to serve Him by emulating the conduct of His emissaries, Una, Prince Arthur, and Coelia and her cohort in the House of Holiness. The obstacles to serving Him and the means of overcoming them are clearly defined, as are the consequences of spiritual success and failure. The emissaries are distinguished by faith in God, by a fervent wish to serve His cause, and by unremitting opposition to evil. The obstacles to emulating them are a metaphysical force of evil, and a tendency in the insufficiently tutored human soul to chaos. The metaphysical force is embodied in a variety of Satan's minions, most potently in Archimago and Duessa. The impulse to chaos expresses itself as the preference of the untutored soul for passion over reason as the guide to conduct. The metaphysical force is vanquished as the soul is instructed in the primacy of reason, and in theological truth. The Red Cross Knight is instructed by Una, and by the inhabitants of the House of Holiness, punished while refusing instruction, or deficient as a student, with spiritual decline, and rewarded, when attentive and fully educated, with human felicity in a world in which God is not, except in rare cases, directly accessible to human beings, but which, through His emissaries, He governs and preserves.

Of *Macbeth* alone of the works discussed nothing salvational can be accomplished, because in *Macbeth* alone inexplicable evil is embodied in the witches, a metaphysical force that cannot be defeated, and in Macbeth, a human being. Therefore, the best that can be hoped for is the defeat of Macbeth. And both embodiments are especially terrifying because nothing is known about their motives: about why Macbeth is intent on murdering Duncan, or about why the witches are intent on tormenting him. Therefore the evil they occasion is horrific. And the Christian force that alone can defeat Macbeth is mustered only gradually; a force strong enough to destroy him.

Duncan murdered, only the need of a Christian force is broached; no such force is mustered. It coalesces, and attacks, only gradually, as the success of the witches at tormenting Macbeth goads him to a homicidal frenzy that Christianity must contend against.

The frenzy is provoked in Macbeth when he realizes that his insistence on having Banquo and Fleance murdered requires that, for the first time, he oppose his will to that of the witches; an action grossly stupid and inexorably fatal.

Fortunately, it provokes also the resolve in the Christian force, which consolidates its strength, encounters Macbeth, and kills him.

But it does not kill, or in any way punish, the witches. They simply disappear.

In the most explicitly metaphysical of the works discussed, *Paradise Lost*, the essential task of human life, to obey and to love the God of the Christian Bible, is made clear by His presence throughout, and by the angels He commissions to aid Adam and Eve: in turn, Gabriel to guard them while they sleep, unaware that a mortal enemy exists, Raphael to teach them everything they must know about that enemy to avoid Falling to him, and Michael to lead them, having Fallen, mournfully but with hope, from Paradise. Raphael, the most instructive of them, explains at exhaustive length, and in vivid detail, who Satan is, why he is intent upon destroying them, and the weapon with which he will assault them.

To arm them against the danger within themselves, he stresses emphatically that, if the tendency of the passions—even of a beautiful and alluring passion—to undermine their conduct is restrained, Satan cannot succeed against them. He assures them that their spiritual and intellectual resources are adequate to both dangers, and that in consequence they are free to choose between God and Satan. And he explains the consequences—respectively, life and death—of their choice. Thus, before they are decisively assaulted, they understand that, to remain indefinitely

Introduction

in the literal and spiritual paradise they inhabit, they have only to remain obedient to God, by remaining alert to their metaphysical enemy, and to the destructive potential of their own emotions. Nonetheless, they opt for disobedience, and suffer its consequences; but consequences mitigated by God's Grace, that responds to their contrition by preserving them from immediate death, and by promising them, and their progeny, on condition of continued obedience, sufficient happiness through human history, and, at its close, transfiguration.

Because no celestial emissaries, and only a child of limited power, exist in *The Scarlet Letter* to guide three sinners toward salvation, at a pivotal moment in their spiritual wanderings God Himself rescues two of them from Satan. (The third has committed irrevocably to serving him.) Often misperceived, even by Hester, as an imp of Satan, Pearl is throughout the voice of conscience, torturing her mother because she has sinned, forbidding both parents the destructive indulgence of deeper sin, and goading her father in particular towards virtue. Because her power, however, is limited, God himself completes her work. Against Hester's depraved conviction, nurtured from unendurable suspicion to confident conviction through seven years of solitude, suffering, and errant thought, that romantic love is more important than God, Pearl cannot effectively contend. Nor can she rescue Dimmesdale from his hypocrisy and cowardice, or Chillingworth, transmogrified from a kindly scholar to a minion of Satan obsessed with destroying the adulterer who has destroyed his life. Against such impulses only God can successfully contend. Therefore He intervenes, when Hester convinces Dimmesdale, in the forest, to abandon Him in favor of herself. At that pivotal moment, every concerned soul in the balance, He suddenly takes possession of Dimmesdale, through the gift of Grace infusing in him the strength to confess his sin in public, and thereby, the hold of evil broken, to rescue Hester from herself, to nullify Chillingworth's satanic destructiveness, to loosen the hold of rage upon Pearl, and to die in felicity, reunited with the good.

In *Crime and Punishment*, God does not intervene directly. Instead, He acts through Sonia Marmeladov, a saintly Christian almost unbearably burdened by private suffering, and unsupported by direct metaphysical assistance, yet charged with the care of Rashkolnikov, a soul profoundly troubled, but stubbornly resolved not to abandon evil. Warped, and intent upon remaining warped, he murders two women for a reason that is only sporadically, almost grudgingly, explained. How he overcomes his own objections to committing the murders, how he the murders the two women, and how he escapes, though only barely, from the scene of the murders, are vividly dramatized. But of why he murdered only an unconvincing meditation on the unbearable oppression of poverty is presented. The murders done, he is attacked by a combination of conscience, self-disgust, terror at being apprehended for murder, and horror at an isolation he has never felt so crushing that he resolves either to confess or to commit suicide. His preference confession, on his way to a police station he does, in a manner of speaking, confess; but then, suddenly, he meets Sonia, and instantly concludes that spiritual union with her—of all people—will afford him the strength to master the attack. And in that delusion he persists long enough for an investigation to unfold that all but establishes that he murdered the two women, and—far more important—for Sonia to gain the access to his soul sufficient to shatter his resistance to taking up the Cross that alone can empower him to begin the long and painful salvational process he must endure.

Of conscience he feels very little until Sonia has shattered his resistance. But the pressure of the investigation is excruciating. And the pressure of Sonia drawing from Christianity, her impregnable fortress, the strength to save him from the Devil in himself, and despite its residual strength in him, eventually to embrace God, is decisive.

How the Devil worked in him—how it convinced him to murder the two women—what, that is to say, his motive was—he explains to Sonia when she has mastered him. And though the Devil rages in him for confessing, and long afterwards, and though therefore he loathes the Cross, he does bear it. And Sonia and the God of Christianity attend him.

To four of the five works thus far only briefly summarized, the idea of spiritual growth is central. The Red Cross Knight, weakened severely by his willful and dangerous abandonment of Una, must struggle, through reunion with her, to spiritual maturity. Because they disobeyed God, Adam and Eve must struggle to regain some measure of the spiritual harmony they enjoyed in Paradise. Dimmesdale must somehow find his way, despite Hester, to God, in the process depriving Hester of her heart's deepest, but evil, desire. And Rashkolnikov must find his way to Sonia through the nihilism that defiles his soul.

Introduction

Only to *Macbeth* is spiritual growth irrelevant, because only Macbeth, of the protagonists noted, is irredeemably of the satanic force.

In all of the works discussed the Christian mandate is embodied in coherent structures. The number of parts into which the structures are divided varies, as does the disposition, construction, and dramatic function of individual parts. And the parts are sub-divided variously into sections. But in every case, structure is crucial to the dramatization of moral value. In every case, that is to say, construction artfully mandates that human beings live as Christians.

Book One of *The Faerie Queene* is divided into two parts. In the first part, the Red Cross Knight, essentially noble but spiritually immature, is almost destroyed by evil; and but for God's Grace, would have been destroyed. In the second part, through a process of spiritual resuscitation he is redeemed, and serves God heroically.

His first encounter with evil in the first part succeeds only because Una intercedes in his behalf. His second encounter fails completely because, inexcusably enraged, he abandons Una; a catastrophic mistake because, deprived of her indispensable spiritual guidance, he sinks more and more deeply into vice more and more transparent, and finally collapses, rescued from death only by God's Grace, but mocked as he degenerates by his conviction that he is growing steadily stronger, and by the contrast between his deepening folly and the steadfastness of Una in confronting evil while undeservedly deprived of his protection.

In the second part, he is rescued from the effects of his folly by Prince Arthur, by Una, and by the inhabitants of the House of Holiness, elevated through a process of suffering and illumination to spiritual maturity; and, thus empowered, defeats the almost invincible dragon long the terror of Una's parents.

In the first encounter in the first part, his impressive zeal is undermined by a tendency to rashness that almost defeats him. Heedless of Una's prudent advice, he rushes into the Cave of the dragon Errour, burning to encounter her. He is almost killed; and would have been, had he not heeded, at the last possible moment, Una's further advice to strangle her. Too kind (and too much in love) to fault his rashness, Una lauds his victory, neglecting to mention the danger of zeal untempered by reason.

Perhaps instructed by the first battle, in the second he is much more restrained; but not, in the end, restrained enough. Roused from sleep in the Hermit's cell by Una (Archimago's sprite, in disguise) offering to enter his bed, indignant at her supposed looseness, he nonetheless curbs the impulse to kill her, instead questioning and reassuring her, and wondering afterwards only whether she is worth defending. Given the subtlety of Archimago's attack, the Red Cross Knight's self-restraint is impressive. It is, however, insufficient the next morning to the spectacle of Una and a young squire (two of Archimago's sprites, in disguise) lewdly embraced. Too enraged to sift, as he had done during the night, the apparently incontrovertible evidence of his senses, he rushes off, reason, intelligence, self-restraint abandoned, will and passion in consequence his guides.

Those guides almost destroy him. Una spurned, almost at once he meets Duessa, her spiritual opposite, and, guided by her, begins his descent from vice through more obvious and dangerous vice to exhaustion and total spiritual defeat. The imperative of chastity at once forgotten, lust at once begins to burn in him. And, his advances encouraged by Duessa, lust is quickly compounded by pride; the combination being, though not adequate at once to stifle every impulse of virtue, sufficient gradually to divest him of strength. Though in heat for Duessa, he defeats Sansfoy. Reason informs him, when he first arrives, that he does not belong in the House of Pride, and keeps him at a distance from Lucifera's cohort. Though that distance diminishes, he defeats Sansjoy. And he concludes at last he must abandon the House. But even his victories weaken him spiritually. Sansfoy defeated, he embraces Duessa, and kisses her ardently. The night before the battle with Sansjoy, he feasts with Lucifera's cohort. And his victory dedicated, on bended knee, to Lucifera, he returns, in state, to the midst of her court, her physicians commanded to heal his wounds. As the Red Cross Knight does not yet realize, even battles in the service of God, fought successfully in degenerate circumstances for morally ambiguous reasons, perforce debilitate. He abandons the House of Pride before dawn, unaware that he has defiled himself, but fully aware that, somehow or other, he has become enmeshed in terrifying danger, and is barely escaping with his life.

As he skulks away, he is accompanied by the mockery warranted by the complacency with which he congratulates himself for increasingly impressive attainment, and by the contrast between his behavior and that of Una.

Introduction

The mockery intensifies as the complacency and the transparency of the evil develop together. Not even the first of his attachments is opaque. Precisely who Duessa is may not be clear when the Red Cross Knight first meets her. But that she is dressed as the Whore of Babylon, and is dallying with Sansfoy, should alert him to her essential character, as should her willingness, on short acquaintance, to be fondled and kissed. The House of Pride is much less opaque, and Lucifera and her cohort are unmistakable. The House shifts precariously on its foundation of sand. Lucifera continuously trumpets her haughtiness, openly leading a parade of the Seven Deadly Sins, and openly consorting with Duessa. Although at the outset the Red Cross Knight distances himself to some degree from the total degeneracy of the House, by the time he has defeated Sansjoy he is at its center, content with its ministrations and praise. After he has escaped its clutches, he regrets having left Duessa behind. And when she finds him, though so debilitated he can barely move, he attempts lewd intercourse with her. The degree of his blindness almost throughout to the House of Pride, and throughout to Duessa, provokes mockery throughout. The evils that threaten his soul are obvious. He fails almost completely to see them; in fact, he considers them testaments to growth. In consequence, he is deservedly mocked, and his standing, at least in potential, as a hero, is undermined.

It is undermined also by the contrast between his degeneration after abandoning Una, and her constancy during her wanderings. That nothing can diminish Una's virtue, or her love for the Red Cross Knight, implicitly censures his immersion in vice, and his love for her; as does the fealty of creatures less impressive by nature than himself inspired by her behavior, and the providential protection she is afforded at need. From the lust of Sansloy she recoils in horror. Unable to wean the satyrs and Sylvanus from idolatry, she leaves them. Uncomfortable with the incomplete devotion of Satyrane to Christianity, and therefore uncertain of the outcome of his battle with Sansloy, she rushes off before the battle ends. She wanders only to find the Red Cross Knight, or to learn what has become of him; when she thinks she has found him (Archimago, in disguise), she melts before him, love abounding; and when Archimago tells her, lying, he is dead, she collapses. The lion forgets his rage in her presence; Sylvanus and his satyres forget their lustfulness; the pagan blood in Satyrane stops flowing. And Providence itself, when her others protectors prove inadequate, intervenes to rescue her from Sansloy. Spiritually flawless, unshakable in love, protected by creatures through the chain of being, she is spurned only, in favor of vice, by the Red Cross Knight. The others instinctively understand her worth. Only he, reason willfully abandoned, concludes that she is less deserving of his attentions than Duessa, Lucifera, and the related attractions of self-destructive vice.

Without help, he is doomed. It is provided, through the Grace of God, at almost the last possible moment. And the help is decisive. Rescued from Orgoglio's dungeon by Arthur, compelled by Una to understand Duessa, and taught by Caelia and her cohort in the House of Holiness the axioms of Christianity, the process of penance, and the ecstasy of vision, the Red Cross Knight gradually attains spiritual maturity, and is in consequence at last prepared, in a battle almost impossibly difficult, to defeat the dragon long the terror of Una's parents, and to be rewarded with Una's hand in marriage.

Arthur's task is the least complex, and the most easily accomplished. As Arthur is a paragon of virtue, and Orgoglio merely a bag of wind, Arthur dispatches him almost without effort, and rescues the Red Cross Knight as easily from Orgoglio's dungeon.

Una's task—to encourage the Red Cross Knight to reformation, by making him aware that Duessa is a devilish whore—is far less simple than she imagines, and far more dangerous. At her behest, he is exposed to the sight of Duessa stripped naked, and understands, in consequence, who she is. But he understands also, before he is strong enough to deal with the insight, how shameful his attachment to her was. And that sense of shame almost destroys him. His conscience roused, but only morbidly, he is devastated by self-loathing, and therefore, in the Cave of Despair, resolves to kill himself.

Aware that she cannot deal with the self-loathing, Una wisely delivers him to the House of Holiness, whose inhabitants complete the complex task of purging his soul of evil, and of inspiring in it confidence and joy. To assure him that no career of self-debasement precludes salvation, he is introduced by Fidelia to the religious mysteries upon which self-reformation depends, and afterwards by Speranza to the hope that God's Grace will favor him. That done, he is subjected to the excruciating, but indispensable, pain of repentance, and, his conscience finally cured, rewarded with a vision of Heaven, and with the welcome news of his royal lineage, and of the sainthood eventually to be conferred upon him. Thus empowered, he leaves the House of Holiness, and journeys with Una towards the dragon afflicting her parents' home.

Introduction

Though the battle with this dragon is almost unendurable, its outcome is a foregone conclusion. Spiritually mature, attended by Una, and by God's Grace, however beleaguered, the Red Cross Knight perforce prevails. And, having prevailed, he has earned, at last, the most radiant of brides, and through his lifetime and afterwards the praise and the reward of eternal bliss due the accomplished servant of God.

Macbeth is divided into two parts. The first part ends at the end of Act Two, Scene Two, with the murder of Duncan by Macbeth. The second part ends at the end of Act Five, Scene Nine, with the death of Macbeth.

The first part is dominated almost entirely by a satanic force that consists of three witches and Macbeth. Nothing opposes it. The second part successfully opposes it as regards Macbeth (though not as regards the witches) because a catastrophic decision to oppose the witches rouses in him a homicidal outburst that gradually mobilizes a Christian force that kills him.

That the witches are satanic is established by their terrifying first appearance, and underscored both by their second appearance, and by the horrific portent in the contrast between Banquo's attitude towards them and that of Macbeth. Banquo is terrified, and almost at once suspicious that they are satanic, hesitates even to address them. By contrast, Macbeth, whose spiritual identification with them is established at once by linguistic echo, demands that they speak to him, fixated by their prophecy that he is to become king of Scotland; a response that Banquo correctly attributes to fear, entirely unaware that the fear is not of regicide, that Macbeth is resolved to commit, but of being convicted of, and punished for, regicide.

Macbeth's resolve is especially harrowing because his wife misunderstands both herself and her husband, and therefore goads him into murdering Duncan the night he arrives at their home. She imagines mistakenly that she can stifle the womanly compassion that militates against murder, and, that done, participate in the murder of Duncan; of necessity, because, though she correctly supposes that her husband wants Duncan dead, she mistakenly supposes that he must be taught to dissemble, and that he is too kind-hearted to commit murder. She stumbles almost by accident upon the reason Macbeth hesitates—his fear of being convicted of, and punished for, regicide. And by brushing that fear—indeed, that terror—contemptuously aside, she seals Duncan's fate; unaware that her husband needs no instruction in dissimulation, as his first encounter with Duncan shows, and that his lust to murder far exceeds her own.

Dagger in hand, intent on murdering not only Duncan, but also his son Malcolm, Macbeth is impeded by no force opposed to the Devil's. That force, Banquo warns him, always intends and fosters destruction. And in a tableau immediately before Macbeth enters on his way to the regicide, Banquo hesitates to put his armor aside, wary of even thoughts that bedevil the night.

But Banquo's hesitation is not a force, any more than his suspicion about the witches was. To the moment of the regicide, the only force that exists is that of the Devil.

In the second part, that force is undiminished. But a number of facts that perhaps prefigure a Christian counter-force appear. And because, driven by an astonishingly stupid impulse that is not explained, Macbeth opposes his will to that of the witches, they assault him, destroy his self-esteem, and prompt the sickening homicidal rampage that gradually coalesces a Christian force that destroys him.

Immediately after Duncan is murdered, a number of facts that foreshadow that force appear. A porter opens the Gate to Hell, to admit condemned sinners. Banquo affirms his trust in God. Malcolm flees to England, to muster a force against Macbeth. And Heaven, troubled by the regicide, unleashes unnatural convulsions in nature.

The impulse in Macbeth appears at once, in Macbeth's resolve to murder Banquo and his son Fleance; a resolve that, as he soon realizes, dooms him, because it opposes his merely human will to evil to the metaphysical will to evil of the witches.

No such opposition exists as regards the murder of Duncan. As Macbeth knows, the witches are indifferent to how the crown passes from Duncan to Macbeth. They do not care if he murders Duncan, or if, as he knows is an option, he does nothing, as he did nothing to become the Thane of Glamis and of Cawdor. But as he also knows, they have in effect told him that he must not murder Banquo and Fleance—that, indeed, he cannot kill them, because they have prophesied—in effect, decreed—that the crown is to pass from Macbeth to Banquo's children. Thus, in resolving to murder Banquo and Fleance, Macbeth is challenging the witches—in effect, opposing the will of a devilish human being to the will of creatures metaphysically devilish.

Introduction

Why Macbeth does that is not known. But the consequences of doing it are; they accrue inexorably.

That the first and lasting consequence is his deepening panic at having challenged the witches is underscored by the self-deception that marks the first half of his soliloquy after he is crowned king, and by an unbearable fear that gainsays his apparent self-control in his encounter with the murderers he recruits to dispatch Banquo and Fleance. The self-deception is based on his nonsensical analysis of Banquo. And the fear, that shakes him (and his wife) during the day, and infests his dreams (and hers) at night mocks his self-control. In his wife the fear, it turns out, bespeaks that she is ravaged by conscience. In Macbeth it bespeaks his almost immediate and sickening recognition that challenging the witches was a catastrophic mistake.

That they sent the ghost of Banquo to torment him is probable; that Macbeth is convinced they sent him is certain. And that, having endured its two appearances, it is certain also that he resolves to go immediately to them, presumably to protest that they exposed him as Banquo's murderer, but in perverse fact to hear the witches repeat what they told him the first time they met—that Banquo's progeny, not his, would inherit his throne—that their will, not his, would prevail—that they have defeated and crushed him.

That underscored, a rage to murder as often as he can and almost at random erupts in Macbeth, whose first innocent victims are Macduff's wife and children.

Macbeth thus completely berserk, a force, thus far only foreshadowed, must be mustered at once to march against him.

That that force will be entirely Christian is established in a long encounter between Macduff and Malcolm, in which Malcolm tests Macduff by presenting himself as irredeemably profligate, but then reveals that he is a paragon of Christian virtue; then asserts correctly that King Edward the Confessor, a Christian saint, Siward, an ideal Christian warrior leading ten thousand soldiers, and God's angels have assembled to destroy Macbeth.

His death is debased by staggering mockery, for almost to his last breath accepting at face value the pronouncements of the witches. Though in his final meeting with them he damns anyone stupid enough to believe anything they say, almost to the end of his last battle he is convinced he is invulnerable, because they have assured him he cannot be defeated until forests move, or until he confronts an enemy not born of woman.

Literature as Witness

Paradise Lost is divided into three parts. In the first part, the metaphysical forces, Satan and God, who contend for the soul of mankind are contrasted, and battle for the first time. Then Adam and Eve are made aware that Satan exists, and that he intends to destroy them, and schooled exhaustively in how to defend themselves against him. In the second part, they Fall to him. And in the third part, the consequences of their fall, to him, to them, and to the world, accrue.

The first part underscores that Satan is unredeemably loathsome. Driven by unbounded pride to depose God, his rebellion defeated, he resolves to spite Him by destroying mankind. The disgust and the terror evoked by his effort are absolute, and are mitigated only by the ironic laughter of which he is almost unremittingly the butt.

The centrality of pride in Satan's mental life, and its consequences, are dramatized at once. Precluded by egotism from accepting God's rule, and seething therefore with envy and rage, with a cohort of cunningly seduced angels he provokes a war. Easily defeated, and therefore more deeply enraged, he vows implacable enmity to God, whom he plans to spite by seducing the creatures God has created to supply the place his rebellion has left vacant.

The plan takes shape as Satan lies enchained on the burning lake in Hell, recovering from the battle in Heaven, and is furthered during the council scene he manipulates in Pandemonium, and during his journey through Chaos to the upper world. To all objections to the plan he is willfully deaf. God, at best his peer, and perhaps, he thinks, his inferior, having humiliated, disgraced, and defeated him, must suffer. And if He is invulnerable to direct attack, He must suffer the loss of His treasured new creation, mankind. That its archetypes have done him no harm is irrelevant. God, he is convinced, has spited him. Therefore he will spite God, by destroying them.

The horror evoked by his implacable resolve is undermined only by the laughter roused by his blindness. The Prince of Darkness is, it turns out, also the most imperceptive of princes, in all but two instances ludicrously unaware that he remains God's slave wherever he is, whatever he plots. Convinced he is free, he is, merely and laughably, an unwitting pawn.

The Master who moves him, at will and entirely without effort, is his absolute spiritual opposite. Prompted by compassion, tolerance, and incomprehensible love, God appears surrounded by light (perhaps *is* light),

Introduction

and invites opposition to His stern edict against Adam and Eve, for whom He has created a radiant world.

God is presented in light (perhaps *as* light), the metaphorical analogue to the moral radiance that prompts Him to accede, in the colloquy in Heaven, to the Son's petition that He forgive mankind for its catastrophic trespass. Though His indignation is entirely warranted, and though the demands of justice, He insists, must be satisfied, He is easily persuaded to deal with the trespass mercifully, to insulate Adam and Eve with His race from the most dire consequences of their hideous disobedience. And the colloquy done, the exquisite world created for them, seen for the first time, testifies to His enduring regard for them.

The metaphysical forces between whom Adam and Eve must choose contrasted, they move towards Eden, the first to destroy them, the second to save them. The destroyer, his malice focused by his first experience of the beauty of mankind and its habitation, arrives in Eden first, his resolve steeled especially by envy, and by regret grounded in self-pity and rage. More horrifying than in his first appearance, because an actual, rather than a projected, threat, spying on the unsuspecting couple, crouched as a toad at Eve's ear, he is easily repulsed and imprisoned by Gabriel, and dismissed with an effortless shrug of God's hand. The victory, however, is inconclusive, because Adam and Eve, unaware even that an enemy intent on destroying them exists, have not participated in the struggle to defeat him.

Because they will soon be compelled to participate, because they will be morally bound to do so, they are taught by Raphael who Satan is, why he will persist in the effort to destroy them, and precisely how his attack will occur. Thus forewarned, and in consequence fully forearmed, they will be responsible for the choice they will be compelled to make between their implacable enemy and their loving protector.

Beyond question, Satan will attack again. And, though God could protect them again while they slept, they can attain freedom as human beings only through the exercise of moral choice. Therefore they are instructed, and left free to choose.

The instruction is conveyed by Raphael, in two narratives far more effective as learning devices than abstract discussion, because dramatic and gripping, especially when heard, as they are by Adam and Eve, for the first time; and then in a disturbing narrative by Adam, that Raphael interprets. From the first narrative, the story of the rebellion in Heaven, Adam and Eve learn, by following Satan in action, the depth of his adamant evil. From the second, that recounts the Creation, they learn the depth of his envy and homicidal hatred, of themselves in particular, because God intends to elevate them to his place in Heaven, to rule wisely the world created to soothe Him for his rebellion. And from Adam's own narrative of his first meeting with Eve, as interpreted by Raphael, Adam is warned to beware of the tendency that exposes him most disturbingly to attack, his habit of lapsing from reasoned self-command when confronted with the allure of Eve. Husband and wife review the lessons taught by the first two narratives, and Adam reviews the lesson of the third, both thus acknowledging that they have understood Raphael completely, and implicitly confirming that they have been forewarned, and will, in consequence, be morally bound to accept responsibility for their conduct when Satan next attacks.

In the second part, the attack occurs, and Adam and Eve succumb to Satan. The major cause of the defeat is Adam, who panders, at two crucial moments, to the tendency Raphael warned him to control, through uxorious dotage affording his wife a degree of independence obviously dangerous, and then resolving to share the lethal consequences of her folly.

The first moment occurs during the morning of the Fall. Not having heard the soliloquy that precedes Satan's attack, Adam and Eve cannot know the most important day of their life has begun. But they know their enemy is lurking somewhere, and Adam in particular is alert enough to insist that Eve, weaker than he is, remain at his side. She does not do so, because, unable to withstand her wheedling censure, his arguments frustrated by stubborn accusations, Adam allows her, for the first time, to work by herself.

His arguments are models of cogent exposition. Her responses are simple: he does not trust her, he does not respect her, he does not love her. And she begins to cry. To these responses he opposes no defense. Crushed to have hurt the feelings of the woman he loves more than anything else, anxious to appease her and to restore her good cheer, reason notwithstanding, he dismisses her to death.

And when she returns, he resolves to join her in death. Drunk with delight, convinced she is attaining godhead, Eve offers the fruit of the forbidden tree to her husband utterly unaware of the consequences of doing so. Adam accepts, and eats, undeceived, aware that he is eating death. Because he cannot, he insists, live without her, he prefers her company, even in death, to continued life bereft of her. She is more important, in short, than God. Therefore he prefers her to God.

Introduction

Therefore his culpability far exceeds hers. Eve sins to secure her husband's unqualified love. Knowledge for its own sake does not tempt her. She desires it only because she feels her husband cannot love her completely unless she becomes his intellectual peer. She deserves to be pitied; because her husband does love her completely, because she has been tricked into thinking he does not, and therefore into eating from the tree, by an enemy she cannot successfully oppose, and because, though she pursues it sinfully, her desire is touching. Adam deserves no equivalent pity. His duty is clear. He knows—or should know—that, provided he remains obedient to God, his well-being, with or without Eve, is assured. The willful insistence that not even God can replace Eve in his uxorious affection precludes extenuation on his behalf. In eating of the fruit, as in allowing his wife to work by herself, Adam knew he was acting in despite of reason and duty. He cannot evade the consequences of those actions.

In the third, and last, part, the consequences accrue, to Satan, and to Adam and Eve. Satan is punished directly, quickly, and without mercy. By contrast, the punishment of his mortal victims is indirect, slow, and tempered with mercy so abundant, once earned, as in effect to convince Adam that, for himself and for his progeny, the Fall was fortunate.

Turned, like his cohort, at the moment of his imagined triumph at Pandemonium into a helplessly writhing serpent, Satan is dismissed with the ironic contempt that has mocked him throughout. Adam and Eve are treated with compassion, and eventually with uplifting respect; but only after, through an act of self-construction rooted in love, they have earned the compassion, and in consequence the respect.

Staring balefully at one another after the Fall, disgusted with the lust that has suddenly overwhelmed them, their souls polluted with anger, hatred, suspicion, discord, they deserve nothing, and are soothed by little. A brief visit by the Son assures them they will not die at once. But the salvation He speaks of is merely potential, and is far less impressive dramatically than the horrors that surround them. The world itself is in convulsion. And Satan and his cohort, though punished in Pandemonium, will soon be free, as Sin and Death already are, to ravage the earth. Against these sudden and lasting upheavals not much can be done; and nothing at all, until Adam and Eve, reconciled in love, are in consequence empowered, to the extent that fallen mankind can be, to contend against the evils of a fallen world.

Slowly, haltingly, the reconciliation occurs. And in consequence the balm it has earned them is applied. Pledged once again to one another in love, and deserving therefore once again of God's love, they are visited, at His command, by His angel Michael, who assures them, if they remain obedient, they and their progeny will be strengthened against evil to the end of time, and thereafter will dwell, for eternity, with God.

Michael's assurance is rendered in his narrative, in closing, of human history. Through it Adam learns (and will inform Eve, who is asleep) that the power of evil, heightened by the Fall, and the diminished capacity of mankind to oppose it notwithstanding, eventually, through God's Grace, mankind will triumph, Satan, his cohort, Death and Sin, will be destroyed, and a transfiguration will occur dazzling enough in effect to warrant the conclusion that the Fall was in effect the fortunate prelude to a spiritual elevation almost beyond the heart's desire. Reassured and revived by Michael's narrative, and ecstatic at the distant prospect it augurs, weakened by sin, but trusting in God and full of sober hope, hand in hand with his wife, Adam passes from Eden into the mundane world, and eventually, he and his progeny obedient, into an eternity of bliss.

The Scarlet Letter is divided into three parts. In the first and second parts, two irreconcilable views of reality are juxtaposed: in the first part, Hester Prynne's, in the second part Arthur Dimmesdale's. In the third part, the views clash, and the wrong view—Hester's—prevails. Therefore God intervenes in behalf of Dimmesdale's view.

In the first part, Prynne begins, despite herself, the process of grasping her commitment to Satan in a modern form. Unshakably convinced, though nominally Christian, that passionate love, even when, as in her case, adulterous, is more important than God, and certain therefore that Romanticism is superior to Christianity as creed, but unable, because they terrify her, to confront the conviction or the certainty, she struggles, although only intermittently, and without conviction, to conform to a code of human conduct alien to her essential being. In the second part, Arthur Dimmesdale, unshakably convinced of the truth of Christianity, struggles to conform his life to its dictates, the obstacles to doing so his cowardice and hypocrisy, and the satanic assaults upon his soul of Roger Chillingworth. In the third part, Hester and Dimmesdale meet, to debate the merits of Romanticism and Christianity. Because, over seven years of introspection, isolation, and suffering, Hester has located within herself the perverse strength not only to accept her conviction, but also to ground it in ideology, and to act upon it, and because Dimmesdale, during the same seven years, has squandered

INTRODUCTION

his strength in self-defeating efforts to cleanse his soul, and in warding off Chillingworth's attacks, Hester defeats, quickly and with ease, the man she regards on principle as her husband, passionately loves, and longs to reclaim. The consequences of her victory, at once dramatized, being horrific, and no human agency being available to contend against it, God intervenes, by empowering Dimmesdale to defeat, finally, not only Hester, but his own weakness, a potentially decisive weakness in his daughter, and the hideous malice of Chillingworth, his tormentor.

To assure that Hester will enter the debate neither commended for her ideology, nor unambiguously condemned as an apostate, the first part stresses both her sin and the conditions, social and psychological, that nonetheless rouse sympathy in her behalf.

That Hester has sinned is underscored in both sections into which the first part is divided: the day Hester is exposed on the scaffold to public ignominy, and the three years that follow that day. The opening chapter announces a tale of human frailty. Standing on the scaffold, Hester is contrasted to the Virgin Mary. And Pearl is referred to as a child of sin, because she was conceived in sin. Beyond question, Hester is guilty of the deepest sin against the sanctity of marriage, and should be punished severely.

She should not, however, be tortured. Because she is, and for two additional reasons, a carefully measured degree of sympathy mitigates the censure warranted by her sin. As Christians, the townspeople and authorities of Salem are obliged to punish Hester with compassion and restraint. Instead, in both sections of the first part, they torment her, continuously and without pity, as they exhibit her and her infant on the scaffold, and revile her wherever, during the three years afterwards, the crabbed spirit of Puritan rigor moves them do so, underscoring the pollution of her loathsome soul, and applauding themselves for exemplary forbearance and Christian charity, in exhibiting Hester, half-mad with despair, and her infant daughter, for merely three hours, and for resolving merely to deprive them forever afterwards of human society.

Hester's apparently sincere desire not to sin again also rouses sympathy in her behalf, as does the failure of both the townspeople and the authorities of Salem to grasp her adamant opposition to Christianity. That the penitential regimen of penance she adopts to avoid further sin is almost entirely unconnected to conscience—that she is, indeed, almost never bothered by conscience—is easily overlooked, especially as the regimen itself seems impressive. And her defense of the superior sanctity of the heart's desire is presented only once, in Christian language which stresses so emphatically Hester's horror at her own thoughts, and in consequence her frenzied need to suppress them, that its standing as a defense is apparent only to the most painstaking scrutiny. To everyone, including almost always herself, Hester seems, if not a Christian, at least a penitent resolved to be bound by Christian morality, and therefore deserving, despite her sin, at least sympathy, and perhaps even respect.

Her essential indifference to both the morality and the creed is underscored by the contrast between her outlook and that of Dimmesdale, the focus of the second part. Dimmesdale is immovably devoted to Christianity, unshakably convinced of its truth, devastated by his hideous lapses from its dictates, and hounded by their consequences almost into madness and non-being.

By nature unable and unwilling to live without a creed, Dimmesdale finds in Christianity the perfect framework for his high intelligence, love of humanity, purity of sentiment, and fitness to experience even revelation. But the intensity of his devotion to God dooms him, when his soul is corrupted, to an equivalent intensity of self-disgust; compounded because, the slave of cowardice and hypocrisy, he refuses to endure the public debasement that alone, as he knows, would restore his soul in purity to its Maker. His spirit drained, by his own weakness, and by the dastardly assaults of Chillingworth, to which the weakness exposes him, over a period of seven years he ceases almost to be a human being, and disqualifies himself as an advocate in debate for the creed to which he is utterly devoted.

The adultery, his initial sin, never ceases to torment Dimmesdale, and neither does his cowardly refusal to disgrace himself, and in consequence to lose his lofty standing, by enduring the humiliation of public confession, or his habit on inserting into his sermons mock-confessions certain, as he knows, to be misinterpreted by his congregants and fellow-clergy as superiority in virtue. Because he understands precisely how he has defiled himself, and because the Romish remedies he applies—vigils, fasts, self-flagellation—prove, as he realizes, worse than useless, seven years of unremitting self-torment destroy his self-esteem, provide Chillingworth, Satan's minion, access to his soul, and drive him inexorably towards madness and despair. On the scaffold, at midnight, in the seventh year, he is almost unhinged. Racked by self-loathing, exhausted, desperate, he can barely stand, much less debate the woman who loves him, and who, aglow with satanic

Introduction

strength, proposes confidently, as the balm for his soul, a degenerate creed irreconcilably at odds with his own.

Despite his unfitness to participate in it, when, in the third and closing part the debate occurs, in the forest, the satanic impulse in Hester defeats him, quickly and easily. To the extent possible the indictment of Hester is mitigated. But that her impulse is satanic is underscored throughout.

Dimmesdale submits quickly to Hester, physically, spiritually, and intellectually. He asserts, briefly and without conviction, the imperatives of Christianity. But, his head pressed against her bosom, and assured he will not leave Salem alone, his vigor restored by her erotic strength, he resolves to abandon his creed for hers, in essence to prefer, as Hester does, Satan to God.

For the consequences of his resolve neither he nor Hester can escape censure. As he walks from the forest back to town, he restrains himself, but only barely, from demonstrating in destructive action his allegiance to his new master, whose identity he knows, and to whom, for the first time, he has consciously pledged his soul.

Nothing can obscure Hester's responsibility for the catastrophe that has suddenly overwhelmed Dimmesdale. And during the forest scene itself the censure of her is almost unsparing. Nature condemns her. The author, speaking in his own voice, condemns her. Pearl, her daughter, condemns her. And Dimmesdale's thoughts on his walk back to town condemn her. The only mitigating pleas on her behalf are entered before she enters the forest, and are based on her supposed weakness as a woman, and on the existence of an evil more black than her own. Because she is a woman, she can supposedly speculate upon complex questions of creed only with her heart; and as her heart has been frozen for seven years, her speculations are inevitably confused, and the impulses they loose in her therefore deserve pity. As she prepares to enter the forest, the confusion prevents her even from realizing what her impulses are, what emotion will erupt when she meets Dimmesdale, or what plan she will offer him. She is a woman pitifully misled by her yearning for love. Chillingworth, whom she meets, knows precisely what evil he intends, and pursues it methodically. Hester, by contrast, knows not what she does.

Especially therefore, she must be restrained. And because no human agency exists to restrain her, God takes the task upon Himself, through an act of Grace converting Dimmesdale's defeat to victory, and divesting all concerned human evil of strength. The Election Day sermon passes from

Heaven through Dimmesdale's soul, is transferred to paper by his pen, and spoken by his literally enraptured mouth. Nothing of it is his own. The voice of God speaking mysteriously through his voice, it silences every competing voice, and restores his soul, and the equilibrium of his world. The truth of God proclaimed in public, in the sermon itself, and in Dimmesdale's triumphant public self-debasement, Dimmesdale returns in joy to his Maker, Hester suffers the defeat she must, the hold of rage upon Pearl is broken, and Chillingworth's satanic strength vanishes. The greater glory of God affirmed, only Hester's long life remains, untouched unfortunately by the consolation of Christianity.

Crime and Punishment is divided into three parts. In the first part, to test a nihilistic theory, Rashkolnikov murders two women; though, as the theory is mentioned only in passing, and as other motives apparently compelling but in fact superficial are vividly dramatized, why he murdered is far from clear. In the second part, almost crushed by the pressures, internal and external, created by the murders, he resolves either to confess, or to commit suicide; and is kept from acting on that resolve only by the appearance of Sonia, who, for reasons not at once apparent, suddenly strengthens him, and thus renews his commitment to his theory (still not revealed as central to his conduct, or even discussed), and his will to persevere despite the pressures. In the third part, the pressures intensify, and Sonia, whose grounding in Christianity he misjudges completely despite the transparency of her behavior, gradually draws him towards God. In consequence, the will to persevere in satanic nihilism (at last discussed, in detail) destroyed, Rashkolnikov surrenders, and begins the journey, through confession and suffering, to life as a penitent of the God of Christianity.

In the first part, because the apparently compelling motive of rage at injustice and poverty is presented forcefully, and because the underlying motive to the two murders is not even broached, attention is focused almost exclusively upon the process through which the rage overcomes the only force that obstructs it, conscience. In Rashkolnikov conscience, it turns out, is at the moment weak, and rage is volcanic. During the rehearsal at the outset of the first part, Rashkolnikov asserts that he would never commit so dastardly a crime as murder. And in a terrible dream he tries to prevent the murder of a horse. But these expressions of moral restraint are quickly, and without much effort, nullified, by three related events that convince Rashkolnikov that, whatever the objections to radical action, he must act. Those events—his discussion with Mr. Marmeladov, Sonia's father, of

INTRODUCTION

her fate, a letter from his sister, Dunya that establishes, as Rashkolnikov at once grasps, that she is doomed to Sonia's fate, prostitution, and the sudden appearance of the embodiment of that fate, a young girl apparently just raped—by convincing Rashkolnikov that poverty prevents him from opposing effectively the pervasive injustice about to overwhelm his sister and mother, so infuriate him that, conscience brushed furiously aside, he hatchets two women, one completely innocent, to death.

Only the conversation he overhears in a restaurant weeks before he commits the murders hints that his fury does not explain the murders completely. And the hint is tentative, and overwhelmed by the rage that convulses him. That the nihilistic theory central to the conversation reflects a governing commitment in Rashkolnikov cannot therefore yet be known, or even suspected. The fury is central; its hidden well-spring is not.

The murders committed, in the second part Rashkolnikov struggles against immensely powerful pressures that undermine his resolve to avoid detection and punishment for his crime. The struggle almost ended in defeat, he is rescued by the appearance of Sonia, through whom (for reasons not explained until the third part) the resolve, almost shattered, suddenly and inexplicably becomes very powerful.

The internal pressures that assault him are conscience and self-disgust; the external, the pressure of an unbearable, unprecedented sense of isolation, and the pressure of a police investigation. The murders done, conscience does not disturb him at all until, despite himself, it becomes, under the instruction of Sonia, an unendurable pressure. And self-disgust becomes a pressure only once, when he realizes that he is a failure as a nihilist. By contrast, the far more debilitating pressures, often juxtaposed,—the sense of solitude, and the pressure of the investigation of the murder—never relent. Exiting the police-station for the first time, and looking up at a church cupola, Rashkolnikov feels suddenly cut off from the company of human beings, doomed forever to a solitude he has never felt, and cannot endure. To escape, he drifts, for three days, in and out of consciousness; and wakes, on the fifth day after the murders, to find the feeling almost unbearably intensified. Tortured by the unbridgeable distance between himself and Razumikhin, Zamyotov, and Luzhin talking in his room, and by the terrifying accuracy of their discussion of the murders, exhausted and desperate, Rashkolnikov rushes out of the room, resolved either to commit suicide or to confess to the police. And, suicide rejected, he does, in a manner of speaking, confess; to Zamyotov, in a restaurant, and to workers, at the scene of the crime. His strength depleted, in particular by the sense of isolation, and by the police, convinced, as he imagines, of his guilt, he sees no alternative to confession and imprisonment.

Suddenly, however, his strength is restored, and through the prospect of the most unlikely of alliances. In the turmoil and horror of Marmeladov's death, Rashkolnikov seems to find salvation, in a bond with Sonia, at the moment inexplicable, formed in his mind the moment he sees her. For reasons explained (to his detriment) only in the third part, Rashkolnikov is at once convinced that he and Sonia are identical of soul, and that, allied with her, he can defeat decisively the pressures tormenting him. He therefore returns, astonishingly energized, to the struggle against them.

In the third part, he is decisively defeated. To the pressures tormenting him from the outset, the devastating force of Sonia's Christianity is gradually, and to his vast surprise, added. By this total force he is finally crushed, and left, to his abhorrence, but ultimately to the benefit of his soul, to surrender, to the Christian imperatives of suffering and penance, and therefore to life as a Christian.

Against the pressures familiar to him, Rashkolnikov struggles with intelligence and courage. Though he must not defeat them, his character is not diminished by the strategy he devises against the isolation, or by the adroitness of his opposition to Porfiry, whose interrogation tortures him. In the struggle against Sonia, by contrast, he is mocked; as he is for adherence to the theory, at last discussed in detail, that impelled him to murder. Unshakably convinced for far too long that only Sonia—of all people—shares his nihilistic commitment, and therefore that only she can share and mitigate his isolation, he allows her free access to his soul, thus assuring his eventual defeat. And because he is firmly convinced of the merit of his commitment, he espouses it confidently in the face of evidence that refutes it utterly. Both convictions warrant mockery, the indignity appropriate to his failure to see that spiritually Sonia is his polar opposite, and that his theory is abhorrent nonsense.

Throughout the third part, Rashkolnikov struggles against the isolation, and against the torture inflicted by Porfiry. Aware that the murders have cut him off from human society, and that the proximity of people he loves will therefore torment him unendurably, he grasps at once that he must remove Dunya and his mother from his life. Therefore, in two encounters with them, acting, despite enormous pressure, with self-discipline

Introduction

and cunning he cuts them off. And against Porfiry he perseveres through two excruciating interviews, alert to his inquisitor's sadistic stratagems, though horribly debilitated by defending himself against almost fiendish torture. By both struggles his energy is sapped, and he is brought closer, as he must be, to defeat. In both, however, his struggles, though in the service of darkness, are impressive.

His struggles, by contrast, against Sonia, and in defense of his theory, warrant sardonic mockery. From the moment he sees her to almost the moment she masters him, Rashkolnikov insists that, because she is his spiritual twin, Sonia must share his isolation and fate. That he clings to this fantasy is bleakly destructive of his stature. Everything he has been told and seen of her argues beyond question that Sonia is unshakably Christian, that her soul is unblemished by the Cross she bears in the service of God, that her life is virtually an embodiment of the Christian Bible, upon which alone she relies, and which sustains her, through everything. That being so patently the case it almost cannot be misunderstood, Rashkolnikov's insistence that Sonia is essentially a murderer, and therefore is doomed to his company as a murderer, is so astonishingly imperceptive, it debases him especially when, granted access by his blindness to his soul, Sonia begins the work of salvation that he abhors.

When finally, in the first of their interviews, Rashkolnikov discusses the article in which he expounded his theory, Porfiry mocks it openly. So do people and events he consistently misconstrues. His theory necessitates that the death of Marmeladov, one of the vermin who should supposedly be disregarded, stepped over, or crushed, is inconsequential, as is the death of Mrs. Marmeladov, almost vermin. This conclusion he states explicitly to Sonia (without mentioning her parents by name) in expounding his theory in her room, between the scene of the funeral meal for her father, and the scene in which her mother dies. Sonia, horrified, expounds the explicitly Christian objection to Rashkolnikov's conclusion. It is underscored also by the two scenes that surround and refute his exposition. Though the guests at the funeral meal for Sonia's father are far from perfect, they behave impressively, especially when confronted with Luzhin. They are not vermin; not even, though despicable, is Luzhin. They do not deserve to be stepped over, or crushed. And Mrs. Marmeladov, half demented, is noble in death, suffused with love, and enraged at injustice; like the guests at the funeral meal, she is basically sacred, basically worthy of respect, and of love. Her stature is obvious. The stature of the others is obvious. Blinded by his degenerate theory, Rashkolnikov misunderstands them completely.

His strength gone and his theory refuted and mocked, despite himself Rashkolnikov confesses, and takes up his Cross. He does so angrily, under protest, his commitment to his theory almost intact. But finally, no other option exists. Exhausted by the struggle against overwhelming pressures inside and outside of himself, his will to persevere destroyed by Sonia, he reclaims his mother's and sister's love, kisses the earth he has sinned against, sits down at an assistant superintendent's desk, and, the Devil in him notwithstanding, begins the journey to the God of the Christian Bible, and therefore to life.

What Rashkolnikov has not yet begun to learn—how to live—is taught not only in *Crime and Punishment* and in the other works discussed in this book. As this introductory chapter has shown in summary, and as the remaining chapters will show in comprehensive detail, Spenser, Shakespeare, Milton, Hawthorne, and Dostoyevsky are centrally concerned to define and to dramatize a code of conduct imposed by transcendence to which human beings must adhere.

In every case that code is Christianity.

Chapter Two

The Faerie Queene (Book One)

IN HIS FIRST EFFORT as a knight of God, the Red Cross Knight is impressive both in spiritual stature and in reasoned self-command. But he is not quite impressive enough. Though by nature suited to serve as God's warrior, to serve effectively he must subordinate his passions strictly to reason. And he cannot yet do so consistently. Because he is youthful in every sense of the term, in the first of his battles against evil ardor usurps self-command, and in the second, though almost throughout self-command thwarts impressively a devious evil, in the end it is usurped by disgust at vice. In both cases the passion that usurps reason is commendable. Nonetheless, the usurpations weaken the Red Cross Knight, and expose him to additional evils against which he proves increasingly unable to contend.

His dress and his manner argue equally, at his first appearance, that the Red Cross Knight is, at least in potential, heroically impressive. "Ycladd in mightie armes" bequeathed him from "many a bloody field" (1.1.),[1] on his breast "a bloodie Crosse ... The deare remembrance of his dying Lord" (1.2), he has been dressed, though a novice, in the most venerable of armor for the most serious of God's tasks. "Right faithfull and true ... in deede and word" (1.2), sober in mood and without fear he seems preeminently suited to such tasks. And he desires ardently to undertake them, his heart continually yearning, as he rides, "To prove his puissance in battell brave" (1.3).

Because he is a novice, who "armes till that time did ... never wield" (1.1), he is almost defeated by an obvious evil, and is defeated by a devious one. In both encounters, though he performs impressively, a laudable

---

1. Edmund Spenser, *The Faerie Queene: Book One*, edited by Carol Kaske and Abraham Stoll (Indianapolis: Hackett, 2006). All references are to this edition.

emotion undermines his reason, endangering him, and thus his capacity to serve his cause.

The dragon Errour, the first of his antagonists, is unambiguously evil, and must obviously be attacked. But, as Una warns, the attack must be mounted with sober deliberation, "least suddaine mischiefe ye too rash provoke" (1.12). Impatient, however, of deliberation, and of Una's further warning that, as "the perils of this place I better wot than you," he consider the "wisdome" (1.13) of proceeding warily, "full of fire and greedy hardiment" (1.14) he plunges into Errour's cave. He is almost destroyed; and would have been, had Una not advised him, as he "strove in vaine" (1.18) in Errour's grip, to "Strangle her, els she sure will strangle thee" (1.19).

Errour defeated, Una, supportive perhaps to a fault, celebrates the "great glory" her beloved has won on his "first adventure" (1.27), passing in silence over the danger to which his emotion, though laudable, exposed him. As she might to his benefit have pointed out, even zeal in God's service, praiseworthy in itself, undisciplined by reason, leads almost to disaster. Because he is "youthfull" (1.14), fire and hardiment even in God's service, fatal to God's enemy, are almost fatal to him as well.

In the second of his encounters they injure him severely. Because he proceeds by deceit rather than overtly, and because he attacks when the Red Cross Knight is weakened and off-guard, Archimago is far more dangerous an enemy than Errour. Perhaps instructed by his experience with Error, the Red Cross Knight is far from rash in his encounter with Archimago. In fact, almost to the end of the encounter his mind remains impressively predominant. But at the end it is undermined, once again by a laudable emotion, to much more dire effect than before.

It is impossible at the outset to know who Archimago is. To Una as well as to the Red Cross Knight, "sober he seemde, and very sagely sad . . . and voide of malice bad" (1.29). The ambiguity of "seemde" is minimized by an apparently gracious reception, which leaves the Red Cross Knight "well content" to follow "that goodly father" (1.33) home; as apparently he should be, because in his "litle lowly Hermitage" the pious old man is "dewly wont to say His holy things each morne and eventyde" (1.34). Not even Una, who knows the Cave of Errour at a glance, suspects that Archimago is in fact "A bold bad man" (1.37) capable of unleashing subtle evil at the moment it will function most effectively.

That moment is the dead of night, when the Red Cross Knight, "all forwearied" (1.32) of his fight with Errour, and deprived of intellectual guard by sleep, is most susceptible to unconscious suggestion. Sleeping "soundly void of evil thought," he is attacked with "guyle" and "usage sly" (1.46) by a fabricated "dreame of loves and lustfull play, That nigh his manly hart did melt away, Bathed in wanton blis and wicked joy" (1.47). Una, he dreams, is entering his bed with lustful intent. His response is impressive. Within the dream—even within his unconscious being, usually devoid of reasoned restraint—he is disgusted by the sudden transformation of Una from a virtuous princess to "a loose Leman to vile service bound" (1.48). The "great passion" within the dream is either "unwonted" lust, or "wonted feare of doing ought amis" (1.49). And when the safeguard of conscious intellect is roused, it rushes almost at once to his defense. Startled, on waking, to find "Una" (Archimago's minion disguised as Una) at the side of his bed, apparently ready to enact the dream, "All cleane dismayd . . . and half enraged . . . He thought have slaine her in his fierce despight." Still only a moment removed from sleep, and therefore not yet fully governed by reason, he moves to strike her. Reason, however, manages to restrain him. His "hastie heat tempring with sufferance wise," in a remarkable display of self-control "He stayde his hand," and, proceeding in a sober, measured fashion, "gan himself advise To prove his sense" (1.50), by questioning her in a kindly but rigorous fashion. Unconvinced by her "doubtfull" (1.53) responses, he lies in bed "long after" she is gone, not regretting an opportunity lost, but

> musing at her mood,
> Much griev'd to think that gentle dame so light,
> For whose defence he was to shed his blood.
> (1.55)

Even Archimago's attempt to trouble him again, when he does at last return to sleep, with lascivious dreams "all was vaine" (1.55). Safe in moral excellence and reason, he lies, though troubled, still secure.

He does not, unfortunately, remain secure long. Returning to the attack, Archimago suddenly awakens him again, "with fearful frights" (2.4) and apparently indisputable proof of depravity: Una (once again, Archimago's minion) and a young squire (another minion) "full closely ment In wanton lust and leud embracement." Once again, the Red Cross Knight restrains his first impulse, to kill them both "in his furious ire." But he does so "hardly," and only at the old hermit's insistence, for the essential damage to his mind has been done. "The eye of reason was with rage yblent" (2.5). That decisive wound inflicted, he dresses "hastily" (2.6), and rushes off, "Pricked with wrath and fiery fierce disdaine" (2.8). As before, the emotion that moves him is laudable: disgust at immorality, and the need to distance himself from its effects. But, also as before, it undermines him. Reason abandoned, new mentors suddenly attend him: "Will was his guide, and grief led him astray." He disappears "Still flying from his thoughts and gealous feare" (2.12), hurrying inevitably towards catastrophe.

It meets him at once, in the person of Duessa, who begins at once the process by which, with his full consent and cooperation, he descends from vice through deeper vice into a vortex of guilt and self-disgust that almost destroys him. Reason blinded by rage and grief, he is guided by increasingly degenerate will: by a growing conviction that, whatever his desires, they should be fulfilled. To the detriment of his spiritual wellbeing, they are fulfilled. And thus he deteriorates, falling precipitously from lust through pride, to a wish, suffused with self-pity, to die, and at last, self-respect completely lost, to the horrific resolve of self-destruction.

As he falls, he is censured not only directly for the degeneracy in which he participates, but also, indirectly, through irony. During the first motions of the fall, increasingly blind to moral truth, he delights increasingly in what he takes to be progressive elevation. He succumbs to evils increasingly obvious, finding them, despite their increasingly patent degeneracy, increasingly attractive. And he is consistently blind to the stark contrast, underscored by explicit statement, and by the juxtaposition of Una's involvements to his own, between the women he takes up with and the woman he has abandoned. Because he is by nature impressive and inexperienced, because his stature as potential hero must be preserved, and because his antagonist's arts are "devilish" (2.9), as often as possible the irony directed against him is muted. And it ceases the moment he begins to grasp the damage he has caused. But while it persists, it deepens the sense of the damage he has inflicted, upon himself and upon a spotless woman who loves him unshakably, and whose enemy he is bound in honor to defeat.

The lust attacks him almost at once. A glance at Duessa, at her first appearance, unquestionably tells him exactly who she is. It would not have required the counsel of Una, or the contrast between her appearance and Duessa's, to discover that the woman riding towards him, bedecked like the Whore of Babylon (2.14), and entertaining an obviously degenerate lover "With faire disport, and courting dalliance . . . all the way" (2.14) is not the virtuous woman of Proverbs. Why he does not dismiss her with contempt may be guessed at once. The explicit explanation is deferred for a moment, so that his reputation may be preserved for the duration of his encounter with Sansfoy. To that encounter he is, though weakened, still sufficient. As vice takes possession of the soul by degrees, the strength of virtue dissipates. Therefore, to defeat a "faithlesse Sarazin" whose shield plainly proclaims "Sansfoy," and who plainly "cared not for God...a point" (2.12) is still within the Red Cross Knight's power. But as his motive in rushing into battle is mixed, so is the consequence. In part he fights for the glory of God; but in part also, as Sansfoy does, "prickte with pride And hope to winne his Ladies hearte" (2.14). The previous night, the lascivious dream, though abhorrent to his ethical sense, "nigh his manly heart did melt away, Bathed in wanton blis and wicked joy" (1.47). Having seen, as he supposed, Una "knit" (2.4) with the squire in that bliss, and will now his guide, he now finds wantonness deeply attractive, as his response to Duessa's tale of her relationship with Sansfoy shows. The tale is obviously suspicious and contrived, as a moment's reflection would have made clear. But he does not reflect. As she proceeds, "Melting in teares" (2.22) from improbability to more obvious improbability,

> He in great passion al this while did dwell,
> More busying his quicke eies her face to view,
> Then his dull eares to heare what shee did tell.
> (2.27)

His reason yblent, the Red Cross Knight is thus weakened even by an action impressive in itself. The enemy of God is quickly dispatched; but in part in the service of lust in God's warrior. The consequence of further involvement with Duessa is thus clear. Unless he is warned to withdraw, and does, deepening weakness, and incapacity for battle, perforce await him.

The warning, issued at once, but disregarded, results only in a deepened immersion in lust. As he travels with the woman "his falsed fancy ... takes To be the fairest wight that lived yit" (2.30), he is warned by the harrowing story of Fradubio to beware of her nature and of her devilish arts (2.40–42). That he disregards the warning almost completely is understandable. Fradubio's history reflects his own only imperfectly. Duessa is so cunningly disguised Fradubio himself fails to recognize her. And even the suspicion roused for a moment in the Red Cross Knight by Fradubio's story, a glimmer of insight Duessa notices, is used to destructive effect against him. "Full of sad feare and ghastly dreriment" (2.44), he tends to the wounds of the bleeding trees. Duessa alertly pretends to faint, and then enjoys his kindly ministrations, as, ostensibly in his anxiety to revive her, but in fact to fan his growing heat, he "oft her kist" (2.45).

Thus, even an act of kindness, to Fradubio or to a lady in apparent distress, enmeshes the Red Cross Knight in lust more deeply than ever. And the lust, in turn, drags him inevitably down to more debilitating vice. It is no small thing for a knight betrayed in his youth by a woman to be encouraged by an apparently more beautiful and more willing woman; to fight for her, and to minister to her distress. It is cause for complacency, even for pride. And therefore, Duessa roused from her faint, he proceeds with her, inevitably and to disastrous effect, to the House of Pride.

In appearance and in conduct, it is far more transparent than even Duessa. And yet, despite some lingering reservations, neither the House nor its monarch and her cohort rouses in him an appropriate response; inevitably, because the weaker he has grown, the more susceptible he has inevitably become to increasingly obvious evil. Had he seen the House at the outset of his journey, his reason intact, and Una at his side, he would have spurned it at once with contempt, or have attacked it with righteous zeal. That strength, however, squandered in lust, he enters willingly, because he belongs; and, increasingly at home through a sickening stay, leaves a broken shell of himself, humiliated, frightened, deservedly a moment from almost fatal defeat.

The House itself is only marginally deceptive. And its mistress, Lucifera, is not deceptive at all. The House cannot be quite accurately appraised from the front, because "all the hinder parts, that few could spie, Were ruinous and old, but painted cunningly" (4.5). But enough of its perilously "weake foundation" is visible to warrant pause. Though "so faire a mould," the House totters uninvitingly "on a sandie hill, that still did flitt And fall away . . . That every breath of heaven shaked itt" (4.5). To sober judgment Lucifera would be even less inviting. That "Of griesly Pluto she the daughter was, And sad Prosperina, the Queene of helle" (4.11), and that "rightfull kingdome she had none at all . . . But did usurpe with wrong and tyrannie" the realm she manipulates not "with lawes, but policie" (4.12), may not be apparent. Her haughtiness, however, is unmistakable. She sits on her throne "a mirrhour bright" continually in hand, "Wherein her face she often vewed fayne" (4.10), barely condescending with "loftie eyes" and "disdainefull wise" (4.14) to acknowledge the debased obeisance of petitioners.

The unfitness of both mistress and place is obvious even to the Red Cross Knight. But, badly weakened, he cannot muster an appropriate response. He finds "that great princess too exceeding prowd, That to strange knight no better countenance allowd." And he notices even the suspiciously warm welcome accorded Duessa by Lucifera's cohort, delighted "All kindnesse and faire courtesie to shew, For in that court whylome her well they knew." As therefore "the stout Faery mongst the middest crowd Thought all their glorie vaine in knightly vew" (4.15), he must understand that he ought to leave, preferably not in Duessa's company. But he does not leave, because, infected with the sins of the place, he does not want to. He entered willingly, in the company of his adored Duessa, "on humble knee Making obeysaunce," and declaring ridiculously but in degenerate truth that he had come Lucifera's "roiall state to see, To prove the wide report of her great Majestee" (4.13). And so, to his rue, he will prove it, his strength steadily ebbing as he remains, doomed by his will to deepening and increasingly ironic self-debasement.

It unfolds in the procession that at once occurs, and in the subsequent encounter with Sansjoy. The procession serves no dramatic function; it exists exclusively to mock the debasement of the Red Cross Knight. And the encounter demonstrates, as did the encounter with Sansfoy, but much more emphatically, that to a soul already weakened by vice even zeal in God's service can be harmful.

The ghastly participants in the parade of the Seven Deadly Sins (4.16–38) who ride out on their hideous mounts, and return to the House are presented only so that the Red Cross Knight may see them clearly, and disregard almost completely not only what they portend, but also the menace in the burden they draw: the Devil himself "upon the wagon beame ... with a smarting whip in hand" driving them, and in the wagon Lucifera, in place of honor "Emongst the rest"

> the false Ladie faire,
> The foule Duessa, next unto the chaire
> Of proud Lucifer', as one of the traine.
> (4.37)

The total spectacle—the perfectly focused, vivid tableau—engages completely the undivided attention of the Red Cross Knight, virtually demanding that he flee for his life. He does not, however, flee. Aware of some essential impropriety,

> that good knight would not so nigh repaire,
> Him selfe estraunging from their joyaunce vaine,

Whose fellowship seemd far unfitt for warlike swaine.

(4.37)

He thus improves his moral position, withdrawing from "the middest crowd" (4.15) among whom he stood on entering the House of Pride. The improvement, however, is only marginal. Obviously he should leave, not stand aside. But to leave is to abandon not only the joyaunce vaine of pride, but the anticipated joyaunce of Duessa, the woman for whom, despite the indisputable evidence he ignores, he still lusts. To abandon her—as, perhaps, despite the beginning of his insight into it, to abandon pride—he must resubmit will, his perverted guide from the moment he discovered Una's supposed lewdness, to the discipline of reason, abandoned at that moment. That he refuses to do. Therefore he is doomed to the depredations of will, as, with the appearance of Sansjoy, it draws him inexorably closer to destruction.

That the pagan warrior must be fought is self-evident. His "heathnish shield, wherein with letters red, Was writt Sansjoy" (4.38), and his "burning ... rage" (4.39) at the Red Cross Knight define his character unmistakably. Both the preparations for the combat, however, and its aftermath demonstrate, as did the combat with Sansfoy, that, in his weakened condition, even a battle in the service of God further weakens the Red Cross Knight. His "noble hart" burning with "virtuous thought, And ... with childe of glorious great intent," tormented through the night before the battle by "flaming corage ... Still did he wake, and still did watch for dawning light," avid to bring forth "Th' eternall brood of glorie excellent" (5.1). And in the battle, unlike Sansjoy, who "for vengeance ... did long," he longs for "praise and honour" (5.7). Thus, beyond dispute, "th' one for wrong, the other strives for right" (5.8). But he is not therefore immune to harm. He prepares for the battle, as does Sansjoy,

> in joy and jollity
> Feasting and courting both in bowre and hall;
> For Steward was excessive Gluttony,
> That of his plenty poured forth to all:
> Which doen, the Chamberlain, Slowth, did to rest them call.
> (4.43)

During the battle, he avoids defeat through the ludicrous error of misunderstanding Duessa, who shouts to his enemy, about to triumph, "Thine the shield, and I, and all!" (5.11). Convinced the shout is intended for him, and in consequence "mov'd with wrath, and shame, and Ladies sake" (5.12), he dispatches Sansjoy, unaware of his folly in thinking Duessa has come to his aid, or is sincere in exclaiming, after the battle, "The conquest yours; I yours; the shield, and glory yours" (5.14). Finally—and perhaps worst—the battle done, he dedicates his victory to Lucifera. Utterly forgetful of the glorious intent that drew him to battle, "he goeth to that soveraine Queene; And falling her before on lowly knee, To her makes present of his service seene" (5.16), thus aligning himself, explicitly and totally, with the worst of the evils he has thus far encountered.

That alignment underscored vividly by the procession back from the battlefield to the House of Pride, the Red Cross Knight, despite his victory over wrong, is almost prostrate, stripped almost completely of spiritual strength, and therefore, left to his own resources, at dire risk of lasting defeat. His obeisance accepted, the haughty queen "marcheth home, and by her takes the knight " (5.16), now not merely mongst the middest rabble, but lifted above them by degenerate accomplishment, and therefore legitimately the object of their applause. As they recognize, following their queen "with great glee, Shouting, and clapping all their hands on hight," her newest minion belongs at her side. He is, moreover, fitly the object of their ministrations. His wounds deserve their attention, his suffering their solicitude. Therefore their most "skilfull leaches" (5.17) attend him, restoring him to their notion of health. And Duessa, fitly esteemed among them, sits by his bed, weeping "full bitterly" (5.17).

He cannot be especially far from destruction. Not yet even aware of his peril, even if it is somehow impressed upon him, he will, in all likelihood, lack the strength to rescue himself from it, or, even that done, to combat effectively subsequent evils. And therefore, in the absence of outside help, he may well be doomed.

The awareness arrives just in time; as a gift, however, not as a consequence of his own exertions. And because it is partial, sufficient to divest him only of pride, but—astonishingly, given the intimate connection between the two sins—not of lust, and because he has been terribly weakened, it is sufficient only to delay his collapse, and only for a single ironic moment.

As he lies, recovering (as he imagines) in bed, his Dwarf, providentially "wary" (5.45) in his behalf, discovers a dungeon crammed with Lucifera's discarded minions. Seeing their suffering, and apparently struck by their resemblance to himself, he is finally roused to self-preservation. But he has barely the strength even for that. The escape he manages is deeply humiliating, and in its aftermath he is openly mocked, to the very moment he is crushed by defeat.

Though condemned for various permutations of pride, "most of all, which in that dungeon lay" are remarkably similar to the Red Cross Knight, in that they

> Fell from high Princes courtes, or Ladies bowres,
> Where they in ydle pomp, or wanton play,
> Consumed had their goods and thriftlesse howres,
> And lastly thrown themselves into these heavy stowre.
>
> (5.51)

Apparently sensing the similarity, the Red Cross Knight is spurred finally to action, but of a thoroughly unimpressive sort. The warrior who began his career in confidence, dreading nothing, "but ever ... ydrad" (1.2), and yearning continually "To prove his puissance in battell brave Upon his foe" (1.3), is now, his confidence shattered, afraid; and slinks away, still wounded, completely unfit, as he knows, for combat. Though still too weak to travel, because "his woundes wyde Not throughly heald unready were to ryde" (5.45), he rises early, the dungeon in mind, terrified to remain "in peril of like painfull plight," and under cover of darkness sneaks off "by a privy Posterne," fearful of discovery; for, as he knows, no longer able to defend himself, "doubtlesse, death ensewd if any him descryde" (5.52). A more ignominious exit cannot be imagined. And almost incredulous laughter attends it, the inevitable response to his regret, on escaping, that Duessa is not with him, to the resurgence of his lust the moment she reappears, and, the lust having stripped him, metaphorically and in fact, to his final defeat.

Looking back at the House of Pride, still hardly daring to believe he has escaped, he breathes a great sigh of relief (6.1). And yet "sad he was, that his too hastie speed The fayre Duess' had forst him leave behind" (6.2). The astonishing self-deception reflected in this sadness, by exposing the Red Cross Knight to an order of ridicule he has not before deserved, undermines severely his standing as even in potential a hero. The same effect is produced more dramatically when Duessa, pursuing "Her hoped pray," finds him. Left "Wearie" (7.2) almost to total exhaustion by his self-debasements, his very slight remaining strength "turnd to feeble frayle" by the charmed fountain from which he unwittingly drinks (7.4–6), he nonetheless musters the degenerate energy to pay "goodly court... still to his Dame," and before long, full closely ment with her, is "Pourd out in loosnesse on the grassy grownd, Both careless of his health, and of his fame" (7.7). That, the House of Pride clearly seen, he should still burn in lust for Duessa, blind to her intimate bond to its inhabitants in general, and in particular to its despicable mistress, would be inconceivable, were he still capable of seeing anything as it is—that is, through the eye of reason. That eye, however, still blinded by will, he sees no more than his passions permit; and in consequence, almost impotent, yet persistent in lust, indifferent to his essential self, loathsome in his degeneracy on the ground with his whore, he is, as his inevitable doom approaches, openly and deservedly mocked.

The doom appears in the person of Orgoglio, who, though nothing more than a huge bag of wind, disposes of him with laughable ease; understandably so, considering how completely, in his misadventures, he has disposed of himself. Caught, ridiculously, with his trousers almost literally down, his "unready" (7.7) weapons cast imprudently aside, devoid of strength, "haplesse, and eke hopelesse... Disarmd, disgraste," and—most important by far—"inwardly dismayde," scarcely able to "weeld his bootlesse single blade" (7.11), with which he strikes not a single blow, in the shortest and most shameful of his battles he is knocked senseless in the first onslaught by the giant, who then "in a dongeon deep him threw without remorse" (7.15).

He deserves to be there. He deserves, in fact, the disaster that, but for the Grace of God, would have crushed him. Struck by the giant with horrific force, "were not hevenly grace that did him blesse, He had been pouldred all as thin as flowre" (7.12). He deserves, moreover, the mockery that has increasingly attended him. Implacably his own enemy from the moment he foolishly abandons Una, increasingly and amidst growing danger at war with himself, and increasingly blind to his deepening peril, though essentially noble and therefore deserving of measured sympathy, as he degenerates he deserves to be increasingly censured, in part through the leveling medium of irony.

The censure is imposed not only directly, but indirectly as well, in the juxtaposition of Una's narrative to the Red Cross Knight's; the absolute contrast between her conduct and his underscoring dramatically not only his initial folly in casting her off, but its inevitable consequence, deepening folly. Her steadfastness indicts him as powerfully as does its spiritual antithesis, his instability. Because the possibility that Una will succumb either to lust or to pride is nil, the charge against the Red Cross Knight cannot be underscored by showing her resisting those vices. Instead, the waverings of the Red Cross Knight are contrasted to three salient dramatic facts: the unshakable persistence of Una's love, shown in her unrelenting search for him, in her willingness to forgive him, instantly and without reserve, for every unkindness, and in her grief at imagining that he has been hurt or killed; the self-restraint and insight of a carefully positioned group of characters who, sometimes in defiance of their essential natures, steadfastly revere and protect Una, and whose individual and cumulative presence therefore underscores by dramatic juxtaposition the blindness and abject folly of the Knight in misinterpreting her nature and in consequence abandoning her; and the concern of Providence itself to protect her. If Una is unshakably, unwaveringly in love, if her protectors understand who she is, and guard and adore her, sometimes in despite of themselves, and sometimes even at the risk of their lives, and if God himself watches carefully over her, what censure must the Red Cross Knight deserve, for preferring to her spotless company degenerate involvement with destructive whores? As he blindly, willfully, stupidly pursues his own destruction, this question, answered not only by the drama itself but also periodically by explicit statement, perforce mocks him as, his spiritual strength more and more completely sapped, he falls more and more completely apart.

To preserve as much of his stature as possible, the extenuating argument that almost anyone in his circumstances would have been duped is twice offered in his behalf. And episodes of story-telling unrelated to him deflect attention from his spiritual degeneration. But neither device accomplishes much. The argument is countered with censure of his conduct. And the story-telling occurs only twice. The effort, as he collapses, to shore him up argues primarily an impulse to pity a young, inexperienced, still perhaps essentially noble warrior not yet quite certain to be destroyed.

The unwavering persistence of Una's love is continually stressed. The sudden disappearance of the Red Cross Knight leaves her "in despayre" (3.2). And, though "Forsaken, woefull, solitaire," she instantly begins "Far from all peoples preace, as in exile, In wildernesse and wastfull deserts . . . To seeke her knight" (3.3). Wandering in search of him, she lies down in the woods, unable to sleep, instead lamenting and weeping

> For the late losse of her deare loved knight,
> And sighes, and grones, and evermore does steepe
> Her tender brest in bitter tears all night.

(3.15)

When Archimago appears disguised as her beloved, she rushes towards him "with faire fearfull humblesse" (3.26), "weeping" (3.27), recrimination nowhere in her thought, afraid only that he may have ceased to love her, or that she may somehow have displeased him; possibilities that, like his absence, have been a kind of death.

> "Much feared I to have ben quite abhord,
> Or ought have done, that ye displeasen might,
> That should as death unto my deare heart light:
> For since mine eie your joyous sight did mis,
> My chearefull day is turnd to chearelesse night,
> And eke my night of death the shadow is."
> (3.27)

She welcomes him, her "light, and shining lampe of blis" (3.27), without insisting—without even suggesting—that he explain his absence. And the suspiciously vague explanation he offers seems to her "due recompence Of all her passed paines." Because to a true lover "one loving howre For many years of sorrow can dispence . . . she speakes no more Of past" (3.30), enthralled to have him back. Later, she remains completely indifferent to the ministrations of the satyrs, her woodland guardians, because

> she, all vowed unto the Redcrosse Knight,
> His wandring peril closely did lament,
> Ne in this new acquaintance could delight.
> (6.32)

And when, once again duped by Archimago in disguise, she concludes that her knight has been killed in battle,

> her tender hart so thrild,
> That suddein cold did ronne through every vaine,
> And stony horrour all her senses fild
> With dying fitt, that down she fell for paine.
> (6.37)

Her grief profound in proportion to her love, she is only with difficulty "wonne from death" (6.37).

Her protectors, though unaware of the preeminence of such love, or even that it radiates continually from her, grasp instinctively the rare preeminence of a nature from which *something* exquisite flows. And they are never tricked, as the Red Cross Knight is, into thinking her capable of spiritual treachery. Therefore they guard her, as he does not, with a perfect faithfulness that underscores, by contrast, his willful, foolish, shameful doubts.

The first of her protectors, the lion she meets while wandering in the woods, though of its nature wrathful, bows instinctively to Una's virtue, and appoints itself, unshakably, her guardian. His native impulse, like that of the lion bearing Wrath in the procession of the Seven Deadly sins (4.33), is to attack, enraged. And he does attack, intending "To have attonce devour her tender corse." But miraculously, he finds his "His bloody rage aswaged with remorse, And, with the sight amazd, forgat his furious force" (3.5), and submits himself to his intended victim, "in yielded pride and proud submission" (3.6). The contrast between this behavior and the willful fickleness of the Red Cross Knight is so stark not even Una can forbear to note it.

> "The Lyon, Lord of everie beast in field,"
> Quoth she, "his princely puissance doth abate,
> And mightie proud to humble weake does yield,
> Forgetfull of the hungry rage, which late
> Him prickt, in pittie of my sad estate:
> But he, my Lyon, and my noble Lord,
> How does he find in cruell hart to hate
> Her, that him lov'd, and ever most adord
> As the God of my life? why hath he me abhord?"
> (3.7)

Though she cannot quite bear to admit it, her questions are rhetorical, because all explanations of her beloved's behavior, especially when juxtaposed to the behavior of the lion, obviously condemn him. The lion, by nature unable to reason, nonetheless grasps the "beautie . . . And simple truth" (3.6) of Una, transcends itself, and remains, until it dies protecting her (3.41–42), "as a strong gard Of her chast person" (3.9). By contrast, his reason blinded "with rage" (2.5), the Red Cross Knight willfully abandons her, flying "with wrath and fiery fierce disdaine" (2.8) to the company of a whore, ridiculously unaware that his heart has hardened, that a paragon of virtue still, with diminishing justification, adores him as the God of her life, and that he abhors her utterly without cause.

Her second protectors respond to her precisely as the lion does, transcending their natures in sensing her preeminence, and instinctively devoting themselves to her service. Licentious by nature, the "Fauns and Satyres" (6.7) who rescue her from Sansloy, thunder-struck by a loveliness whose deeper meaning they lack the intelligence to understand, but whose implications for their conduct they instantly, though only intuitively, grasp, forgetting themselves submit to her at once, steadfastly intent on securing her from harm. A "rude, mishapen, monstrous rablement" (6.8), in almost every circumstance "wyld" (6.9) and "barbarous" (6.12), dazzled by "her beautie bright" (6.9) they are suddenly, though a "salvage nation" (6.11), filled with "compassion . . . pity and unwonted ruth" (6.11), and, laying aside their "rustick horror" (6.11), bow down before her (6.12) and "worship her as Queene" (6.13). Their master, "old Sylvanus" (6.7), to whom they escort her, is as impressed. His first response is, of course, lustful. Gazing at her, he "burnt in his intent" (6.15). That fire, however, is soon banked by a confused amazement that guarantees her safety, even from him. She so far eclipses all of his lovers (6.15) that he cannot decide who she is. Sometimes he half-imagines she is Venus, but realizes she cannot be, because "Venus never had so sober mood." And she is not Diana, whom sometimes she seems also to resemble (6.16). But that she is a goddess of some sort, or some semblance of the "flowre of fayth and beautie excellent" (6.15) he cannot conceptualize he somehow senses. And therefore, apparently to him, as to his cohort, she is an astonishing presence, to be protected and revered. She is certainly not, as to the Red Cross Knight, a creature capable of disloyalty, lust, or deceit. To the satyrs' credit, and to his shame, that possibility never occurs to them.

The third and last of Una's protectors underscores indirectly the dangers the satyrs could have posed for her, and underscores yet again the power of her beauty—the embodiment of her spiritual excellence—to inspire devotion. "A Satyres sonne" (6.21), in recounting his own conception through rape, Satyrane offers a cautionary view of what Una might have suffered from his kinsmen. His mother, seeking her errant husband, was seen one day in the woods by a satyr, who

> chaunst her wandring for to find;
> And, kindling coles of lust in brutish eye,
> The loyall linkes of wedlocke did unbinde,

And made her person thrall unto his beastly kind.
(6.22)

Only the lasting respect she commands from everyone (except, ironically, the Red Cross Knight) with even an instinctive impulse to decency secures Una from the outrage suffered by Satyrane's mother. It also assures the fealty of Satyrane, who removes her, at her request, from the salvage nation, and battles Sansloy, when "that proud Sarazin" suddenly reappears, "the memory Of his leud lusts, and late attempted sin" (6.46) revived, burning once again to assault Una's virtue.

Because Satyrane is closer in character to the Red Cross Knight than of Una's other protectors, his conduct is perhaps an especially galling rebuke to the Knight. But it is neither a more explicit nor a more forceful rebuke. Because he is "a noble warlike knight . . . Plain, faithfull, true, and enimy of shame," a warrior who "ever lov'd to fight for Ladies right" (6.22), the contrast between his protectiveness and his compeer's willful neglect of duty constitutes a particularly stinging indictment. But the other contrasts—between the conduct of the Red Cross Knight and that of the lion, and of the satyrs—argue as openly and as powerfully against him, as does the evidence of Una's enduring love, that his stupid, willful, spiritual waverings diminish him severely, and warrant the mockery he unwittingly endures.

The argument is completed by a theological fact to which he remains consistently blind: that Providence helps those whose faith remains firm. The contrast between the evidence of this fact in Una's adventures and the absence of equivalent evidence in his misadventures closes the dossier of rebuke against him.

Completely defenseless because abandoned by her knight, Una is at once provided with the lion that protects her against all danger until it is destroyed by Sansloy. At that moment in unprecedented peril, because for the first time threatened by a degenerate passion, Sansloy's "lust" (3.41), and no means of rescue apparent, as she cries out pitifully the question is asked, "Who now is left to keepe the forlorne maid From raging spoile of lawlesse victors will?" (3.43) To all appearances, no one is left, and the forlorne maid is therefore doomed. Finding that blandishments, which he first attempts, have no effect, Sansloy resolves to force himself upon her. But is it possible—theologically possible—that Una will be raped?

Ah heavens! that doe this hideous act behold,

> And heavenly virgin thus outraged see,
> How can ye vengeance just so long withhold,
> And hurle not flashing flames upon that Paynim bold?
> (6.5)

To rescue her no "witt of mortal wight Can now devise" an adequate plan. God, however, can, and does. "Eternal providence, exceeding thought, Where none appeares can make her selfe a way" (6.7). Apparently for no reason, but in fact in response to the will of God, the satyrs appear, and Una is safe, basically because she deserves to be safe. Her faith perfect, she is provided, at need, with protection always adequate. For wandering in the woods, and for combatting the relatively trivial evil of Corceca, Abessa and Kirkrapine (3.16–23), the lion is protection enough. To neutralize the far more serious evil of lust, the band of "rude, mishapen, monstrous" (6.8) satyrs, far more powerful than the lion, are adequate. And to rescue Una in turn from the satyrs, who cannot, despite her best efforts, be cured of the profound evil of idolatry (6.19), the most powerful of her protectors, a noble knight, Satyrane, is provided. In no circumstance will perfect faith be abandoned. The implication for the Red Cross Knight is unmistakable. He has stupidly abandoned Una; God, in His infinite wisdom, has not abandoned her. His own faith perilously weak, God seems temporarily to have abandoned him.

In the face of the total rebuke to him, and of the mockery it warrants, if he is not to be dismissed as at least in potential a hero, it is necessary to preserve as much of his stature as, given his descent towards self-destruction, can be preserved. The effort to do so centers largely upon the argument that his enemies are cunning and powerful enough to dupe almost anyone; an argument presented on two occasions, but undermined by a forceful statement of the counter-argument.

That Archimago can fool almost anyone is clear. Having cunningly "divided into double parts" the guests at his hermitage, he boasts with cause about "his devilish arts, That had such might over true meaning hearts" (2.9). His power "by his mighty science" to assume "As many formes and shapes in seeming wise, As ever Proteus to himself could make" (2.10) is especially formidable. Una's failure to recognize him when he appears during her wanderings is understandable. Disguised as her beloved (3.26–32), "when he sate upon his courser free, Saint George himselfe ye would have deemed him to be" (2.11). And when he appears as "a weary wight forwandring by the way" (6.34) to devastate her with the news that her beloved is dead, neither she nor Satyrane suspects deceit. Duessa also is difficult to discover. By her own boastful admission "I, that do seem not I . . . the daughter of Deceipt and Shame" (5.26), she confuses even Night, who, though almost grudgingly, admires her skill:

> "In that fayre face
> The false resemblaunce of Deceipt, I wist,
> Did closely lurke; yet so true-seeming grace
> It carried, that I scarse in darksome place
> Could it discerne, though I the mother bee
> Of falsehood, and roote of Duessaes race."
> (5.27)

That duplicity capable of deceiving the "most aunctient Grandmother of all," a creature who grasped even "the secrets of the world unmade" (5.22), should be capable of deceiving the Red Cross Knight is understandable. In fact, the question is asked rhetorically, could anyone withstand her craftiness in evil?

> What man so wise, what earthly witt so ware,
> As to discry the crafty cunning traine,
> By which deceipt doth maske in visour faire,
> And cast her colours, died deepe in graine,
> To seeme like truth, whose shape she well can faine,
> And fitting gestures to her purpose frame,
> The guiltlesse man with guile to entertaine?
> Great maistresse of her art was that false Dame,
> The false Duessa, cloked with Fidessaes name.
> (7.1)

This question, asked a moment before the Red Cross Knight, in punishment of his self-debasement in lust and pride, is crushed by Orgoglio, is the most formidable effort to extenuate—indeed, almost to excuse—his trespass. It does not, unfortunately for his reputation, succeed. The description of him at this point as "guiltlesse" is far too generous, as the evidence thus far presented shows; in particular, the evidence that occasions irony. Almost all of that evidence is embedded in drama, that is almost always more weighty than statement. And the statement is undercut long before it appears, by a warning issued to the Red Cross Knight as he rides with Duessa towards the House of Pride.

Young knight whatever, that does arms professe,
And through long labours huntest after fame,
Beware of fraud, beware of ficklenesse,
In choice, and chaunge of thy deare-loved Dame,
Least thou of her believe too lightly blame,
And rash misweening doe thy hart remove:
For unto knight there is no greater shame
Then lightnesse and inconstancie in love:
That doth this Redcrosse knights' ensample plainly prove.
(4.1)

Because this indictment of the Red Cross Knight, presented towards the outset of his career of self-debasement, reverberates throughout it, he cannot, towards its close, be excused as the dupe of even so diabolical a deceiver as Duessa. Neither in her first appearance nor in her behavior in the House of Pride is she especially cunning, or difficult to descry; and nothing about her seems like truth. The Red Cross Knight is deceived because he is young and fickle, because he blames Una too lightly, because he is rash and therefore misweening, because he is light and inconstant in love; and therefore, as his actions unmistakably prove—all of his actions, before and after the indictment is presented—he should, though he does not, feel the most profound shame. The charges against him can be reduced to some degree. But the diabolical cunning of his external enemies and the impulse to pity both innate and potential nobility notwithstanding, they cannot be dismissed.

The effort to deflect attention from him through story-telling essentially unrelated to his career, a device employed only twice, accomplishes almost nothing. Duessa's journey to the underworld, to Night (5.19–44), draws attention completely away from him, as does the recounting of Satyrane's history (6.20–29). But neither interlude allows him to be forgotten for long, or softens for long the total rebuke of the degenerate conduct that has led inevitably, from passion through increasingly unsavory passion, to total and apparently irreversible defeat.

As he is dragged "sencelesse" (7.15) to Orgoglio's dungeon, the rebuke attends him. "Haplesse, hopelesse, and inwardly dismayed" (7.11), deservedly humiliated, imprisoned and mocked, his career from the moment of abandoning Una the incontrovertible witness against him, he inspires pity, in measured degree, because he is innately noble and potentially heroic, but he cannot be otherwise shielded from his own history, that indicts him directly as it unfolds, and indirectly, Una's history juxtaposed to it. His intellect blinded by rage and grief, he abandons her, lightly, rashly, shamefully, preferring to her simplicity and truth the destructive allurements of lust and pride; and, increasingly blind to their increasingly obvious effects and consequences, and therefore, as he should be, increasingly mocked, he descends inevitably through self-abasement to defeat. As he does so, the woman who loves him, totally, ardently, longing only for the delight of his company, seeks him everywhere, surrounded by guardians who protect her—his task—because he has run off, and who appear, in response to her every peril, at the command of God. Against these histories, his own and Una's, his reputation cannot be protected, even by the generously intended but inaccurate assertion that particularly cunning devils have duped him. He lies, senseless, in Orgoglio's dungeon because he deserves to. And if he is rescued, it will be not through his own strength, which is gone, but through the Grace of an infinitely loving God.

That Grace begins its ministration the moment the doors of the dungeon slam shut, operating through increasingly gifted spiritual healers: in turn, Prince Arthur, Una, and the sacred inhabitants of the House of Holiness. Arthur performs two relatively simple tasks, rescuing Una from her only moment of spiritual instability, and rescuing the Red Cross Knight from the dungeon; moreover, his actions and history evoke both rebuke and hope for the Knight, censuring him for the last time, but implying strongly he may yet be capable of heroic action. Una performs the more difficult task of expanding the Knight's consciousness, encouraging him to review and to evaluate his past, the indispensable first step in his spiritual resuscitation. Unfortunately, she is not quite adequate to this task, and in consequence leads him almost to disaster. The various inhabitants of the House of Holiness perform flawlessly the most difficult task, purging the corruption in his soul, and rewarding him afterwards with a vision of Heaven, prophetic insight into his destiny, and knowledge of his royal lineage. The total ministration complete, and the Knight therefore invincible spiritually, in a battle nonetheless profoundly draining he defeats an almost invincible evil, and, a final effort by his old enemies thwarted—with ease this time, because he is complete—he attains, as he should, the reward of Una's love.

THE FAERIE QUEENE (BOOK ONE)

That Grace preserves the Red Cross Knight from destruction in Orgoglio's dungeon, and directs the process of his regeneration, is established at once.

> Ay me! how many perils doe enfold
> The righteous man, to make him daily fall,
> Were not that heavenly grace doth him uphold,
> And stedfast truth acquite him out of all.
> Her love is firme, her care continuall,
> So oft as he, through his own foolish pride
> Or weakness is to sinfull bands made thrall:
> Els should this Redcrosse knight in bands have dyde,
> For whose deliverance she this Prince doth thither guyd.
> (8.1)

Beyond question, "heavenly grace" alone keeps the Red Cross Knight alive in Orgoglio's dungeon; unprotected by her, he would "in bands have dyde" there. Nor is her solicitude confined to the dungeon. She alone will direct his regeneration: "acquite him out of all," and assure his "deliverance." Her motive is, as always, mysterious. She acts in behalf of fallen human beings because, for reasons beyond their grasp, "Her love is firme, her care continuall," and enfold them with an unremitting intensity utterly beyond their imagination. Her agents are various; but all of them are subject entirely to her direction. She guides Prince Arthur to Orgoglio's dungeon, so that his task may be performed. She then guides Una in the performance of her task, and the inhabitants of the House of Holiness in theirs. No act of spiritual reconstruction occurs—or could occur—without her continual love and care. Without her, no one, not even the essentially "righteous man," could hope to survive.

The first of her agents, Prince Arthur, appears at the instant he is needed. Though after hearing of the disaster at Orgoglio's Una is "long tost with stormes," and wanders "many a wood, and . . . many a vale" (7.28) before "At last" (7.29) meeting Arthur, in narrative time she meets him almost immediately after the Red Cross Knight is imprisoned in the dungeon (7.15). Only two short descriptions—of Orgoglio's hideous gift to Deussa (7.16-18), and of Una's grief at the disaster (7.19-28)—intervene. And Arthur's appearance is not accidental. Though apparently Una "chaunced by good hap" (7.29) to meet him, because in a universe governed completely by God's will chance cannot in fact exist the parenthesis that glosses the

Red Cross Knight's collapse against the Tree of Life during the battle which completes his adventures—"It chaunst, (eternall God that chaunce did guide)" (11.45)—glosses also the appearance of Arthur, which is no more fortuitous than the appearance of the lion, that "It fortuned" (3.5) sprang from the woods to protect Una, or the appearance of the satyrs, explicitly ascribed to "Eternall providence" (6.7). Arthur appears because the operation of Grace requires his appearance. And he appears at once because it wishes its ministration to begin at once.

Before he can attend to the Red Cross Knight, Arthur must minister to a credible but surprising deterioration in Una. Her response merely to the sight of the dwarf bearing her beloved's discarded armor is understandable. A woman in love, before the dwarf can attempt to explain "Thrise did she sinke adowne in deadly swownd" (7.24). And though, the explanation absorbed, she "strove to maister sorrowfull assay" (7.27), for a long time afterwards, as might be expected, "evermore, in constant carefull mind, She fedd her wound with fresh renewed bale" (7.28). The effect of that bale is, however, given her history, entirely unexpected: a decline in her faith. Her grief at the defeat of the Red Cross Knight festering secretly, she begins to imagine that he cannot be redeemed by any agency, and in consequence begins to despair. To relieve her, Arthur must therefore gain access to the "secret sorrow" (7.38) underlying her pain, and by allaying it diminish her hopelessness. At first she refuses to discuss the sorrow, convinced that doing so will only deepen it. Predictably, however, Arthur prevails.

> "But griefe," (quoth she) "does greater grow displaid,
> If then it find not helpe, and breeds despaire."
> "Despaire breeds not," (quoth he) "where faith is staid."
> "No faith so fast," (quoth she) "but flesh does paire."
> "Flesh may empaire," (quoth he) "but reason can repaire."
> (7.41)

Because she is essentially healthy, and therefore able, despite her sorrow, to follow Arthur's arguments clearly, her spiritual balance is easily restored. His "goodly reason and well guided speach" impress her mind so quickly and so forcefully that without additional hesitation she unfolds "the secrets of my griefe," before long confident that his "wisdome" or "prowesse" (7.42) will somehow aid her, and relieved that his intelligence and "chearefull words" have swiftly "reviv'd her chearelesse spright" (7.52).

Una comforted, Arthur turns to the second of his tasks, as simple: defeating Orgoglio, and rescuing the Red Cross Knight from his dungeon. That Arthur will prevail against Orgoglio is obvious. Though "An hideous Gaunt, horrible and hye" (7.8), Orgoglio is merely a "monstrous masse of earthly slyme, Puft up with emptie wynd" (7.9), and defeats the Red Cross Knight with ease only because the Red Cross Knight has defeated himself. Arthur, by contrast, at his first appearance seems invincibly warlike (7.29–34), and bears a wondrous diamond shield impervious even to satanic deceit:

> No magicke arts hereof had any might,
> Nor bloody wordes of bold Enchaunters call;
> But all that was not such as seemd in sight
> Before that shield did fade, and suddeine fall.
>
> (7.35)

That against a knight obviously "goodly" (7.29), and possessed of weaponry obviously charmed Orgoglio will stand no chance is clear to Una, who confidently accepts Arthur's invitation, as he dismounts before Orgoglio's castle, to observe him in battle. Earlier, as Satyrane and Sansloy had fought, Una had "fledd farre away, of that proud Paynim sore afrayd" (6.47), prudently unconvinced that Satyrane would prevail. When Arthur, by contrast, "badd the Ladie stay" (8.2), she does so. Although she watches "from farre, In pensive plight and sad perplexitie, the whole atchievement of this doubtfull warre" (8.26), she does not run off, no doubt convinced that Arthur will triumph. This conviction resonates in Orgoglio from the outset; "dismaid" at the sound of the Squire's horn calling him to battle, he hurries from his chambers "With staring countenance sterne, as one astownd, And staggering steps" (8.5). His premonition is wellfounded. Though he fights impressively, he is badly wounded almost at once. Arthur finds time during the battle even to relieve his Squire, in distress. And when he falters, the veil on his wondrous shield is uncovered, "The light whereof, that hevens light did pas" (8.19), striking Duessa's "fruitful-headed beast ... stark blind" (8.20) and unmanning Orgoglio, who "has redd his end In that bright shield" (8.21).

Orgoglio dead, Arthur is appropriately praised by Una as a "fresh budd of vertue springing fast" (8.27), but cautioned unnecessarily. "Your fortune maister eke with governing" (8.28), she instructs him. Nothing in his behavior warrants such instruction. In victory he shows no unbecoming pride. He treats Ignaro with forbearance and respect. Though for a moment annoyed at his "sencelesse speach, and doted ignorance," having observed him carefully "He ghest his nature by his countenance, And calmd his wrath with goodly temperance" (8.34). The "pitteous plaints" (8.38) of The Red Cross Knight "with percing point Of pitty deare his heart . . . thrilled sore" (8.39). And nothing—"nether darknesse fowl, nor filthy bands, Nor noyous smell"—can deter him from the rescue,

> But that with constant zeal and corage bold,
> After longe paines and labors manifold,
> He found the meanes that Prisoner up to reare.
> (8.40)

From first to last, as counselor and as warrior, Arthur behaves perfectly. And thus his presence is an implied rebuke to the behavior of the Red Cross Knight. It also, however, by implication offers hope that the Knight may one day fulfill his potential.

Both the rebuke and the hope derive from the similarity between the men. Both are introduced performing their quintessential tasks: impressively armed, avidly in search, as God's warriors, of evil, confidently, fearlessly, resolved to defeat it. And both are champions of virtuous women, to whom their labors are fervently pledged. As the Red Cross Knight is bound to rescue Una's parents from the dragon that plagues them, so Arthur is bound to succor the woman who in his enchanted dream offered her love, and whom he now forlornly seeks: the "Queene of Faeries," blessed— "happy," in Una's opinion—to have found "Mongst many, one that with his prowesse may Defend thine honour, and thy foes confownd" (8.16). The Red Cross Knight has stumbled badly. The presence of Arthur, who has not, thus shames him, by dramatic contrast underscoring his disastrous self-debasements. At the same time, however, it offers hope. Though exhausted and helpless, the Knight, because essentially like Arthur, may yet prove the object of his gracious Master's particular care.

Una, the second agent of that care, begins her work even before Arthur exits, and continues it thereafter with the best of intentions; however, because her method is faulty, with almost fatal results. Correctly convinced, perhaps in part by her own experience, that a clear assessment of the history that has almost destroyed him is the indispensable first step in the Red Cross Knight's self-reconstruction, Una sets that history before him; but far too vividly, and far too abruptly, for his soul, in its weakened condition, to bear. Beyond question, he must confront his mistakes. But the danger that confronting them all at once, and starkly, may rouse a self-loathing beyond endurance, does not occur to her; nor does she imagine the hideous resolve such self-loathing may provoke.

Una's conviction that self-assessment is therapeutic perhaps derives, at least in part, from its therapeutic effect upon herself. But she neglects to consider that her situation is essentially different from the Red Cross Knight's, in that, unlike him, she is completely sinless; and that therefore a method that strengths her may weaken him—perhaps even provoke him to self-destruction.

As she perhaps recalls, Una was rescued from at least the prospect of despair through the apparently simple expedient of retrospection. Having persuaded her to reason with him, and in consequence to prevent her grief from decaying into despair (7.41), Arthur gently persuades her "to disclose the breach Which love and fortune in her heart had wrought" by recounting her "story sad" (7.42). In consequence her spiritual balance is restored. Because nothing but the recounting (7.43–51) and Arthur's subsequent offer (7.52) of assistance separate Una's intense grief and the revival of her "chearelesse spright" (7.52), it is reasonable to assume that the story, sad itself, prepares her to accept Arthur's offer, and that, looking back, she is perhaps aware of its restorative effect, and concludes that a similar recounting could similarly effect the Red Cross Knight.

The reason it cannot completely eludes her. Because she is sinless, nothing in her history can provoke in her either shame or guilt, and therefore retelling it, especially to someone apparently capable of aiding her, rouses hope. Because she is in love, and forgiving by nature, she prefers to think that the Red Cross Knight was, like herself, the victim of satanic deceit rather than an active, willful participant in sin; and therefore, perhaps, imagines introspection will revive him, as it has revived her. She assures Arthur that "an Enchaunter bad His sence abused, and made him to misdeeme My loyalty" (7.49), that "false Duessa . . . Mine onely foe . . . with her witchcraft, and misseeming sweete, Inveigled him to follow her desires unmeete" (7.50), and that therefore Arthur must "Ne let that wicked woman scape away, For she it is, that did my Lord bethrall" (8.28). That the Red Cross Knight is, at the minimum, blameworthy never occurs to her. And therefore the possibility never occurs to her that confronting his history may rouse in him impulses indispensable to self-reformation, but dangerous if not skillfully governed. Because she knows nothing of such impulses—of guilt and shame—or of the potentially morbid complexity of conscience, their spiritual source, she shows him at once, and without preparation, the cause of his fall, apparently confident that the insight will strengthen him.

It almost kills him. Lying exhausted in Orgoglio's dungeon, he petitions for a quick death; but only, his conscience still dormant, to end the agony of "dying every stound" while yet living "perforce in balefull darkenesse bound." His "piteous plaintes and dolours" in the dungeon do not bespeak his willingness to acknowledge responsibility for his plight. He wants to die not because he has, in his opinion, done anything wrong, but because for "three Moones" (8.38) he has been locked in darkness, deprived of pleasure; including, presumably, the pleasure of Duessa, about whose nature he still knows nothing. He petitions not, in fact, for death, but only, self-pityingly, for release from internment.

The deeper petition—the cry, from the depths of his being, for death—begins only as he is compelled to acknowledge that in significant measure he has betrayed himself, and in consequence to confront, long before he is prepared to do so, an unendurable sense of guilt and shame; a sense whose very existence he fails, through a dangerous interval, to notice.

The acknowledgment and the self-confrontation are forced upon him, ironically, by Una. Blind to the possible consequences of her action, and impelled, no doubt, at least in part by a jealous wish finally to discredit a rival's love, against the prudent but inconsistent advice of Arthur she insists that Duessa be stripped naked in the presence of the Red Cross Knight. Arthur cautions Una sensibly that "The things, that grievous were to doe, or beare . . . to renew . . . breeds no delight." Unhappily, he also directs the attention of the Red Cross Knight to the most grievous of those things, "that wicked woman in your sight, The roote of all your care and wretched plight" (8.45), and asks if he wants her killed or not. Una, disregarding Arthur's caution, and the fact that his question was not directed at her, insists upon an option not suggested by Arthur, and profoundly dangerous to the Red Cross Knight's health: that the wicked woman be stripped "naked all" (8.46), so that at last the Knight can see, beyond the possibility of continued self-delusion, who she is.

She could not have served the man she loves less effectively. A moment removed from Orgolgio's dungeon, "A ruefull spectacle of death and ghastly drere" (8.45), unable to stand, unable to view "th' unwonted sunne," his body shrivelled, "all his vitall powres Decayed" (8.51), as she herself notes, of his very "selfe . . . berobbed" (8.52), how can he be expected to endure the enormity of his own sin, set suddenly and with inescapable starkness before his eyes? The sight of Duessa naked is so ugly it cannot be completely described by a "chaster Muse" (8.48) even to a disinterested audience. Yet Una insists that it be fully observed by the Red Cross Knight in his most debilitated moment, and that he absorb, at once and unflinchingly, its total significance.

> "Such then" (said Una,) "as she seemeth here,
> Such is the face of falshood: such the sight
> Of fowle Duessa, when her borrowed light
> Is laid away, and counterfesaunce knowne."
> (8.49)

It is an awful mistake. Burdening a sinner almost too weak to stand with full disclosure of the willful, ludicrous, shameful misapprehensions that plunged his soul into increasingly serious and obvious evil, increasingly to his own detriment and the detriment of a loving and innocent woman he had pledged in sacred honor to defend must, if the sinner is by nature decent, rouse in him, sooner or later, a self-loathing he may well be hard-pressed to survive. And the threat to his survival will be compounded if, for any significant interval, the self-loathing remains completely unnoticed.

And such an interval does occur, because Una, though aware of her beloved's debility, fails to trace it to its hidden source, and therefore gravely underestimates its strength. She and "that faire crew of knights" remain in Orgoglio's castle for a time, "To rest them selves, and weary powres repaire" (8.50), and leave only

> when their powres, empayrd through labor long,
> With due repast they had recured well,
> And that weake captive wight now wexed strong.
> (9.2)

Even when they set forth, "weighing the decayed plight And shrunken synewes of her chosen knight," she recognizes that he is "yet weake and wearie" (9.20). But she fails (as he does) to grasp the subterranean source of the weakness: the morbid festering in his soul of conscience. And unaware therefore of its virulence, she cannot protect him against it as it surfaces, intent on his life.

The failure is understandable. As they travel together, no sign of his conscience appears. The Red Cross Knight, still completely inexperienced in introspection, in all likelihood is unaware it exists. His usual business is fighting evil, and perhaps restored, in his opinion, to health, he returns as a matter of course to that business. Una also, for whatever reason, is not alert to conscience as a danger. Therefore when it surfaces with the appearance of Sir Trevisan, and begins its assault, it does so unobserved, and therefore almost to fatal effect.

Its strength is astounding. Though its effects and method are fully revealed before the assault, the Red Cross Knight is not in consequence empowered to confront it, nor does Una realize, until almost too late, that he cannot oppose it unassisted.

Neither Trevisan's unhinged condition nor his unmistakable warning moves the Red Cross Knight to caution; to the contrary, they rouse him to indignation and to almost fatal rash action. Though still "armed" (9.21), Trevisan flees as though from "Infernall furies" (9.24), their near-success against him evident in the "hempen rope" (9.22) still around his neck. His heart "blood-frosen," his "boldnes" (9.25) crushed by "uncouth dread" (9.22), obviously "of him selfe . . . afrayd" (9.23), before he speaks he has issued, through his appearance, a dire warning that his speech compounds. He and Sir Trewin were attacked, he says, by "A man of hell that calls himselfe Despayre" (9.28), who preyed upon their disappointment in love, and whose only weapon was "wounding words," which he used to catastrophic effect:

> He pluckt from us all hope of dew reliefe,
> That earst us held in love of lingring life;
> Then hopelesse, hartlesse, gan the cunning thief
> Perswade us dye, to stint all further strife.
> (9.29)

If the Red Cross Knight is similarly vulnerable, Trevisan warns, "like infirmity like chanunce may bear" (9.30).

But that is impossible, the Knight responds. Uninstructed by Trevisan's appearance, he disregards his speech as well, waving aside Despair's method with the rhetorical question, "How may a man . . . with idle speach Be wonne to spoyle the Castle of his health?" (9.31) Obviously, in his opinion, he cannot be. And so he rushes headlong into the miscreant's cave, confident that against mere idle speech he must prevail.

He escapes with his life, but only barely. By gradually, subtly, and apparently in kindness drawing his conscience forth to consciousness, Despair argues, as his most generous friend, that only death suits his history: that, the shame and guilt hidden thus far from himself acknowledged, he will realize that he no longer deserves to live; that he must rescue himself from the deepening shame and the deepening guilt that would inevitably poison, more and more horribly, continued life; and that the means of self-rescue have been set, in a gesture of compassion, before him. Because he proceeds at once to conscience, Despair deflects the Knight's zeal at once. And because he proceeds only gradually from a general to a starkly personal discussion of guilt and shame, the lethal intent beneath his cunning show of compassion never becomes apparent to his victim.

Having entered the cave, Sir Trewin's corpse, still warm, before him, burning with "firie zeal . . . in courage bold Him to avenge," the Red Cross Knight asks Despair indignantly whether justice does not demand "With thine owne blood to price his blood, here shed in sight?" (9.37) The question is "foolish" and "rash," he replies, because justice obviously demands that in general "he should dye who merites not to live," and demanded in particular the death of Sir Trewin, driven to despair by "his owne guilte mind, deserving death," and in consequence anxious in death to find "ease, that liveth here uneath" (9.38). The mere mention of a guilty mind silences the Red Cross Knight long enough for Despair to argue that, perhaps unconsciously, having committed some sin as vile as Trewin's, he also longs for "eternall rest And happy ease," regrets bitterly that he "further from it daily" (9.40) wanders, and has censured Despair for magnanimously helping Trewin to achieve it because he is "Most envious" and perversely "joyest in the woe thou hast" (9.39). Confronted suddenly with his own conscience, the Red Cross Knight "much wondred at his suddeine wit" (9.41). As the confrontation is still oblique, he still manages a sensible response: that God, and not human beings, should decide when they die (941). But this response, a single sentence of only three lines, barely interrupts Despair's argument, that proceeds quickly through a strained theological assertion that suicide is destiny (9.52) to the insistence that whoever "hath missed the right way, The further he doth goe, the further he doth stray" (9.43); an insistence particularized with catastrophic effect as Despair turns to the Red Cross Knight's past. Since he unquestionably has missed the right way, Despair asserts, addressing him directly, "Thou, wretched man, of death hast greatest need, If in true ballaunce thou wilt weigh thy state" (9.45). And to aid in the balancing, he sets before him, to crushing effect, the weights that must be placed in the scales. Is "the dungeon deepe" (9.45)

> wherein he lay not weight enough?
> "Is not enough, that to this Lady mild
> Thou falsed hast thy faith with perjuree
> And sold thy selfe to serve Duessa vild,
> With whom in al abuse thou hast thy selfe defild?"
> (9.46)

Finally, his conscience is before him, unendurably. Completely unaware of Despair's motive in exposing it to his consciousness, he stares at the details of his guilt and shame, and, finding them unbearable, rushes away in disgust from himself, towards the easeful solution of his magnanimous friend, whose "subtile tong" (9.31) has done the work Trevisan warned in vain it would do.

> The knight was much enmoved with his speach,
> That as a swords poynt through his hart did perse,
> And in his conscience made a secrete breach,
> Well knowing trew all that he did reherse,
> And to his fresh remembraunce did reverse
> The ugly vew of his deformed crimes.
> (9.48)

The lethal consequence accrues at once. In his desperation "weake and fraile, Whiles trembling horror did his conscience daunt, And hellish anguish did his soule assaile" (9.49), able to see "nought but death before his eies" (9.50), he takes the dagger held out by Despair, and "At last, resolv'd to work his finall smart" (9.51), lifts up his hand to destroy himself.

That Una intercedes only at this last possible moment demonstrates that, because of a limitation of insight, she is not fit to aid him further. That Despair is an evil is evident both from his appearance, and from his arguments, that Una, standing with the Red Cross Knight, hears. It must therefore be the case that, until the last possible moment, she does not understand the danger those arguments pose to the Knight; otherwise, she would beyond question have opposed them sooner. For too long, she fails to suspect that his conscience is active, or that it may be turning morbidly against him. That Trevisan's story does not provoke such suspicion is understandable. Despair did not attack his conscience, or that of Sir Trewin.

Both men were driven to "bitter byting grief" by disappointment in love (9.29); Sir Trewin by a "proud" woman who "joyd to see her lover languish and lament" (9.27), and Sir Trevisan by circumstances not specified. Neither knight seems to have participated through willful transgression in his own descent towards self-destruction. Therefore Una should not be criticized for failing to associate the attack they endured with a potential danger to The Red Cross Knight. But the nature of Despair's attack upon the Knight is clear from the outset, and should have roused Una to protest at once. As has been shown, Despair focuses at once upon conscience; and, though subtly and gradually, yet clearly enough upon the conscience of the Red Cross Knight in particular. Una nonetheless permits his crushing arguments to unfold, neither opposing their defects nor encouraging the Knight to action. By simply remaining at his side in silence almost to the instant of irreversible disaster, she demonstrates that, for the first time, spiritual counsellors more gifted than herself must be brought to his aid.

The dagger wrested from his hand, Una at last understands clearly the underlying cause of his almost unendurable spiritual anguish, and the only effective means of uprooting it. For the first time "enraged rife" (9.52), she asks heatedly, "In heavenly mercies hast thou not a part?" (9.53). The question is rhetorical; as Una knows, "Where justice growes, there grows eke greater grace, The which doth quench the brond of hellish smart" (9.53). The hellish smart, she now understands, is her beloved's conscience, diseased because uninstructed in Grace. Of course he has sinned. Of course conscience must therefore plague him, or he will never be whole. But as it does so, it itself must grasp, and assure him, that to even the darkest, the most hideous of sins, the Grace of God—heaven's mercy showered mysteriously upon the undeserving—is always, miraculously, more than sufficient.

Thus, to be cured, the Red Cross Knight must be taught the Grace of God; not the theoretical construct, but the reality from whose radiance alone he can draw the strength somehow to endure an excruciating process of self-reconstruction that will leave him at last spiritually complete. Through proper instruction, this reality must be set at the center of his being, and the lessons that flow inevitably from it patiently absorbed.

Una cannot offer such instruction. She can, however, bring him to it: to an "aunciant house . . . Renowmd throughout the world for sacred lore And pure unspotted life" (10.3), where the last, and by far the most gifted, of his spiritual healers, the inhabitants of the House of Holiness, await him. Empowered "thorough grace" (10.1), they function flawlessly, first instructing the Red Cross Knight in the religious mysteries upon which all melioration depends, then leading him, compassionately but with fixed resolve, through the process of self-reconstruction, and rewarding him, finally, with a dazzling vision of heaven itself, a prophetic statement of his place there as saint, and a deeply flattering recounting of his lineage.

To assure the sense will not linger that Una was insufficient as a counsellor to her Knight, she is attended, as she steps, for the moment, aside, by a splendid and richly deserved encomium. Dame Caelia herself, the mistress "grave and hore" of the House of Holiness, "Whosoe onely joy was to relieve the needes Of wretched soules, and helpe the helpelesse pore" (10.3), embraces her, exclaiming,

> "O happy earth,
> Whereon thy innocent feet doe ever tread!
> Most vertuous virgin, borne of hevenly berth,
> That, to redeeme thy woefull parents head,
> From tyrans rage and ever-dying dread,
> Hast wandred through the world now long a day,
> Yett seassest not thy weary soles to lead."
> (10.9)

This tribute paid, the healing of the Red Cross Knight begins, with instruction in two articles of faith upon which all spiritual progress depends. At Una's behest, he is into the "schoolehous plaste" (10.18) of "the eldest" (10.12) of Caelia's daughters, Fidelia (Faith). She teaches the indispensable first lessons, her text the "sacred Booke, with blood ywritt, That none could read except she did them teach," her insights "heavenly documents . . . That weaker witt of man could never reach; Of God; of grace; of justice; of free-will" (10.19). She teaches, in short, lessons beyond the range of human intelligence: that God exists; that Grace attends the stumblings of human beings; that God is just; that human beings are free to choose between evil and good. None of these lessons can be taught to the satisfaction of the human mind. But until they are learned, in despite of the mind, the human soul cannot be cleansed. Until the Red Cross Knight is taught by Fidelia simply to believe that the mysterious, infinite love of God embraces and irradiates all of reality, he cannot understand against whom he has sinned, and therefore to whom he must render his account.

But that understanding can itself be dangerous, because it rouses conscience more starkly than ever; and therefore conscience, once again near desperation, must once again be soothed, not this time for a moment by Una, but lastingly, by a second article of faith. Never before has the Red Cross Knight understood so clearly that God loves without reserve; but never before has he been, in consequence, so "Greev'd with remembrance of his wicked wayes." In fact, "prickt with anguish of his sins so sore . . . he desirde to end his wretched dayes; So much the dart of sinfull guilt the soule dismays" (10.21) him. But the guilt may now be rendered less desperate than in the Cave of Despair by the instruction of Fidelia's sister, Speranza (Hope). From her the Knight gains "comfort sweet," the hope that the Grace of God may be conferred upon him: that God may love without reserve *him*.

Though sweet, it is a tenuous comfort. That he feels it is fortunate; "Els had his sinnes, so great and manifold, Made him forget all that Fidelia told" (10.22). But as nothing has yet spurred him to action, his underlying malady—"that disease of grieved conscience" (10.23)—remains untouched:

> the cause and root of all his ill,
> Inward corruption and infected sin,
> Not purg'd nor heald, behind remained still,
> And festering sore did rankle yett within.
> (10.25)

Faith and Hope having, however, also taken root, a lasting cure is, for the first time, possible; and, with his active cooperation, is "in short space" (10.27) effected. The process he engages with the "Leach . . . Patience" (10.23) to endure is so painful that "often . . . like a Lyon he would cry and rore, And rend his flesh, and his own synewes eat" (10.28). But he does endure it; and an old process—"Amendment"(10.26), "Penaunce . . . Remorse . . . Repentance" (10.27)—produces an old, salvational result. Spiritually whole, he is returned by Patience and Repentance to Una, "Who, joyous of his cured conscience," rewards him with her first kiss.

He has earned it; as he has earned the additional rewards at once provided: the assurance that he will prevail against Una's worst enemy, a vision of Heaven, the splendid news, prophetically imparted, of his eventual beatification, and the flattering news of his royal descent. Completely "recover'd" (10.29), therefore whole, and in consequence prepared to rescue Una's parents, he is at last in actuality, not merely in potential, capable of opposing the most powerful of evils. To signify his decisive growth in strength, the third of Caelia's daughters, Charissa (Charity), appears. The emblem of fecundity in good deeds, she undertakes, at Una's behest, to school the Knight in the means of producing them (10.33), thus in effect foreshadowing his triumph over the dragon holding Una's parents hostage. In addition, as the most exquisite of rewards, Charissa "to heaven . . . teacheth him the ready path" (10.33). At her behest, he is led by Mercy along a difficult, "narrow way" (10.34) to "an holy Hospitall," where, surrounded by the "seven Bead-men" (10.36), she instructs him with such "great industree" that soon

> so perfect he became,
> That, from the first unto the last degree,
> His mortall life he learned had to frame
> In holy righteousnesse, without rebuke or blame.
> (10.45)

Thus etherealized, he is led, once again by Mercy, to the "sacred chappell" where the "holy man" (10.46) Contemplation resides, rapt by such "Great grace" that "God he often saw from heavens hight" (10.47). At Mercy's behest, Contemplation leads him along "A little path that was both steepe and long, Which to a goodly Citty led his vew . . . the Citty of the greate king" (10.45), wherein he sees, in settings so lovely "earthly tong Cannot describe, nor wit of man can tell" (10.45), angels descended "From highest heven in gladsome companee" wandering about "As commonly as frend does with his frend" (10.51) In this place, his earthly work done, he will wander as commonly, Contemplation informs him, "emongst those Saints whom thou dost see . . . a Saint . . . Saint George of mery England" (10.51).

Dazzled by the vision and by the prospect of sainthood, The Red Cross Knight understandably wonders if he may be excused from fulfilling his obligations to Una, and simply enter heaven at once. Though that is impossible, Contemplation assures him (10.62–63), he may wish to know, as a gift in parting, that, though "now accompted Elfins sonne" (10.60), in fact he is descended "from ancient race Of Saxon kinges" (10.65) and thus by lineage as well as by nature noble.

The knowledge of his lineage, though no doubt flattering, cannot heighten the Red Cross Knight's self-esteem. The total ministration to his soul complete, his self-esteem is complete. He is complete. And therefore God's, Grace continuing to attend him, he cannot be defeated by any evil, however potent. The attention devoted by Arthur, Una, and the saintly inhabitants of the House of Holiness to his ailing soul, plagued by himself and by external evil, has driven from it sickened conscience. That root

The Faerie Queene (Book One)

malady cured, and the recovered soul enraptured with vision and flattered with sainthood and royal descent, no force of evil can hope to defeat him, no temptation, however cunning, to seduce him. He moves towards the dragon at Una's palace, and to the final assault of Archimago and Duessa, God with him, impervious to defeat.

That the victory over the dragon, though a foregone conclusion, nonetheless proves almost impossibly difficult underscores in closing the overwhelming significance of Grace. Never has the Red Cross Knight been stronger. Never, nonetheless, has his need of God's assistance been greater. The dragon is almost invincible. Therefore, except as God shields him, his peril, his own strength notwithstanding, is dire.

On the first day of the three-day battle, he is almost touched by both fear and despair. The mere sight of his horrific opponent makes "the Redcrosse knight nigh shake with feare" (11.15). The fire flaming from its enraged mouth "Him all amazd, and almost made afeard" (11.26). And by nightfall he feels so "Faynt, wearie, sore, emboyled, grieved, brent" that "death oft he did desire" (11.28). Not far from defeat, he falls back, "It fortuned" (11.29), into "The well of life" (11.29). This apparent fortune is, beyond question, as elsewhere (3.5,7.29,11.45), the operation of Grace. The dragon "clapt his yron wings as victor" (11.31) in vain. And Una's prayers through her nightlong vigil (11.32), though welcome, are needless. Completely revived by the waters of the well, the Red Cross Knight awakens in the morning in theological fact "new-borne" (11.34), "baptized" by the "holy water" (11.36). On the second day once again almost defeated in battle, he is once again saved, apparently by chance. This time, however, the meaning of chance is explicitly glossed. His body almost scorched by the dragon's fire, "It chaunct, (eternall God that chaunce did guide)" (11.45) he stumbles back against "The tree of life" (11.46). Once again, Una's nightlong prayers are needless. The chaunce is God, his indomitable aid. As even the dragon understands the third morning, watching in dismay the Knight "himselfe so freshly reare, As if late fight had nought him damnifyde" (11.52), his situation is hopeless. Against the Red Cross Knight alone he might have prevailed. Against God he is doomed.

The dragon destroyed, the Knight is tendered the dazzling reward he has earned not only for freeing Una's parents, but for reshaping his soul to enduring excellence. Strong, through God's Grace, at the broken places, he is fit, for the first time, to gaze on the "blazing brightnesse" of Una's literally indescribable "celestial" beauty (11.23), and to be bound to that brightness in wedded bliss.

At last, because he has earned it, he has everything. And because he is whole, and perfectly betrothed, the final assault upon his soul, though by enemies profoundly strong in evil, poses no threat. He and Una understand it at once, and almost without effort shrug it off (12.25–35). A woman with a message, he informs Una's parents, who intends to disrupt the banns is a witch, infamous for satanic duplicity. And the cunning messenger, Una informs them, is the black magician Archimago, in disguise. Nothing could be simpler than to discover them, now; nothing simpler than to disarm and imprison them.

The banns are renewed. Una's father ties "to the knight his daughter deare . . . With sacred rites and vowes for ever to abyde" (12.36). And the enchanted groom "Thrise happy man . . . himselfe did hold,"

> Possessed of his Ladies hart and hand;
> And ever, when his eie did her behold,
> His heart did seeme to melt in pleasures manifold.
> (12.40)

The way to her heart and hand has been long. Betrayed by passion, willful, blinded, he stumbled, and fell, and, but for the Grace of God, would beyond question have died along the way, his mission aborted, his lineage, his nobility, his calling disgraced. Though self-abandoned, for reasons beyond human understanding he was not abandoned by the God of Christianity, who lifted him gently, guided his painful return to life, opened his eyes for a moment to heaven and prophetically to his beatification, and stood by, as his shield, through the desperate battle that left him at the canopy with his celestial bride, at last the warrior and the servant of God he was meant, from the outset of his journey, to be.

Chapter Three

Macbeth

THE HALLUCINATORY FRAGMENT OF a scene that introduces the three witches (1.1.1–12)[1] establishes at once and beyond dispute that they are profoundly dangerous; that self-protective human beings therefore interact with them at their peril; and that Macbeth in particular, whom they intend to meet (1.1.8)

> When the hurlyburly's done,
> When the battle's lost and won
> (1.1.3–4)

interacts with them at his peril.

Their second appearance (1.3.1–78) minimizes only slightly the danger they pose. Because his wife does nothing more than scorn the request of one of them for chestnuts, a sailor is tortured mercilessly:

> I'll drain him dry as hay:
> Sleep shall neither night nor day
> Hang upon his penthouse lid;
> He shall live a man forbid.
> Weary sev'nnights nine times nine,
> Shall he dwindle, peak, and pine:
> Though his bark cannot be lost,
> Yet it shall be tempest-tost.
> (1.3.18–25)

That both of the witches' first appearances are dire warnings to self-protective human beings is thus manifest.

1. William Shakespeare, *Macbeth* (London: Arden, 1966).

That in their second appearance they encounter not only Macbeth, whom they are seeking, but also Banquo, whom they have not mentioned, underscores the essential difference between the two men: that though for a moment he is tempted, Banquo protects himself by fear consonant with Christian faith, whereas Macbeth, a devotee from the outset of the Devil, not only does not fear them, but commands them to talk with him.

The instant they appear, Banquo is fearful and suspicious of them, and though tempted for a moment by their apparent largesse to Macbeth, by the time they vanish understands that they are emissaries of the Devil.

The fear and suspicion strike him at once, and prompt his virtually rhetorical questions:

> What are these,
> So wither'd and so wild in their attire,
> That look not like th' inhabitants o' th' earth,
> And yet are on it? Live you? And are you aught
> That man may question? You seem to understand me,
> By each a once her choppy finger laying
> Upon her skinny lips: you should be women,
> And yet you beards forbid me to interpret
> That you are so.
> (1.3.39–47)

Their bizarre attire and features are the visible facts that prompt his essential questions: Are the witches indeed inhabitants of the earth—that is to say, human? Are they alive? And may human beings safely interact with them? And those questions he almost certainly regards as rhetorical.

As he is considering them, at Macbeth's command the witches burst out talking by showering upon him apparently splendid prophecies:

> 1 *Witch.* All hail, Macbeth! Hail to thee, Thane of Glamis!
> 2 *Witch.* All hail, Macbeth! Hail to thee, Thane of Cawdor!
> 3 *Witch.* All hail, Macbeth! that shalt be king hereafter.
> (1.3.48–50)

For a moment Banquo wavers, asks, and is told what prophesies will apparently ennoble him:

> 1 *Witch.* Hail!

2 Witch. Hail!

3 Witch. Hail!

1 Witch. Lesser than Macbeth, and greater.

2 Witch. Not so happy, yet much happier.

3 Witch. Thou shalt get kings, though thou be none:

(1.3.62–67)

By the moment afterwards, however, when the witches have vanished, his self-protective caution has returned, and he is asking, again in all likelihood rhetorically, whether they have fed himself and Macbeth "the insane root That takes the reason prisoner?" (1.3.84–85)

A moment later, when Angus and Rosse enter and address Macbeth as Thane of Cawdor (1.3.100–106), all of Banquo's doubts about who the witches are, and whom they serve, disappear with an exclamation beyond question rhetorical: "What! Can the Devil speak true?"(1.3.107) Thereafter he is unambiguously God's servant, as his first undertaking—to warn Macbeth of the peril he confronts—demonstrates. To Macbeth's assurance that, because the witches predicted correctly that he would become Thane of Cawdor, Banquo can trust their prediction that *his* children will become kings (1.3.118–120), Banquo replies with a dire warning:

That, trusted home,

Might yet enkindle you unto the crown,

Besides the Thane of Cawdor. But 'tis strange:

That o'ftentimes to win us to our harm,

The instruments of Darkness tell us truths;

Win us with honest trifles, to betray's

In deepest consequence.

(1.3.120–126)

Because Banquo knows that the prophecies of the witches "tell us truths"—for example, the truth that Macbeth will become king—by "enkindle" he can mean only "prompt by satanic means." That he does not associate the warning with himself must bespeak his conviction that God will protect him from the instruments of Darkness. And that he does associate the warning with Macbeth must bespeak at least a suspicion that Macbeth may be vulnerable to those forces.

He is far more than vulnerable to them; he is inextricably bound to them; a hideous fact reflected in a verbal echo. At their first appearance the witches exclaim, "Fair is foul, and foul is fair" (1.1.11). The first words Macbeth utters are "So foul and fair a day I have not seen" (1.3.38). And that his speech reflects, as theirs does, evil intent is clear when, Angus and Rosse having exited, he asserts in an aside that the evil intent is murder.

That assertion is preceded by Banquo's puzzled observation that something about the witches' prophecy to Macbeth apparently frightens him. Of Macbeth he asks, "Good Sir, why do you start, and seem to fear Things that do sound so fair?" (1.3.51–2) And to the witches he notes, "He seems rapt withal" (1.3.57). The aside confirms that he is afraid, and explains what the fear feels like, but not what he is afraid of.

> [Aside] This supernatural soliciting
> Cannot be ill; cannot be good:-
> If ill, why hath it given me earnest of success
> Commencing in a truth? I am the Thane of Cawdor:
> If good, why do I yield to that suggestion
> Whose horrid image doth unfix my hair,
> And make my seated heart knock at my ribs,
> Against the use of nature. Present fears
> Are less than horrible imaginings.
> My thought, whose murther yet is but fantastical,
> Shakes so my single state of man,
> That function is smother'd in surmise,
> And nothing is, but what is not.
> (1.3.139–142)

The prophesy of the witches does not merely frighten Macbeth; it unfixes his hair—it sets his heart knocking at his ribs—it so shakes his manhood that he cannot function. In short, it terrifies him. And it does so by rousing in his imagination an evil fantasy the more horrific the more deeply it takes root, and that he nonetheless resolves to actualize. The evil is murder, of a particularly heinous sort; though Duncan is not mentioned by name, regicide. The witches are indifferent to how he actualizes it; they simply prophesy that he will become king. And he knows that, as he became the Thane of Glamis and the Thane of Cawdor without committing evil, so he may attain the throne:

[*Aside*] If Chance will have me King, why, Chance may crown me,
Without my stir.
(1.3.144-145).

Yet within hours, the terror of regicide roused in Macbeth's imagination suddenly vanishes, why that happens is explained, and Duncan is dead.

It vanishes because in response to a question from her husband Lady Macbeth eradicates it. She does not understand either of them very well. But she does understand what will spur him to murder. Therefore, from the moment she enters to him, Duncan is doomed.

That she does not understand herself very well is demonstrated by her response to Macbeth's letter heralding the arrival of Duncan. Convinced that her womanhood prevents her from murdering, she instantly commands infernal assistance:

> Come, you Spirits
> That tend on mortal thoughts, unsex me here,
> And fill me, from the crown to the toe, top full
> Of direst cruelty! make thick my blood,
> Stop up th' access and passage to remorse;
> That no compunctious visitings of Nature
> Shake my fell purpose, nor keep peace between
> Th' effect and it!
> (1.5.40-47)

The evidence that she understands herself insufficiently, if at all, is three-fold: that she expects a change so astounding—perhaps even impossible—to occur—and at once—simply because she commands it to occur—and by spirits she can identify only vaguely; that she issues the command three times in her soliloquy (above, 1.5.47-50, 50-54), as though uncertain it will be obeyed; and that the intensity of her wish to feel no "remorse," no "compunctious visitings of Nature," bespeaks the fear—almost the conviction—that she will be tortured by conscience.

Her understanding of Macbeth is not more impressive.

That she thinks mistakenly that he is inept at deception is established by the lecture she reads him on the rudiments of deception immediately after he has masterfully deceived Duncan. On entering Macbeth's castle an instant before Macbeth greets him, Duncan says, speaking of Cawdor, just executed,

> There's no art
> To find the mind's construction in the face:
> He was a gentleman on whom I built
> An absolute trust -
> (1.4.12–14)

and is addressed by Macbeth with such apparent humility and joy that he cannot imagine his assassin is before him. And this master of deceit she instructs

> To beguile the time,
> Look like the time; bear welcome in your eye,
> Your hand, your tongue: look like th' innocent flower,
> But be the serpent under't.
> (1.5.62–65)

She thinks, mistakenly also, that however he may covet its rewards, Macbeth is too kind-hearted to commit murder. Thinking of him in soliloquy, she says:

> Yet do I fear thy nature:
> It is too full o' the milk of human kindness,
> To catch the nearest way. Thou wouldst be great;
> Art not without ambition, but without
> The illness should attend it: what thou wouldst highly,
> That wouldst thou holily; wouldst not play false,
> And yet would wrongly win; thou'dst have, Great Glamis,
> That which cries, "Thus thou must do," if thou have it;
> And that which rather thou dost fear to do,
> Than wishest should be undone.
> (1.5.16–24)

Because what fear unhinges Macbeth as he fantasizes about murdering Duncan has not yet been explained, Lady Macbeth's apparent assumption that it is ethical—even religious—in nature—that he blanches at assassinating Duncan in "The Lord's anointed Temple" (2.3.69)—is understandable. That she thinks he is "too full o' the milk of human kindness" to commit murder, because by nature he acts "holily" demonstrates that her understanding of him is meager at best.

Unfortunately, she does understand, from Macbeth's necessarily oblique letter to her, that he is burning to murder Duncan; and that therefore she may be able to persuade him to stifle human kindness and act unholily. And she is able to do, because she locates and eradicates, the fear that has been preventing him from murdering.

His letter is addressed to "my dearest partner in greatness" (1.5.11–12), obliquely but clearly his partner in murder. She understands, speaking to him, as it were, in soliloquy, that the task is one "which rather thou dost fear to do, Than wishest should be undone." And when he enters, they agree what "This night's great business" (1.5.67) is.

Suddenly, however, Macbeth balks. In a decisive soliloquy, he renounces murder; though only until he explains what the terror is that from the outset has kept him from murdering; a terror that Lady Macbeth eradicates when he shares the explanation with her.

The soliloquy (1.7.1–28) condemns assassination for three reasons, discussed in ascending order of ethical, social and religious significance, but is concerned seriously with only the first, and least significant, of them, and with the third, though only as it deepens the terror of the first.

First, assassins are always caught.

> If it were done, when 'tis done, then 'twere well
> It were done quickly: if th' assassination
> Could trammel up the consequence, and catch
> With his surcease success; but that this blow
> Might be the be-all and the end-all- here,
> But here, upon this bank and shoal of time
> We'd jump the life to come.—But in these cases,
> We still have judgment here; that we but teach
> Bloody instructions, which, being taught, return
> To plague th' inventor: this even-handed Justice
> Commends th' ingredience of our poison'd chalice
> To our own lips.
> (1.7.1–12)

If we were not caught, we would risk even Divine justice after death. But we are always caught.

Second, it is unethical to assassinate a relative, a king, and a guest:

> I am his kinsman and his subject,

Strong both against the deed; then as his host
Who should against his murtherer shut the door,
Not bear the knife.
(1.7.13–16)

And third, murder is a deadly sin, certain to be not only, as noted above, merely unmasked, but publically damned by emissaries of God, especially if the victim is so pious that

> his virtues
> Will plead like angels, trumpet-tongu'd, against
> The deep damnation of his taking-off;
> And Pity, like a naked new-born babe,
> Striding the blast, or heaven's Cherubins, hors'd
> Upon the sightless couriers of the air,
> Shall blow the horrid deed in every eye,
> That tears shall drown the wind.
> (1.7.18–25)

Apparently convinced by the three reasons to desist, he tells Lady Macbeth, who enters as his soliloquy ends, "We will proceed no further in this business" (1.7.31). Infuriated, she launches two attacks: that he is simply afraid of acting (1.7.35–45), and that she is not (1.7.37–59). Both attacks he simply shrugs off. But then he asks a question that proves he has never taken seriously the second and third reasons in his soliloquy. The question is simple: "If we should fail?" (1.7.59) Her answer is simple:

> We fail?
> But screw your courage to the sticking-place,
> And we'll not fail.
> (1.7.60–62)

And the proof is simple: if he had taken the second or the third reason in his soliloquy, or both of those reasons, seriously, he would, though convinced he would evade secular detection, nonetheless have desisted from murdering Duncan because he would have thought, correctly, that murdering him was unethical, or profoundly sinful, or both.

So the mystery of what exactly has from the outset been terrifying Macbeth is resolved. Banquo notices correctly that the witches terrify Macbeth; but does not know what he is terrified *of*. Lady Macbeth thinks, mistakenly—ludicrously so—that Macbeth is "too full o' th' milk of human kindness" and always aspires to act "holily." In fact, a moment just after he murders Duncan aside, his terror is entirely mundane: the terror of being unmasked as a murderer.

Reassured by his wife and therefore confident, two brief acknowledgments that terror attends the murder he is about to commit notwithstanding, Macbeth moves resolutely towards the fatal bedroom.

Just before he meets Banquo, he acknowledges the terror, but seems fully in command of it.

> I am settled, and bend up
> Each corporeal agent to this terrible feat.
> Away, and mock the time with fairest show:
> False face must hide what the false heart doth know.
> (1.7.80–83)

The fact, he acknowledges, is terrible. But it is settled; as are the duplicity and the commitment to evil. Even his limbs are resolute.

Similarly, as the soliloquy ends with him striding towards Duncan, asleep, he acknowledges "the present horror . . . of the time" (2.1.59) .But, as in the context above there was nothing of a terror that unhinges, or even prevents careful attention to a task at hand, so here there is no sense of "horror."

To the contrary, whether the dagger he sees is real or a figment of his imagination interests him as a question, until he concludes, "It is the bloody business which informs Thus to my eyes." (2.1.48–49) And nothing of terror disturbs his description of the murder in the night he is walking through:

> Now o'er the one half-world
> Nature seems dead and wicked dreams abuse
> The curtain'd sleep: Witchcraft celebrates
> Pale Hecate's off'rings; and wither'd Murther,
> Alarum'd by his sentinel, the wolf,
> Whose howl's his watch, thus with his stealthy pace,
> With Tarquin's ravishing strides, towards his design
> Moves like a ghost.
> (2.1.49–56)

There is horror enough in the time; but none in Macbeth, who knows, because his wife has assured him, that the thing *will* be done when 'tis done, and that therefore he need not be terrified of the only thing that from the outset has terrified him.

That conscience might terrify him he considered only in the third of the reasons in his soliloquy against assassinating Duncan, and appeared there only in relation to his terror of being caught. Its appearance immediately after he murders Duncan is therefore startling, especially because it is unrelated to his terror of being caught, and because it never again appears in him; and is a necessity of dramatic structuring: the foreshadow of an essential contrast between himself and his wife that is underscored increasingly as their doom approaches.

Everything in his tortured conversation with her immediately after he murders Duncan demonstrates beyond question that conscience has unhinged him. Having overheard Malcolm and Donalbain at their prayers, he asks, absurdly, " 'But wherefore could I not pronounce Amen?'" (2.2.30) He is certain "Macbeth shall sleep no more!" (2.2.42) He refuses to return the bloody daggers to Duncan's bedroom and bloody the grooms, because "I am afraid to think what I have done; Look on't again I dare not" (2.2.50-51). He is certain his bloody hands

> Pluck out mine eyes.
> Will all great Neptune's ocean wash this blood
> Clean from my hand? No, this my hand ill rather
> The multitudinous seas incarnadine,
> Making the green one red.
> (2.2.58–60)

And to the sudden knocking at the Gate he shouts, "Wake Duncan with thy knocking: I would thou couldst!" (2.2 .73)

In the tumult that follows the discovery that Duncan has been murdered, virtually nothing shadows Macbeth's triumph. That he kills the grooms so quickly rouses some suspicion (2.3. 100–118). But that suspicion shifts to Malcolm and Donalbain because, for good reason, they abscond (2.4.23–29). And he is not troubled by two foreshadows of retribution: the Porter's speech at the Gate of Hell, that no one, including himself, hears (2.3.1–22); and the upheavals in nature (2.3.55–64, 2.4.1–20) that no one can identify as indicting him. Thus, he has committed the perfect murder:

Duncan is dead, the terror he will be identified as his murderer is nil, and he is king.

That, his terror of being unmasked as a murderer nullified, Macbeth enjoys murdering is consonant with his inextricable bond to the witches. As noted, he admits that chance may elevate him to the crown "Without my stir." And it is obviously imprudent to murder Duncan the night he arrives, unexpectedly, at his castle, at once, without formulating even the rudiments of a sensible plan. But he is so avid to murder that he cannot restrain himself. And when Duncan announces that

> We will establish our state upon
> Our eldest, Malcolm; whom we name hereafter
> The Prince of Cumberland.
> (1.4.37–39)

he resolves to murder Malcolm also:

> [Aside] The Prince of Cumberland!—That is a step
> On which I must fall down, or else o'erleap,
> For in my way it lies.
> (1.5.48–50)

And by inference he will murder Donalbain as well, who will otherwise succeed his brother Malcolm to the throne.

How these two murders are to be planned and executed Macbeth does not consider. But that he will o'erleap Malcolm and Donalbain by murder is beyond question:

> Stars, hide your fires!
> Let not light see my black and deep desires;
> The eye own eye wink at the hand; yet let that be,
> Which the hand fears, when it is done, to see.
> (1.5.50–53)

The delight in Macbeth's commands to the stars and to his own eye and hand are, beyond question, the murderer's delight.

Had Macbeth been satisfied with what he had accomplished in respect of Duncan, he might well have evaded retribution indefinitely. But he is not satisfied. And therefore he is doomed.

Though it is not immediately evident, the cause of the dissatisfaction—that Banquo is alive—is suicidal, because Macbeth's obsession with murdering him requires that, for the first time, he oppose his will to the will of the witches.

In his first soliloquy after he is enthroned, Macbeth argues that two facts underlie the obsession. The first fact is non-existent; the second is ominous.

> To be thus is nothing but to be safely thus:
> Our fears in Banquo
> Stick deep, and in his royalty of nature
> Reigns that which would be feared: 'tis much he dares;
> And, to that dauntless temper of his mind,
> He hath a wisdom that doth guide his valour
> To act in safety. There is none but he
> Whose being I do fear; and under him
> My Genius is rebuk'd; as, it is said,
> Mark Antony's was by Caesar.
> (3.1.48–56)

That Macbeth seems not to realize nothing in this portrait of Banquo describes him–that Banquo is not royal of nature, dauntless, wise, valorous, or fearful—that his virtues do not so clearly rebuke those of Macbeth that he must be murdered—seems inexplicable; unless the speculation is warranted that he wants to murder again to feel again the pleasure of murdering.

The secnd fact is ominous because it requires Macbeth to oppose the witches, directly, for the first time, because

> Prophet-like
> They hailed him father of a line of kings;
> Upon my head they plac'd a fruitless crown,
> And put a barren scepter in my gripe,
> Thence to be wrench'd with an unlineal hand,
> No son of mine succeeding. If 't be so,
> For Banquo's issue have I fil'd my mind;
> Only for them; and mine eternal jewel
> Given to the common enemy of man,
> To make them kings, the seed of Banquo kings!
> Rather than so, come, fate, into the list,
> And champion me to th' utterance!

(3.1.58–71)

The arrogance, the hubris, the suicidal stupidity of this outburst cannot be too emphatically underscored. Never in his dealings with Duncan did Macbeth disobey the witches. They prophesied that he would become king, but were indifferent to how the elevation would occur: to whether or not he murdered Duncan. Here, by contrast, he disobeys the witches; indeed, declares war against them. They must, he demands, annul the prophecy that they enunciated with perfect clarity during their first encounter with Macbeth and Banquo, that Banquo recalls with perfect clarity: that the crown

> should not stand in thy posterity;
> But that myself should be the root and father
> Of many kings.
> (3.1.3–5)

That, Macbeth demands, must never be. The posterity must be his, not Banquo's. He, not Banquo, must be the root and father of many kings. And they must consent to that, or he will enlist fate in his battle against them.

To that ultimatum the witches respond by torturing Macbeth unbearably.

His downfall begins with his decision to nullify the witches' prophesy by having Banquo murdered; at once, because his apparent composure when instructing the two murderers who will dispatch him (3.1.72–139) masks a torment more intense than his opening soliloquy indicates; a torment that neither he nor his wife can, for different reasons, endure. In Lady Macbeth's opinion, though their situation is dire, nothing can be done about it. In her opinion,

> Nought's had, all's spent,
> Where our desire is got without content.
> 'Tis safer to be that which we destroy,
> Than by destruction dwell in doubtful joy.
> (3.2.4–7)

But brooding upon what cannot be undone is futile:

> Things without all remedy
> Should be without regard: what's done is done.
> (3.2.11–12)

Macbeth disagrees. In his opinion, a crucial task must be completed:

> We have scorch'd the snake, not kill'd it:
> She'll close, and be herself; whilst our poor malice
> Remains in danger of her former tooth.
> (3.2.13–15)

Wife and husband are brooding about different matters: she, about Duncan, who is dead, he about Banquo, who is not dead. That difference notwithstanding, both eat their meals

> in fear, and sleep
> In the affliction of these terrible dreams,
> That shake us nightly. Better be with the dead,
> Whom we, to gain our peace, have sent to peace,
> Than on the torture of the mind to lie
> In restless ecstasy.
> (3.2.18–22)

The terrible dreams that nightly shake Lady Macbeth, about which nothing can be done, are, it will be revealed, dreams of conscience roused by murder committed. Those that shake Macbeth nightly, and about which, in his opinion, a great deal can be done, are of murders that infuriate him because not yet committed. As he tells his wife:

> O! full of scorpions is my mind, dear wife!
> Thou know'st that Banquo, and his Fleance, lives.
> (3.2.36–37)

Whatever happens to Lady Macbeth, he will be free of the terrible dreams; as soon as the scorpions are dead; despite what the witches have prophesied.

Therefore he has Banquo murdered. And though he is deeply unsettled that Fleance has escaped, he is too young to threaten him for years.

> Then comes my fit again: I had else been perfect;
> Whole as the marble, founded as the rock,
> As broad and general as the casing air:
> But now, I am cabin'd, cribb'd, confin'd, bound in
> To saucy doubts and fears.
> (3.4.20–24)

Fortunately, however,

> The worm that's fled,
> Hath nature that in time will venom breed,
> No teeth for the present.
> (3.4.28–30)

But that there are teeth elsewhere never occurs to him; so he can delight in his murder for barely a moment before he is unhinged when the witches suddenly show their teeth, by evoking the terror he cannot bear: the terror of being exposed in public as a murderer.

"The chief guest" (3.1.11) at a state dinner in Macbeth's palace hours after Banquo is murdered suddenly appears. He is late. He sits down in Macbeth's place. No one but Macbeth sees him. Macbeth, shattered, screams—at Banquo's butchered ghost: "Thou canst not say, I did it: never shake Thy gory locks at me." (3.4.49–50) And, having motioned, Banquo will no doubt speak as well, and accuse—a likelihood Macbeth pretends he is indifferent to:

> Why, what care I? If thou canst nod, speak too.-
> If charnel-houses and our graves must send
> Those that we bury, back, our monuments
> Shall be the maws of kites.
> (3.4.69–72)

The ghost does not speak; he simply disappears. But Macbeth is terrified that he may return—that whatever has conjured him may conjure him again—as often, and whenever, it wants to:

> the time has been,
> That, when the brains were out, the man would die,
> And there's an end: but now, they rise again,
> With twenty mortal murthers on their crowns,
> And push us from our stools.
> (3.4.77–81)

And it does return, to scourge Macbeth a second time within minutes, by convincing him that his confession to murder is, or is certain soon to be, public knowledge:

> It will have blood, they say: blood will have blood:

> Stones have been known to move, and trees to speak;
> Augures, and understood relations, have
> By magot-pies and choughs, and rooks, brought forth
> The secret'st man of blood.
> (3.4.121–125)

Whom Macbeth's company, and the world, will identify as his victims does not interest him. Because they do not yet know even that Banquo has been murdered, they will fix first on Duncan; thereafter they will know that he murdered Banquo also. Related matters interest him to obsession: that his tormentors defeated him quickly and without effort, simply by toying with his unbearable terror, and can continue to torture him, whenever they want to, unopposed; that opposing them was, from the outset, worse than stupid; and that because he opposed them, he is doomed to, at the least, a life of torment.

As he tells his wife after the ghost of Banquo disappears for the second time, he knows who his tormentors are. He knows also that what they will tell him will crush him. And he is intent on hearing it as soon as possible:

> I will tomorrow
> (And betimes I will) to the Weird Sisters:
> More shall they speak; for now I am bent to know,
> by the worst means, the worst.
> (3.4. 131–134)

As Macbeth correctly supposes, his tormentors are the three witches. He intends to speak with them "tomorrow . . . betimes," convinced that they, "the worst means, " will impart to him the "worst" news.

Macbeth knows the witches are tormenting him, because he opposed his will to theirs by murdering Banquo. He knows that they are the worst of adversaries because he realizes, too late, that no human can oppose them. And he knows the news they impart will be the worst because it will inflict the worst, the most unbearable, torment.

At the end of his conversation with his wife, Macbeth hints at a resolution that seems inexplicable. He is, he tells her,

> in blood
> Stepp'd in so far, that, should I wade no more,
> Returning were as tedious as go o'er.
> Strange things I have in head, that will to hand,

Which must be acted, ere they may be scann'd.
(3.4.135–139)

In fact, he has so far murdered only two people. So he is talking obliquely about a pool of blood he will be wading in, apparently with deepening satisfaction as it deepens:

> My strange and self-abuse
> Is the initial fear, that wants hard use:
> We are but young in deed.
> (3.4.141–143)

That Macbeth is unmistakably referring to a homicidal orgy that he initiates almost at once is strange indeed, because his motive seems inexplicable. His satisfaction cannot be related to the delight he felt in murdering Duncan, because that delight was contingent on his not being unmasked as Duncan's murderer; a contingency that is permanently precluded by what amounted to his public confession, when the ghost of Banquo appeared, to at least the murder of Duncan. And the possibility that he lashes out spitefully at random because he is disgusted at himself for having been crushed so effortlessly by the witches can be no more than speculation, because it is supported only by the juxtaposition of his resort to the orgy and the realization that the witches have crushed him effortlessly because, as he says, he is "bent to know, By the worst means, the worst."

Whatever his motive for the orgy of murder, that his torment will be hideous is underscored by the grisly potion the witches prepare for their last encounter with him, in their cave, that contains, among other ingredients,

> Nose of Turk, and Tartar's lips;
> Finger of birth-strangled babe,
> Ditch-deliver'd by a drab,
> Make the gruel thick and slab:
> Add thereto a tiger's chaudron,
> For th' ingredience of our cauldron.
> (4.1.29–34)

Macbeth's entry, ostensibly a demand, is in fact a death-song. It is followed, in turn, by the witches' prophesy that he will prove invulnerable to human enemies, and a dramatic reiteration of the death-song.

The death-song underscores that Macbeth is completely aware of the power of the witches to destroy, and thus that he has stupidly condemned himself to unbearable suffering:

> I conjure you, by that which you profess,
> Howe'er you come to know it, answer me:
> Though you untie the winds, and let them fight
> Against the churches; though the yesty waves
> Confound and swallow navigation up;
> Though bladed corn be lodg'd, and trees blown down;
> Though castles topple on their warders' heads;
> Though pyramids, and palaces, do slope
> Their heads to their foundations; though the treasure
> Of Nature's germens tumble all together,
> Even till destruction sicken, answer me
> To what I ask.
> (4.1.50–61)

Macbeth's ostensible demand that the witches answer his question about Banquo's progeny and the royal succession is in fact his admission that the witches are omnipotent as regards him; that they intend to torture him forever, as sport; that they will perforce succeed; and that therefore, as he now realizes, too late, his opposition to their prophesy was suicidal from the outset. If he is convinced, and the fact is, that they can untie the winds, confound navigation, blow trees down—if, in fact, they can so tumble nature that destruction sickens—torturing him to death is a trifle; a trifle that mocks him horribly.

The total message of the eleven apparitions that Macbeth encounters is that he can live a natural lifetime, but crushed by the unremitting awareness of his stupidity. The warning of the first, that he "Beware of Macduff!" (4.1.71) is nullified by the apparent assurance of the second that "none of woman born Shall harm" him (4.1.80–81), and of the third that

> Macbeth shall never vanquish'd be, until
> Great Birnam Wood to high Dunsinane hill
> Shall come against him.
> (4.1.92–94)

"Sweet bodements! Good!" (41.96) he exclaims of the first three. But because he has come to the cave to hear, not sweet news, but "By the worst means, the worst"—that he deserves to be tortured for the profound stupidity of opposing his will to that of the witches—he demands that the remaining eight apparitions underscore that stupidity, and a self-disgust it perhaps rouses in him.

The apparitions, though feigning to advise that he "Seek to know no more" (4.1.103), of course oblige. The ghost of Banquo appears, trailed by an apparantly endless line of his progeny. And to the question Macbeth hurls at the witches—"Filthy hags! Why do you show me this?"(4.1.115-116)—the obvious answer is that he demands to see it—to see every iteration of his self-destructive folly.

> A fourth?—Start, eyes!
> What! Will the line stretch out to th' crack of doom?
> Yet another?—A seventh? I'll see no more: -
> And yet the eighth appears, who bears a glass,
> Which shows me many more; and some I see,
> That two-fold balls and treble scepters carry.
> Horrible sight!—now I see, 'tis true;
> For the blood-bolster'd Banquo smiles upon me,
> And points at them for his.—What! Is this so?
> (4.1.116–124)

It is, of course, so. He has perforce been crushed. And therefore he exclaims, as the witches vanish, "Let this pernicious hour Stand aye accursed in the calendar" (4.1.133–134). It is pernicious because it has underscored his realization that he has perforce been a ludicrously incompetent opponent to the witches, and because that realization may have roused a rage that may attend self-disgust directed outward, to random murder. Informed that Macduff has fled to England, he vows to slaughter his defenseless family as the first victims of his resolve that

> From this moment,
> The very firstlings of my heart shall be
> The firstlings of my hand.
> (4.1.146–148)

And almost at once (4.2.1–84) Lady Macduff and her young son are dead, and two possibilities regarding closure are juxtaposed by Rosse, who exits before Macbeth's murderers arrive:

> Things at the worst will cease, or else climb upward
> To what they were before.
> (4.2.24–25)

The slaughter accomplished, things are at the worst. But the first sign of a force that will raise them upward has already appeared, in a conversation between Lennox and another, unnamed Lord that denounces Macbeth as a murderer and describes the mustering of a force against him—a Christian force:

> The son of Duncan,
> From whom this tyrant holds the due of birth,
> Lives in the English court; and is receiv'd
> Of the most pious Edward with such grace,
> That the malevolence of fortune nothing
> Takes from his high respect. Thither Macduff
> Is gone to pray the holy king, upon his aid
> To wake Northumberland, and warlike Siward;
> That by the help of these (with Him above
> To ratify the work), we may again
> Give to our tables meat, sleep to our nights,
> Free from our feasts and banquets bloody knives,
> Do faithful homage, and receive free honours,
> All which we pine for now. And this report
> Hath so exasperate the King, that he
> Prepares for some attempt of war.
> (3.6.24–39)

The spiritual credential of the force thus established by Lennox beyond question, he underscores it with a prayer:

> Some holy angel
> Fly to the court of England, and unfold
> His message ere he come, that a swift blessing
> May soon return to this our suffering country
> Under a hand accurs'd!
> (3.6.45–49)

The unnamed Lord replies, "I'll send my prayers with him." (3.6. 49)

And the army, its sacred task ratified by God, that will destroy Macbeth is, a question regarding Macduff answered, poised to attack him.

The question, whether, having abandoned his wife and children to slaughter, he can be trusted to participate in the attack is answered by recourse to Christianity. He is tested by Malcolm, who pretends so successfully to be far more degenerate than Macbeth that Macduff, dumfounded that Malcolm has, as he imagines, so dishonored his devout Christian parents that he despairs of rescue for Scotland:

> Thy royal father
> Was a most sainted king: the Queen that bore thee,
> Oft'ner upon her knees than on her feet,
> Died every day she liv'd.
> (4.3.108–111)

Impressed by Macduff's "noble passion" (4.3.114) regarding his parents, Malcolm admits him to his army.

Another paean to Christianity is delivered by a doctor in praise of King Edward the Confessor, absent because healing wretches beyond the reach of medical care:

> A most miraculous work in this good king,
> Which often, since my hear-remain in England,
> I have seen him do. How he solicits heaven,
> Himself best knows; but strangely-visited people,
> All swoln and ulcerous, pitiful to the eye
> The mere despair of surgery, he cures;
> Hanging a golden stamp about their necks,
> Put on with holy prayers: and 'tis spoken,
> To the succeeding royalty he leaves
> The healing benediction. With this strange virtue,
> He hath a heavenly gift of prophecy;
> And sundry blessings hang about his throne
> That speak him full of grace.
> (4.3.147–159)

Siward also is a paragon of Christianity:

> Gracious England hath
> Lent us good Siward, and ten thousand men;

> An older, and a better soldier, none
> That Christendum gives out.
> (4.3.189–192)

His army assembled, Malcolm announces that

> Macbeth
> Is ripe for shaking, and the Powers above
> Put on their instruments.
> (4.3.237–239)

The Powers are Christian.
Their instruments are on.
Therefore Macbeth is doomed, as is his wife; their encounters with death juxtaposed to underscore the essential difference between them. Both are more in need of "the divine than the physician" (5.1.72). But Lady Macbeth dies an incompetent penitent, ravaged by conscience, but driven, crazed, to suicide; whereas Macbeth, to almost his last moment a minion of the witches, scorns the divine, regrets only that his deepest fear—the fear of the consequence of being unmasked as a murderer—has been realized, and that therefore he will be universally reviled in a world that must therefore, he asserts irrationally, be meaningless and not worth living in.

That a doctor in Macbeth's castle, having observed Lady Macbeth, declares her mind "infected" (5.1.69) is established by her speech while sleep-walking; a speech obsessed by unbearable guilt regarding murder:

> Out, damned spot! Out, I say!—One; two: why, then 'tis time to do't.—Hell is murky. –Fie, my Lord, fie! A soldier, and afeard? What need we fear who knows it, when none can call our power to accompt?—Yet who would have thought the old man to have had so much blood in him? (5.1.34–39)

"O, damned spot" mocks her response to Macbeth, convinced that not even an ocean could wash clean Duncan's blood on his hand, with the assurance that "A little water clears us of this deed" (2.2.66). And "damned" asserts that murdering has damned her.

"One; two: why, then, 'tis time to do't" refers to Macbeth's instruction to a servant to bid "thy mistress, when my drink is ready, She strike upon the bell" (2.1.31–32), a code instruction for him to proceed to Duncan's bedroom, as is clear from a stage direction that sets the murder literally in motion: "*[A bell rings]* I go, and it is done: the bell invites me" (2.2.62).

"Hell is murky" locates her destination for an eternity of retribution.

"A soldier" refers to nothing specific. But the entire statement—"Fie, my Lord, fie! A soldier and afeared? What need we fear, when none can call our power to accompt?"—must refer to a conversation, not drmatized, in which she assured Macbeth that, though he had been unmasked as Banquo's murderer, no one would dare accuse them of it, because no one would dare call to accompt their power as King and Queen.

Her horrified recollection that Duncan, "the old man . . . had so much blood in him" recalls that she would, she said, have murdered him "Had he not resembled" another old man, "My father as he slept" (2.2.12–13); that is to say, it equates her horror of murdering of Duncan and her horror of patricide.

Having overheard her, the Doctor, fearing suicide, instructs her servants to

> Look after her;
> Remove from her the means of all annoyance,
> And still keep eyes upon her.
> (5.1.72–74)

They do not succeed; crushed by her conscience, and despairing of repentance, she destroys herself.

Macbeth's eulogy misconstrues reality completely. Told that she is dead, he says:

> There would have been a time for such a word.
> To-morrow, and to-morrow, and to-morrow.
> Creeps in this petty pace from day to day,
> To the last syllable of recorded time:
> And all our yesterdays have lighted fools
> The way to dusty death. Out, out, brief candle!
> Life's but a walking shadow; a poor player,
> That struts and frets his hour upon the stage,
> And then is heard no more: it is a tale
> Told by an idiot, full of sound and fury,
> Signifying nothing.
> (5.5.18–28)

It is not true that all men are fools walking through meaningless days to meaningless deaths. It is not true that therefore the sooner one dies, the better. It is not true that observers of life are idiots, or that what they observe signifies nothing. It is true that life is a battle between good and evil. It is true that, as Banquo warned Macbeth,

> oftentimes, to win us to our harm,
> The instruments of Darkness tell us truths;
> Win us with honest trifles, to betray's
> In deepest consequence -
> (1.3.123–126)

It is true that Macbeth is by nature a creature of the Darkness who opposed his will to the will of other such creatures vastly more powerful than he was, who perforce crushed him, with ludicrous ease. It is true that his eulogy to his wife bespeaks not the structure of reality but his gradual realization of what his place in that structure is, and is consequence his despair at having acted as a fool, a poor player, a doomed idiot. It is true that the instruments of Darkness torture him horribly. And it is true that the instruments that destroy him are instruments of Light—of Christian light, apparently powerless against he Darkness itself, but powerful enough to restore social order by disposing of him.

As the forces of Christian light encircle him, he asserts that, though unmasked as a murderer, he is not terrified—his word is "afraid"—of being punished, because he is convinced the assurances of the witches regarding Dunsinane and enemies not born of women will protect him.

That he is afraid is established by the fact that he protests too much that he is not afraid. He asserts that "Till Birnam Wood remove to Dunsinane I cannot taint with fear"(5.3.2–3). He tells himself, "Fear not, Macbeth; no man that's born of woman Shall e're have power over thee" (5.3.6–7), and that therefore he will "never sag with doubt, nor shake with fear" (5.3.10). He drives out a servant because those linen cheeks of thine are counsellors of fear" (5.3.16–17). He orders Seyton, "Hang those that talk of fear" (5.3.36). He asserts again, "I will not be afraid of death and bane, Till Birnam forest come to Dunsinane (5.3.59–60). And he assures himself, "I have almost forgot the taste of fears" (5.5.9).

That he accepts at face value the assurances of the witches is not surprising. Their prophesies that he would be elevated to Thane of Cawdor and then to King have been fulfilled. And he is certain their prophesy that Banquo's progeny, not his, will succeed to throne. Thus, they have never lied to him, and he has therefore no reason to suppose they are lying about

Dunsinane or about enemies not born of women. And because they are only tormenting him for his hubris, but have never hinted they will kill him for it, he has no reason to suppose they want him dead.

But they do want him dead; for some reason not explained; but not, beyond question, because they want to aid the forces of light of Christianity.

But they do aid them, as Macbeth, astounded and infuriated, realizes a moment before an army of Christians descends upon him, and, *ad dei gloriam*, dispatches him to the eternity he deserves.

When a messenger tells him "I looked toward Birnam, and, anon, methought, The Wood began to move," (5.5.34–35), Macbeth begins, at last, to realize he is doomed:

> I pull in resolution: and begin
> To doubt th' equivocation of the fiend,
> That lies like truth: "Fear not, till Birnam wood
> Do come to Dunsinane." And now a wood
> Comes toward Dunsinane- Arm, arm, and out!-
> If this which he avouches does appear,
> There is no flying hence, nor tarrying here.
> (5.6.42–48)

But a moment before Siward enters, he takes heart again, because, he asks himself,

> What's he
> That was not born of woman? Such a one
> I was to fear, or none.
> (5.7.2–4)

And he kills Siward.

But a moment later, Macduff enters with the fatal news that seals Macbeth's doom, and, and explains beyond question how it was effected. The news is that Macduff "was from his mother's womb Untimely ripped" (5.9.15–16). And the witches have confronted him with his executioner:

> Accursed be the tongue that tells me so,
> For it hath cow'd my better part of man:
> And be these juggling fiends no more believ'd
> That palter with us in a double sense.
> (5.8.17–20)

Thus, as he departs for Hell, Macbeth suffers the consequence of murdering that has always terrified him, that the witches wanted him dead is established, and order is restored to Scotland.

But in *Macbeth* alone in the works in this study, all does not end well. As was shown, at the end of Book One of *The Faerie Queene*, Archimago and Duessa are enchained; that is to say, evil had been nullified. As will be shown, at the end of *Paradise Lost*, that it will eventually be nullified is certain. And at the end of *The Scarlet Letter*, and of *Crime and punishment* it is nullified. At the end of *Macbeth* it simply vanishes, untouched—apparently untouchable—by any moral force, including Christianity, and almost completely inscrutable; all that can be known about it—about the witches—being that they will reappear when they want to, that they will torment and destroy anyone stupid enough to oppose what they want, that they will loose as much of Hell as they want to, and disappear again, the worst of nightmares, untouched—untouchable—when they want to. Not even Christianity can successfully oppose them. Nothing can.

Chapter Four

Paradise Lost

THE CONTRAST BETWEEN THE two metaphysical forces—Satan and God—who contend for the souls of Adam and Eve is absolute.

Satan's first appearance defines him. Totally self-ignorant, and therefore from the outset, as almost always, fitly the object of ironic mockery, he seethes in a chaos of revolting emotions essentially unrelated to the human race, but potentially destructive of its spiritual well-being. Adam and Eve are of no direct interest to him. As he is, however, irremediably furious at God, whom he cannot harm, he will attack God's new darlings instead. He has already attacked. He it was

> whose guile
> Stirr'd up by Envy and Revenge, deceiv'd
> The Mother of Mankind; what time his Pride
> Had cast him out from Heav'n, with all his host
> Of Rebel Angels, by whose aid aspiring
> To set himself in Glory above his Peers,
> He trusted to have equall'd the most High,
> If he oppos'd; and with ambitious aim
> Against the Throne and Monarchy of God
> Rais'd impious War in Heav'n and Battle proud
> With vain attempt.
> (1.35–44)[1]

The essential impulse in Satan's being is pride, the unshakable conviction that he is, at the minimum, the equal of "the most High." This

---

1. John Milton, *Complete Poems and Major Prose*, edited by Merritt Y. Hughes (New York: Odyssey, 1957).

conviction prompts the ambition that produces the "impious war" in Heaven. His defeat—inevitable, because his attempt was "vain"—stirs up in him envy, both at his victor, and at the creatures created by his victor to replace him. The envy rouses the impulse to revenge, which, operating through guile, causes the Fall.

Nothing subsequent mitigates or contradicts this opening description. Because he is the leader of his cohort, Satan must be shown as superior to them in stature, in the capacity to wrest resolve from defeat, and, that done, to act with vigor and dispatch. But the superiority in stature is never moral. His resolve is to remain implacable in hatred. He intends to destroy the human race by destroying Adam and Eve. And—most damaging, perhaps, to his standing—because he is almost unfailingly ignorant of himself and his situation, in almost all of his appearances he is ironically mocked. He is, almost always, profoundly dangerous; but also, almost always, a dangerous fool.

Both the danger and the foolishness are evident throughout his first appearance, which is divided into three scenes. In the first, he rallies himself and his cohort from the burning lake (1.44–669). In the second, he convokes and manipulates a conference in Pandemonium (1.670–2.628). And in the third, he journeys from Hell to the upper world (2.629–1055). In each of these scenes, he is superior in resolve, in determination, and in power to his cohort. But he is therefore far more dangerous than they are. And he is consistently ridiculed, as they are not.

When he begins to exhort his followers to rise from the burning lake, Satan announces his intention of wresting "resolution from despair"(1.191). And, through an effort of will, he succeeds. At the very outset "rackt with deep despair" (1.126), he manages nonetheless to rouse himself to action, and through a combination of sarcasm, argumentation, and flattery to rouse his men from the torpor of defeat. By the time he has assembled them, they are relieved to find him "Not in despair" (1.525). The accomplishment is impressive. But nothing else about him is, except his physical appearance as he rises from the lake (1.192–227). And the resolution, by laying the groundwork for his assault upon Mankind, deepens the sense of terror that attends him.

That sense is further heightened by his hideously perverted and destructive tenacity. Grounded immovably in "obdurate pride and steadfast hate" (1.58), he intends, as he informs Beelzebub, to glory forever in his

> unconquerable Will,

> And study of revenge, immortal hate,
> And courage never to submit or yield.
> (1.108–110)

In particular, he intends forever "to pervert" (1.164) God's will, "And out of good still to find means of evil" (1.165). Specifically, he intends to pervert the human race.

In this effort he will be aided by his loathsome cohort. As they assemble at his call, the depredations the worst of them are destined to inflict upon Mankind are reviewed at length (1.300–521), to underscore not only their own malevolence, but that of their leader. The assertion that they were "the fellows of his crime" against God is at once corrected, to "the followers rather" (1.606). And because they were "for his fault amerc't Of Heav'n" (1.609–610), so they will torment Mankind in the service of his hatred and pride. They are merely his minions, the facilitators of his insatiable vengefulness and spite. And so the destruction they inflict upon Mankind is merely the reflection of his "dauntless courage, and considerate Pride Waiting revenge" (1.603–604), of his insatiable hunger to continue at "War, Open or understood" (1.661–662) against God, "perhaps" (1.655)—he is not, at this point, certain—by destroying Adam and Eve. His exhortation to his minions complete, "highly they rag'd Against the Highest" (1.666–667), the projections of his immitigable rage.

Because of its intensity, because it is focused upon Adam and Eve, and because its effects have already been detailed in the histories of his minions, the rage is horrific. Because, however, it blinds Satan to his situation of the moment, and to his ultimate fate, it contributes to the ironic laughter that attends him throughout his first appearance. So incensed that he misjudges ludicrously every essential aspect of his predicament, his pronouncements and behavior therefore so unwittingly droll, his inflated sense of himself derides him. To himself a hero dauntlessly courageous in the face of oppression, in fact he is a fool who sees nothing.

His blindness deflates him throughout. Foolishly hatching the plot in Heaven, "He trusted to have equall'd the most High, If he oppos'd" (1.40–41), apparently unconvinced God would dare to oppose him, and confident He would regret it if He did. Lying immobile on the burning lake, his senses only barely restored, unable to move, he resolves "To wage by force or guile eternal war" (1.121) against his foe. He rises from the lake "glorying to have scap't . . . by [his] own recover'd strength, Not by the sufferance of supernal Power" (1.239–241), ludicrously unaware that he would have lain on the lake forever, "nor ever thence Had ris'n or heav'd his head, but that the will And high permission of all-ruling Heaven" (1.210–212) allowed him to. He asserts hilariously that, as his mind made "a Hell of Heav'n," it certainly "Can make a Heav'n of Hell" (1.255). In Hell, at least, he asserts with confidence, "We shall be free" (1.259), oblivious to the fact that he was not free even to rise up from the burning lake. "Better to reign in Hell," he asserts, "than to serve in Heav'n" (263), ridiculously dismissive of Beelzebub's suspicion that they may be fated to do God "mightier service as his thralls By right of War" (1.149), a suspicion that defines Satan's ultimate role: to be left

> at large to his own dark designs,
> that with reiterated crimes he might
> Heap on himself damnation, while he sought
> Evil to others, and enrag'd might see
> How all his malice serv'd but to bring forth
> Infinite goodness, grace and mercy shown
> On Man by him seduc'd, but on himself
> Treble confusion, wrath and vengeance pour'd.
> (1.213–220)

As his minions approach in martial order, banners raised, spears, helmets, shields, at the ready (1.544–570), roused by his command to hear his exhortation, "his heart Distends with pride, and hard'ning in his strength Glories" (571–573), oblivious to the obvious fact that, in the war against Heaven, martial strength was of no consequence, that it is almost certain to be irrelevant to future contentions, and that therefore the parade of his soldiers is a ludicrous sham. And finally, addressing them, he asserts, unconscious of the irony, that their defeat in battle was God's fault, because He "still his strength conceal'd, Which tempted our attempt, and wrought our fall" (1.641–642).

It is impossible not to fear Satan's strength. It is, however, impossible also not to laugh at him, not to see him as a self-deceived fool. That he can devastate the human race is obvious. But the assurance that he is ultimately not to be feared is provided by the ironic laughter to which he is almost unremittingly subjected. His malice, rooted in pride and spite, may injure deeply. But he cannot, in the end, succeed; he is far too foolish a devil for that.

Both the fear he inspires, and his foolishness, are underscored in the second and third scenes of his first appearance, so that that appearance presents a single statement, thrice repeated, about his character. In the second sene, he manipulates, to chilling effect, the council scene at Pandemonium, and fixes upon Adam and Eve as the objects of his spite. But the heightened alarm in consequence sounded is mitigated by the irony that continues to be directed against him. Similarly, in the third scene, as, the council scene ended, he travels towards the upper world in search of Adam and Eve, fear intensifies. But so does the laughter he fitly endures for continued self-deception.

In the council scene, as in the first scene, so that his position as leader may be confirmed, his superiority to his cohort is stressed, once again in his capacity for resolve and for action, and in his cunning. His struggle against despair, initiated in the opening scene, has ended. When the council convenes, he has been "from despair . . . high uplifted beyond hope" (2.6–7). When it ends, he proposes grandly that his minions remain in relative safety and comfort at home (2.456–462), while he alone "Through all the Coasts of dark destruction seek Deliverance for us all" (2.464–465); an offer they embrace with relief, because without exception they "Dreaded . . . th' adventure" (2.474). And during the council scene, he cunningly manipulates the sentiment of his minions, by allowing options to be discussed at length that he has no intention of adopting, and that will make his own option, presented by Beelzebub, as he stands by, apparently indifferent, seem noble by contrast.

Moloch's option, presented first, is as reckless as he is. Rendered indifferent to annihilation by despair (2.43–50), he proposes another frontal war. To this option Belial, oily of tongue, low in thought (2.112–115), "To vice industrious, but to Nobler deeds Timorous and slothful" (2.116–117), responds with the suggestion that they adjust to their diminished situation, which may with time and custom become bearable, "If we procure not to ourselves more woe" (2.225). Mammon also, "the least erected Spirit that fell From Heav'n" (1.679–680), even in Heaven far more ardently drawn to "trodd'n Gold" (1.682) than to "vision beatific" (1.684), proposes adjusting, so they can "work ease out of pain" (2.261), and dig for "Gems and Gold" (2.271) in Hell. Beelzebub, chary of the "dangerous expedition" (2.342) of once again attacking Heaven, yet more ambitious than the others, proposes that God's most recent creation be attacked instead (2.345–378), as a relatively safe means of gaining more than "Common revenge" (2.371).

The contrast between Satan and all of his minions who speak is striking. Unlike them, he is neither timorous nor slothful; a fact that his silence, as they speak, underscores. His superiority in cunning as well is evident in his use of Beelzebub, whom he has obviously manipulated, as his mouthpiece. In their conversation on the burning lake, Beelzebub speaks to Satan despairingly of "eternal punishment" (1.155) as their inevitable lot. In a subsequent exchange not recorded, Satan somehow convinces him that revenge is a possibility, and that he, rather than Satan himself, should present that possibility to his fellows. "Thus Beelzebub Pleaded his devilish Counsel, first devis'd By Satan" (2.379–380), but not openly imposed by him upon the cohort. The plan approved "with full assent" (2.388), Satan for the first time wonders out loud who will undertake the dangerous journey to the upper world to locate, and to spy upon, Mankind (2.402–416), waits out the silence as his minions sit, fearful and "mute, Pondering the danger" (2.420–421), touts himself as the obvious choice, and then abruptly adjourns the council, "Prudent, lest from his resolution rais'd Others, among the chief might offer now (Certain to be refus'd) what erst they fear'd" (2.468–470).

His performance, a masterpiece of subtle guile, like his capacity for resolve and for action, marks him as the natural leader of his cohort. But as his talents serve only evil, and as the evil is preparing to assault Adam and Eve, the sense of the danger he poses is heightened. Beelzebub's plan in the council scene could have come only from Satan,

> for whence,
> But from the Author of all ill could Spring
> So deep a malice, to confound the race
> Of mankind in one root, and Earth with Hell
> To mingle and involve, done all to spite
> The great Creator?
> (2.380–386)

The question is, of course, rhetorical. A malice so deep could come only from the embodiment of absolute evil, of absolute pride. And as that embodiment leaves the council, to begin his flight through Chaos to the upper world, the sense of alarm inevitably deepens.

To attenuate that sense, the ironic mockery of Satan is continued, as his blindness to an obvious truth persists; a truth expressed by an intellect apparently inferior to his own, that he does not rebut, or seem even to hear. Belial, speaking with absolute clarity, asserts that war,

> open or conceal'd, alike
> My voice dissuades; for what can force or guile

> With him, or who deceive his mind, whose eye
> Views all things at one view? he from Heav'n's highth
> All these our motions vain, sees and derides;
> Not more Almighty to resist our might
> Than wise to frustrate all our plots and wiles.
> (2.187–193)

A more lucid general statement of the inevitable futility of opposing God is unimaginable. All strategies, direct or subtle, inevitably fail, and evoke derision; not only in God, but in anyone in command of the obvious fact that, as God is both omniscient and almighty, nothing can prevail against Him. To ignore that fact is to invite derision. And as Satan does consistently ignore it, he takes wing towards the Gates of Hell mocked by the laughter his stubborn, willful obtuseness has earned.

He fares no better in the third scene. As before, he is impressive—but only in evil, and therefore only as a source of terror. And the mockery persists, because his obtuseness does. Because the journey through Chaos to the upper world will in fact be arduous, if the description of it does not undermine Satan, he may, for the first time, seem unambiguously impressive. Therefore the description is undermined, almost at its outset, as it unfolds, and after it ends. Almost before the journey has begun, the encounter at the Gates of Hell stresses yet again the loathsomeness of Satan's nature, and of his designs against Adam and Eve. Because, the Gates behind him, he struggles towards the upper world, a vile promise to Chaos and to Night highlights his designs. And, the journey concluded, a terrifying consequence of it appears. Moreover, at the Gates of Hell, the ironic laughter against him persists.

That the journey will require significant courage is stated before it occurs, directly, in the assertion that it will be "dreadful" (2.426), and indirectly, in the silence during the council scene of Satan's minions, who "fear'd" (2.470) to undertake it. The perception of their master's courage is muted, however, by the device of conveying him almost at once from Pandemonium to the Gates of Hell (2.629–643). There he displays courage as well, but in a context that undermines it, by dramatizing starkly the evil it subserves.

That Satan is "undaunted" (2.677) by Death rushing towards him, that he "Admir'd, not fear'd" (2.678) the hideous apparition, that at the prospect of single combat against him he "stood Unterrifi'd" (2.707–708)—that he responds to Death with courage—is impressive. Therefore the apparition is at once identified, so that the nauseating tale of his lineage and nature will shift attention from his fearlessness of death to qualities in him almost unutterably vile.

Death, it turns out, to even Satan's vast surprise, is his own son, the offspring of his dalliance with Sin, "the Snaky Sorceress" (2.724) whom also he fails to recognize, and who happens also to be his daughter. To refresh his memory, Sin recounts the sickening tale of her birth, and their courtship, and then of events he has been unaware of, the birth of their son, and his first act, the rape of his mother, that engendered the monsters that creep endlessly in and out of her womb, torturing her without intermission. The hideous tale, told at great length (2.747–814), by obliterating every perception of Satan unrelated to itself, refocuses attention starkly upon his vices; vices then further highlighted by his offer, presented with the "subtle . . . lore" (2.815) that marked his cunning in the council scene, in return for their cooperation to satiate both Sin and Death with feasting upon the human race (2.815–844).

The portrait of Satan familiar from the first two scenes has been restored almost completely to dramatic prominence. It lacks only ironic mockery. And that is supplied by Sin's appeal to both father and son to desist from combat, because it will merely amuse

> him who sits above and laughs the while
> At thee ordain'd his drudge, to execute
> Whate'er his wrath, which he calls Justice, bids,
> His wrath which one day will destroy ye both.
> (2.731–734)

Though Sin cannot distinguish adequately between justice and wrath, and though she is gullible enough, when offered an enticing quid pro quo, to disregard—and later, as will be seen, to forget—her own insight, the insight is nonetheless profound. Essentially a restatement of Belial's insight, it informs Satan that whatever he does will inevitably serve God's purpose, not his own (and that one day he and Death will die). Satan does not, of course, respond. He does not seem to hear Sin, any more than he heard Belial. His foolish self-deception intact, ironic laughter reverberates against him.

The Gates of Hell opened, Satan flies "Undaunted" (2.955) through Chaos. But the offer he makes to Chaos and Night undermines the sense of his courage, as does the reappearance, to gruesome effect, of Sin and

Death. In consequence, the journey done, he alights at last upon the upper world preeminent almost exclusively in evil, accursed, and the curse of the human race.

The offer to Chaos and Night is simple. In return for safe passage to the upper world, he will reduce the region in which the human race lives to its "original darkness and your sway ... and once more Erect the Standard there of ancient Night" (2.984-986). Theirs will be "th' advantage all." For himself he desires only "revenge" (2.987). Chaos and Night of course concur. His family proves as accommodating, in its fashion. Following hastily after their sire, Sin and Death prepare to pave a path through Chaos, to ease the access of his cohort to the human race (2.1021-1033).

The path is essentially the work of Satan, as is every impulse of hatred, spite, vengefulness, envy, and cunning directed by the absolute evil he embodies not only against the absolute, impregnable good who is God, but also against, in their inexperience and vulnerability, the unsuspecting archetypes of their race, Adam and Eve. Against them, excoriated for unspeakable malefactions, projected and done, and mocked ironically for apparently impregnable self-ignorance, Satan is poised. And towards them he hurries. "Accurst, and in a cursed hour he hies." (2.1055)

His invincible antagonist is poised to oppose him, His ultimate triumph inevitable, just, and self-evident; the futility of absolute evil ridiculously oblivious to its limitations sufficient assurance that, its horrible capacity for destructiveness notwithstanding, it is doomed ultimately, as it should be, to destruction.

The absolute contrast between absolute good and absolute evil is rendered metaphorically by an analysis of God's motives, by a display of His flexibility, by a description of the world He has created, and by the assurance offered through an overview of human history that describes the process through which evil will be gradually frustrated and then suddenly destroyed; a description that, by stressing, as usual, Satan's ignorance of the self-evident facts that dominate history, continues the almost unremitting mockery that has undermined him from his first appearance. The hymn to Light establishes metaphorically the absolute contrast between Satan and God. Satan is introduced in the darkness of Hell, and journeys through darkness to bring the darkness of Hell also to earth. Therefore, when "at last the sacred influence of light appears" (2.1034-1035), the poet, having "Escap't the Stygian Pool" (3.14), gives thanks to "the heav'nly Muse" who taught him "to venture down The dark descent, and up to re-ascend,

Though hard and rare" (3.19–21); and, immensely relieved, celebrates the antithesis of Stygian darkness, the "holy Light" (3.1) that suffuses the first appearance of God, or may perhaps be God Himself:

> offspring of Heav'n first-born,
> Or of th' Eternal Coeternal beam
> May I express thee unblam'd? since God is light
> And never but in unapproached Light
> Dwelt from Eternity, dwelt then in thee
> Bright effluence of bright essence increate.
> (3.1–6)

The contrast between this absolute splendor and the "utter . . . darkness" (3.16) of Satan's depravity is reiterated by the absolute contrast between Satan's motives and obduracy and the motives of God and His flexibility. As God, in conversation with His Son, notes, Satan's vengefulness and fury are implacable. An obdurate

> rage
> Transports our adversary, whom no bounds
> Prescrib'd, no bars of Hell, nor all the chains
> Heapt on him there, nor yet the main Abyss
> Wide interrupt can hold; so bent he seems
> On desperate revenge.
> (3.80–5)

God also is incensed at the moment. But Satan's fury is basically the expression of injured pride, whereas God's is the expression of righteous indignation. And whereas Satan, because essentially hateful, is utterly inflexible, God, because essentially loving, can be moved, by His loving Son, towards mercy. Satan abhors reconciliation; God desires nothing more fervently.

God's indignation, both at Mankind and at Satan, is entirely justified. Mankind he created "just and right, Sufficient to have stood, though free to fall" (3.98–99). And He endowed the angels in precisely the same fashion.

> Such I creat'ed all th' Ethereal Powers
> And Spirits, both them who stood and them who fail'd;
> Freely they stood who stood, and fell who fell.
> (3.100–102)

Therefore all those who fall, human or celestial, "themselves ordain'd thir fall" (3.128), and must, to preclude the destruction of justice, be punished. Man, in particular, having fallen, "He with his whole posterity must die, die hee or Justice must" (3.209-210).

But, unlike Satan, God can be placated, soothed, convinced. Satan, deluded, poisoned with hate, and therefore desperately in need of counsel, convinced his peer does not exist, accepts counsel from no one. His followers are simply minions to be commanded, cowed, and tricked. By absolute contrast, God, omniscient, radiant in love, in need of nothing, in fact peerless, welcomes the counsel of his own Son, and is surrounded by a cohort spontaneous in its adoration of Him. By announcing to his Son when most completely incensed that Mankind "shall find grace" (3.131), that "Mercy first and last shall brightest shine" (3.134) upon them, He invites the Son to allay His wrath, and in effect predicts that he will succeed in doing so. Not surprisingly, success requires only one brief colloquy, in which the omniscient Father submits to a transparently rhetorical device, and a test of the Son whose outcome is a foregone conclusion. The Father fulminates against disobedience at length, and mentions in closing an impulse to mercy (3.79-143). The Son disregards the fulmination, focusing in his reply on the "gracious . . . word which clos'd Thy sovran sentence, that Man should find grace" (3.144-145), and on the splendid consequences of that gracious word (3.146-166). God, at once in part soothed, assures the Son that He has spoken "All . . . as my thoughts are" (3.171), and invites Him to suffer for Mankind, still in part "under wrath" (3.275). As the Son, "In whom the fulness dwells of love divine" (3.225), instantly and joyfully agrees to do so. God, delighted that "in thee Love hath abounded more than Glory abounds" (3.311-312), delivers Himself of an enraptured effusion (3.273-343), that prompts an enraptured Gloria from His cohort (3.344-415), the total effusion signaling that He has been effectively calmed. As the angels note with fit exultation, the Son, perceiving His Father "much more to pity inclin'd" (3.405) than to harshness, proceeds quickly and without much effort "to appease thy wrath, and end the strife Of Mercy and Justice in thy face discern'd" (3.406-407). He is able to do so for the simple, exalted reason that, unlike his immovably loathsome adversary, God is more than willing to be appeased. Beyond comprehension suffused with love, He desires Mankind to luxuriate in the light of His Grace.

The absolute contrast between God and Satan is underscored yet again by Satan's response to the breathtaking realm of light through which he passes on his way to Eden. His initial astonishment is blunted at once by destructive venom.

> Such wonder seiz'd, though after Heaven seen,
> The Spirit malign, but much more envy seiz'd
> At sight of all this world beheld so fair.
> (3.552–554)

Before long he is travelling "Undazzl'd" (3.614) through areas "all Sun-shine" (3.616), seething in his own darkness. His adamantine envy of the sunshine reflects precisely his unappeasable hatred of God, and of His world, through which he must pass; a world of light, newly created as a rebuke to him. For the first time, as he travels through it, he and God meet; he in person, and God in His essential element—in perhaps His very essence—Light. And, as He must, God predominates. From the long description of the dazzling world (3.499-621)—the spatial equivalent of the hymn to Light—Satan is almost entirely absent. The intruder will pass. The Light will remain, obscuring the memory even of God's quickly appeased anger, and providing assurance that nothing of the darkness can, in the end, prevail.

That assurance has already been provided in the assertion that all of history, human and divine, is merely the expression in time of God's will. He not only sees, but governs, all of life. Looking down "from his prospect high . . . past, present, future he beholds" (3.77–78). He controls them as well. Satan's machinations "shall redound Upon his own rebellious head" (3.85-86). Perverted by him, Mankind will fall. It will nonetheless find Grace. He will not (3.79-134). The Son, though sinless, in a spectacular act with millennial consequences, will rescue Mankind from the effects of the Fall (3.227-265). He will elect to die for the sins of Mankind. He will arise from death, and at the end of time destroy death, and humiliate Satan once and for all.

> I through the ample air in triumph high
> Shall lead Hell Captive maugre Hell, and show
> The powers of darkness bound.
> (3.254–256)

That accomplished by the Son, on the face of the Father "no cloud Of anger shall remain" (3.262-63), as in Him "wrath shall be no more" (3.264). In the celestial battle for the soul of Mankind, "So Heav'nly love shall outdo

Hellish hate" (3.298), and, history ended, the Son will reign at His Father's side, "Anointed universal King" (3.315–317).

All of that is inevitable. All of that is assured. And to all of that Satan is completely, willfully, hilariously blind. He proceeds to his task with perfect confidence that it will unfold in strict conformity with his will: that, as he rose from the burning lake through his own strength, and "Not by the sufferance of supernal Power" (1.241), so he has traversed Chaos and a world of hated light towards Eden: through his own strength, untrammelled by the will of God. A failure of perception more profound, more gross, more stupid, more deserving of ironic contempt, cannot be imagined. Utterly unaware that he is a puppet, utterly blind to the puppeteer's strings, he does not move, but is moved, by God, his antithesis, towards Eden, utterly deaf to the laughter that attends him.

The brief moment in which Satan tricks the arch-angel Uriel, by dramatizing the approach of absolute evil to the field upon which the first battle between Satan and God for the soul of Mankind will occur, sounds the alarm for God, or for one of His surrogates, to approach as well. For the first time, Satan has gained physical access to Mankind, and through the most unsettling of his devices, guile. Therefore he must be countered at once, by the divine force without whose support Mankind cannot hope to survive. That, immediately after the moment passes, those forces are mustered assures that Satan's initial assault will be defeated. That assurance is especially needful, because for the first time Satan's malice is a clear and present danger, and because, in their first appearance Adam and Eve display a weakness that could, if discovered by Satan, serve his malice. For the first time, that malice is directed actively, rather than as burgeoning plot, against Mankind, its destructive potential underscored by an horrific soliloquy that forecasts all of Satan's responses to Mankind, and that is not deflated by ironic mockery. And a propensity in both Adam and Eve to be governed by passion, rather than by reason, gradually becomes obvious, a propensity potentially crucial to Satan in future assaults.

Tricking Uriel proves unnervingly easy, because

> neither Man nor Angel can discern
> Hypocricy, the only evil that walks
> Invisible, except to God alone.
> (3.682–684)

Hypocricy his weapon of choice, disguised as "a stripling Cherub" (3.636) anxious to visit God's splendid new world, Satan passes without effort through Uriel's check-point, Uriel in his goodness suspecting "no ill Where no ill seems" (3.688–689). To all appearances innocent, reverent, and avid to adore God's handiwork, Satan handily circumvents an angel not deficient in "wisdom" (3.686), and moves unhampered towards Eden and his intended prey.

He has never been a more immediate menace. Therefore the need to oppose him effectively has never been more immediate or more pressing. The menace and the successful opposition are dramatized in turn.

Satan spies upon Adam and Eve, enraged at their habitation and joy, and, because suddenly hovering as an imminent danger, and for a rare moment aware of both his situation and his motives, not subject to the irony that therefore diminishes, he inspires terror. Therefore the first expression, in a soliloquy in action of his rage is frustrated by celestial guardians aided at need by their omnipotent Master.

The soliloquy (4.1–130) crystalizes his poisonous resolutions, and three related scenes reiterate them grimly. The soliloquy heightens Satan's menace by dramatizing the description of his mind-set presented in his first appearance (1.33–44) at the moment that mind-set comes into existence. It was loathsome to hear that "th' infernal Serpent" resolved to attack Mankind because, defeated in an "impious" and "vain" war against God, and in consequence "cast ... out from Heav'n," his "guile" was "stirr'd up to Envy and Revenge." It is horrifying to be present at the very moment that resolve is formed, and at the scenes in which it is reiterated, and destructive action begins to flow from it (4.131–538). And neither the horror, nor Satan's sudden (though only momentary) understanding of himself and his situation is mocked, as his attack upon Mankind begins, with the laughter that mocked his previous machinations.

The effect of the soliloquy (4.1–130) is perverse and unnerving. For the first of only two times, at its outset conscience stirs in Satan's soul. But it merely intensifies and focuses his malice. Because in consequence he becomes, for the first time, a clear and present danger to Mankind, and also because conscience is attended, as it invariably is, by self-knowledge, his hardened resolve cannot be undermined by ironic laughter. Thus, the soliloquy hardens Satan's already obdurate commitment to evil, and deepens the horror that commitment evokes.

He rebelled, Satan says, because "Pride and worse Ambition" (4.40) incited him against an adversary not only invincible, because "matchless" (4.40), but deserving

> no such return
> From me, whom he created what I was
> In that bright eminence, and with his good
> Upbraided none; nor was his service hard.
> (4.42–45)

Yet, because he was profoundly twisted, "all his good prov'd ill in me, And wrought but malice" (4.48–49), as it did not in "other Powers as great" (4.63) as himself, who "Fell not, but stand unshak'n . . . to all temptations arm'd" (4.64–65). He was no more constrained to sin than they were. "Hadst thou the same free Will and Power to stand?" (4.66) he asks rhetorically, and answers, "Thou hadst" (4.67). Therefore he should, as he knows, "at last relent" (4.79), and through "Repentance" seek "Pardon"(4.80).

His mind illuminated suddenly by conscience, Satan understands (as he will only once again) his situation and himself. Unfortunately, however, conscience provokes, not reformation, but the destructive despair he seemed to have conquered while rising from the burning lake and assembling his cohort. It has merely lain dormant, and now resurfaces, to catastrophic effect:

> Now conscience wakes despair
> That slumber'd, wakes the bitter memory
> Of what he was, what is, and what must be
> Worse; of worse deeds worse suffering must ensue.
> (4.23–26)

Overwhelmed by the wakened bitterness, Satan insists that he cannot repent, because, even if in consequence he were returned by God's Grace to his "former state" (4.94), he would soon "recant" (4.96) and suffer "a worse relapse And heavier fall" (4.100–101). That being the case, and "All hope excluded thus" (4.105), with the loss of hope "Fear" (4.108) and "Remorse" (4.109) excluded as well, he rushes towards Eden, the hideous credo, "Evil be thou my Good" (4.110), fixed for good in his obdurate heart.

Never before has Satan's fury been directed at Mankind. Only now, hardened by conscience, enraged at the deprivation he has inflicted upon himself, does he transfer that that fury from himself to the creatures newly created to replace him, whose Creator he cannot spite directly. Only "now first inflam'd with rage" (4.9) at Mankind does he hurry towards the border of Paradise, contorted with "ire, envy, and despair" (4.115), seething with "Deep malice" and "revenge" (4.123), his gestures "fierce" (4.128), his demeanor "mad" (4.129), his malice focused so sharply on Mankind, and his self-understanding so clear that neither his thoughts nor his hideous plans can be ironically mocked.

And what he sees—a spectacle of domestic and sensual bliss unfolding throughout a radiant day in a setting almost indescribably lovely—by deepening his envy focuses his fury with absolute and chilling precision. He arrives at Eden almost literally mad. When Adam and Eve, having appeared, spoken, and embraced, walk off, he looks after them, livid, intent on murder.

That the spectacle is surpassingly beautiful even Satan admits. Unfortunately, however, the beauty itself inflames his malice. In the first of the three scenes he spies (4.131–287), he gazes down from the Tree of Life upon the Garden of Eden struck "with new wonder" (4.205) at "Nature's whole wealth, yea more, A Heaven on Earth" (4.207–208) stretched out before him, fully aware that "blissful Paradise Of God the Garden was" (4.208–209). But the beauty of even paradisial nature cannot soothe him. The "Vernal delight and joy" (4.155) it inspires being "able to drive All sadness but despair" (4.155–156), he stares at it "devising death" (4.197), viewing "undelighted all delight" (4.286).

Satan's response, in the second scene (4.288–392), to the far more impressive beauty of Adam and Eve is far more intensely and overtly vicious. As before, he feels the beauty. But also as before, his destructive rage is in consequence deepened. Their beauty, unlike that of nature, reflects not only God's exquisite handiwork, but His image as well. "Godlike erect" (4.289), they seem "Lords of all ... for in thir looks Divine The image of thir glorious Maker shone" (4.290–292). He stares at them, as he stared at Eden for the first time, "With wonder," and insists, perhaps with some trace of sincerity, that he could "love" (4.363) and "pity" (4.374) them. But their regal bearing, their resemblance to their Maker, and their obvious harmony as "hand in hand they pass'd, the loveliest pair That ever since in love's imbraces met" (4.321–322), infuriate him beyond endurance. And his "grief" (4.358) at recalling that they have been "Into our room of bliss thus high advanc'd" (4.359) unleashes the hideously sarcastic mock-address (4.375–392) in which he assures them that they must soon exchange Paradise for Hell, and that for the exchange, which "haply may not please" (4.378), they may "Thank him who puts me loath to this revenge On you who wrong me not for him who wrong'd" (4.386-387).

In the third scene (4.393-538), the conversation of Adam and Eve, conducted in love and capped by an embrace, by adding lust to Satan's rage drives him at last to action. The conversation, that begins with religious instruction and proceeds to mutually delightful reminiscence (4.411-491), ends with Eve, "swelling Breast Naked" (4.495-496) upon her husband's breast, enjoying his "kisses pure" (4.502), and their enemy "with jealous leer malign" (4.503) eyeing them "askance" (4.504), consumed with "envy" (4.503) at the sight of them "Imparadis't in one another's arms" (4.506)

> while I to Hell am thrust,
> Where neither joy nor love, but fierce desire,
> Among our other torments not the least,
> Still unfulfill'd with pain of longing pines.
> (4.508-511)

His fury thus compounded by lust, he stalks off, leaving the couple to their "Short pleasures, for long woes are to succeed" (4.535).

Never has the danger he poses been so clear, so imminent, so sharply focused upon Mankind. From the moment he appeared on the burning lake, his incensed resolve somehow to avenge the ignominious defeat inflicted upon his pride by God has been the degenerate reason of his being. But only gradually has the plan of vengeance taken clear form. It is now before him, in specific detail, about to be converted from thought to action. Moreover, for the moment he understands himself and his situation clearly. Especially because the comfort of the irony which previously attended him has in consequence been removed, he is far more dangerous than he has ever been, and the imperative of effective opposition far more pressing.

It has already been mustered, and appears at need. In three scenes the angelic forces, already invoked, quickly surround Adam and Eve. That they do so is especially needful, because a weakness within Mankind has already appeared, that Satan has noticed, that may prove immensely useful to him, and against which Mankind must therefore be as carefully protected as against Satan himself. That, aided by their Master's intervention, the angels ward off, quickly and effectively, Satan's first attack argues that they may be may be able, with equal ease, to protect Mankind against the danger within.

The invocation to the angelic forces appears as a cry for a "warning voice" (4.1)

> that now
> While time was, our first Parents had been warn'd
> The coming of thir secret foe, and scap'd
> Haply so scap'd his mortal snare.
> (4.5–8)

The invocation is almost misleading, in almost implying that Adam and Eve were never to be appropriately warned. They will be warned, explicitly, clearly, and in great detail. But until they are, they must simply to be protected. Therefore the first of their protectors, already alerted, is already seeking additional help. Uriel, noticing the "distempers foul" (4.118) that contorts Satan's face as his soliloquy unfolds, and at once suspicious of "his gestures fierce . . . and mad demeanor" (4.128–129), hurries off to his captain, Gabriel, to inform him of the danger lurking in Eden.

Gabriel, the "Chief of th' Angelic Guard" (4.550), is neither surprised nor upset. In the first of the three scenses (4.539–597), he informs Uriel that infiltrations of Paradise cannot always be prevented (4.382–385), and that he will deal with Satan. Uriel, apparently reassured, returns to his post. As Satan fooled him, he may be able to fool Gabriel. But at least Gabriel will be at Adam and Eve's side. And thus, for the first time, they will be watched not only by an adversary intent on their destruction, but also by a celestial guardian.

Their need of such a guardian is pressing. In the second scene (4.598–851), they end their day in the manner most likely further to infuriate Satan, and further to incite him to destructive action, by contemplating and adoring God, and retiring to a night of connubial bliss. And because, once asleep, they will be completely defenseless against malice, their need of a guardian has never been greater.

The adoration follows the contemplation naturally, its inevitable consequence in uncorrupted souls; and the sexual fulfillment as naturally follows the adoration. Evening having come, Adam explains the significance of rest in God's design (4.610–633). Eve, attentive, but focused, as always, less upon the world than upon the love between her husband and herself, accepts "Unargu'd" (4.636) his explanation, and celebrates the sweetness of all of God's hours (4.640–656), stipulating, however, that none of them "without thee is sweet" (4.656). In response to her brief question about starlight, Adam speaks further of God's design (4.661–688), and they retire to "thir blissful Bower" (4.690), the prayer they offer before entering a reflection of the conversation that preceded and inspired it:

> Thou also mad'st the Night,
> Maker Omnipotent, and thou the day
> Which we in our appointed work imploy'd
> Have finished happy in our mutual help
> And mutual love, the Crown of all our bliss
> Ordain'd by thee.
> (4.724–729)

The substance of their conversation—the work appropriate to day and to night—has become the substance of the beginning of their prayer. As the work of the day has been delightful because of mutual help and love, the prayer continues with a petition that from their love the children "promised from us two" (4.732) may issue. And, the prayer ended, the love that has attended them through the day attends them to the marriage bed, to be expressed in "the Rites Mysterious of connubial Love" (4.742–743); rites deserving of the hymn (4.750–775) that celebrates "wedded Love" (4.750) as the "Perpetual Fountain of Domestic sweets, Whose bed is undefil'd and chaste pronounc't" (4.760–761). Upon that bed they lie, eventually, asleep, while "on thir naked limbs the flow'ry roof Show'r'd Roses, which the Morn repair'd" (4.772–773).

To the totality of their bliss, equally intoxication with love of God and of one another, Satan no longer responds with words. Approaching the bower in which the couple "imbracing slept" (4.771), "Squat like a Toad" (4.800), he whispers into the ear of Eve, "Assaying by his Devilish art" (4.801) either to pollute "her Fancy" (4.802), or to rouse

> At least distemper'd, discontented thoughts,
> Vain hopes, vain aims, inordinate desires
> Blown up with high conceits ingend'ring pride.
> (4.807–809)

Because she is fast asleep, and suspects no harm, Eve can offer no resistance to this first attack of evil against her. Her protectors, however, are already at hand. Dispatched by Gabriel, Ithuriel and Zephon hasten to the Garden. At the touch of Ithuriel's spear Satan starts up in his "own likeness... Discover'd and surpris'd" (4.813–815), his attack aborted. To Satan's answer, "fill'd with scorn" (4.827), when asked who he is, Zephon responds with open contempt, fearlessly "answering scorn with scorn" (4.834), and demanding that he accompany himself and Ithuriel, essentially as a prisoner, to their captain, Gabriel, "whose charge is to keep . . . these from harm" (4.842-843); a demand Satan is powerless to resist, because, as "Zephon bold" (4.854) informs him, he is "Wicked, and thence weak" (4.856). Having already acknowledged as much to himself—having felt, on hearing Zephon's first rebuke, "how awful goodness is" (4.847), and seen "Virtue in her shape how lovely" (4.848), especially by contrast to his own "lustre visibly impair'd" (4.850)—he goes with his captors towards Gabriel cowed by "awe from above" (4.860). That he "seem'd undaunted" (4.850-851) and "went haughty on" (4.858) is mere show. In his first attack, Satan has been defeated, and knows it.

In the third scene (4.861-1015), the humiliation of that defeat is compounded, as Satan's weapon of choice, guile, is scornfully deflected, and as God, indifferent to his multiplied fury, without a word, with merely a gesture, removes him from the Garden.

Eve asleep, he is able, of course, to trick without effort. Against Gabriel's warriors he is far less successful. Though deceived for a moment by his artful disguise and duplicitous talk, Uriel soon sees who he is. Zephon understands at once that the toad is some evil in disguise. And against Gabriel, articulate and shrewd, Satan cannot hope to succeed, because the most powerful of Satan's weapons of deceit, specious argumentation, are useless against him. He is in Eden, Satan explains, to escape the withering pain of Hell (4.885-901). If so, Gabriel replies "Disdainfully" (4.903), where are his minions? "[W]herefore with thee Came not all Hell broke loose? Is pain to them Less pain, less to be fled, or thou than they Less hardy to endure?" (4.917-920) In fact, says Satan, shifting his ground, he came as a spy, in the hope of finding a place on Earth to settle with his minions (4.924-945). To the sudden shift Gabriel assigns the obvious cause: he is dealing with "a liar trac't" (4.949) and a "sly hypocrite" (4.957).

Satan, already "overcome with rage" (4.857) at Zephon's scornful reference to his weakness, further infuriated—"waxing more in rage" (4.969)—at Gabriel's effortless deflection of his guile, and in consequence reduced to threatening violence against Gabriel and his warriors, is finally crushed, for the moment at least, by the intervention of God, who simply "Hung forth in Heav'n his golden Scales" (4.997). Seeing them, Satan, reduced in an instant to impotence, "fled Murmuring" (4.1014-1015).

Had none of his poison seeped into Eve's ear, in his first assault Satan would have been completely defeated. But especially because, as will soon be seen, that is not the case, assistance beyond protection while they sleep must be provided to Adam and Eve, and soon, because in their first appearance a grave weakness within them has appeared, that Satan seems already to have noticed, and that he will certainly use to subvert them, if, as seems likely, he can. The weakness is passion: its primacy in Eve, and Adam's tendency to be diverted by it from intellectual speculation and self-command. That intellect should govern passion has been explicitly asserted only once, in God's insistence that "Reason also is choice" (3.108). It has, however, been asserted implicitly throughout, in the condemnation throughout of the despicable passions that dominate Satan, and even in the lovingly gentle hint of a reproof of God's wrath occasionally audible beneath the surface of His Son's remarks during their colloquy in Heaven. Those implicit assertions suggest that passion of any sort, rather than degenerate passion alone, is capable of subverting proper conduct, even in supernatural beings. That it must be carefully governed in human beings as well is therefore self-evident. And that it seems, from the outset, not to be governed in Adam and Eve is therefore, the danger that surrounds them considered, at least unsettling, and perhaps even ominous.

The primacy of passion in Eve is evident in her first conversation with Adam. Although not deficient in intellect, her interest in it for its own sake is nil. She listens dutifully as Adam, her mentor, instructs her in theology, the subject the Tree of Knowledge, the topic the interdiction of its fruit (4.411–439). She acknowledges his exposition is "just and right" (4.443). But, having disposed of the topic in a sentence (4.440–443), she turns, without pretense of transition, to a topic that interests her far more deeply: her memory of the day she was born, and met Adam (4.444–491). And that memory is enthralling because it juxtaposes two delectable passions: her love of her own beauty, and her love of her husband's love of her. Awakened, she goes, at once and instinctively, to the lake, her mirror, and, "pleas'd" (4.463) with its "answering looks Of sympathy and love" (4.464–465), would have stared into it "till now, and pin'd with vain desire" (4.466), had not a more alluring passion been offered to her, not in Adam's person, "Less winning soft, less amiably mild, Than that smooth watr'y image" (4.479–480), but in his need for her, expressed not only in words, but sensually, in the "gentle hand" (4.488) that "Seiz'd" hers, and to which she "yielded" (4.489). Caught between two passions, she chooses the one that longs for "Thy coming, and thy soft imbraces" (4.471). The choice for her between passion and reason would seem absurd; by instinct drawn to self-love and to the love of a man, she would consider reason no choice at all.

To Adam, by contrast, it seems the obvious choice. "For contemplation... form'd" (4.297), and thus by nature intellectual, he wonders instinctively about the world, as anxious to understand its governance as Eve is to feel she is lovely and loved. Not surprisingly, his first speech is about the world, his exposition coherent, his insight clear, his conclusion reverential. The world observed, the conclusion follows that "the Power That made us" (4.412–413) must be "infinitely good, and of his good As liberal and free as infinite" (4.414–415), it being obvious that he and his wife have done nothing to merit the happiness lovingly bestowed upon them, and that from them the Power that bestowed it can derive no benefit (4.416–418). That being the case, "let us not think hard One easy prohibition" (4.432–433) imposed by the Power as the test of their obedience. Rather, "let us ever praise him, and extol His bounty" (4.435–436), for just cause his devoted, adoring servants.

In itself, and juxtaposed to Eve's, Adam's first speech attests to his commitment to reason, and therefore to his superiority to her. Unfortunately, however, the scene in which the speeches appear attests also to the ease with which her passion undermines his reason. Husband and wife are, in spiritual essence, "Not equal" (4.296). Because he has been formed for contemplation, and she merely for "softness... and sweet attractive Grace" (4.298), he has been granted "Absolute rule" (4.301), and she must accept "subjection" (4.308). But though she does accept it, he does not prevail. Apparently without reservation, she acknowledges him her "Guide And Head" (4.442–443), more than content to enjoy him "Preeminent by so much odds" (4.447) to herself, convinced that his "manly grace And wisdom" exceed her beauty. But in fact her beauty, and not his wisdom, prevails. The memory of her first awakening reverberating passionately within both, and neither, in consequence, content for long with intellectual discourse, their conversation ends, not with further contemplation of God, but with "these two Imparadis't in one another's arms" (4.505–506), kissing sweetly, not thinking.

Their next appearance is more sweet, but as disturbing. As they prepare to enter "thir blissful Bower" (4.690), Adam once again discourses intelligently (4.610–633, 659–688), and Eve once again contentedly acknowledges to her "Author and Disposer" (4.635) that "God is thy Law, thou mine" (4.637). The business of the hour is not, however, intellectual discourse, but bliss. And the ardor with which both anticipate it argues the limitations of reason as guide.

The first encounter between husband and wife is pretty, even touching. The second is charged with metaphysical force. Both encounters are entirely innocent. Because, however, both demonstrate how easily reason can be circumvented, they are also disturbing, perhaps even ominous, forecasts of grief. As Adam says—ironically, just before entering the bower—"Millions of spiritual Creatures walk the Earth Unseen, both when we wake, and when we sleep" (4.676-677). What he does not yet suspect is that one of those creatures burns to destroy him, and will all too soon be spewing fatal poison into his wife's innocent ear. Because of their weakness—their disposition to passion—it can enter, into her, into both. They must therefore be warned of the dangers, without and within, that threaten them both. As the toad has already been at Eve's ear, they must be warned soon.

They are warned at once. Because some poison may already have entered into Eve, a crucial fact Adam fails completely to notice, they must be warned. And as both nonetheless still aspire to a full consent, they deserve to be warned. That being the case, a God who loves them and therefore wishes, in His infinite Grace, to protect them from harm, must have them warned—as soon as possible, very clearly, and in minute detail.

The warning begins the next morning, when they awake, and is extended through an exhaustively instructive day. Through a narrative of Satan's ignominious rebellion in Heaven against God, they are shown, in vivid, dramatic detail, precisely who their adversary is; and then told precisely why he burns to destroy them, and precisely how he plans to attack (5.1-759). The narrative completed, they verify that they have absorbed its meaning. The warning thus apparently complete, the narrative of Creation, apparently unrelated to the warning, is presented in detail (7.59-640). It is not, however, unrelated. By underscoring the beauty of the Creation, and God's motive as Creator, the second narrative in effect explains, in dramatic detail, rather than merely as a statement in passing, why Satan is implacably intent upon destroying Mankind. And finally, to complete the warning, precisely how Satan will attack is discussed in detail (8.204-653), rather than merely as a statement in passing, so that, this closing discussion ended, Adam and Eve understand clearly—and verify that they understand clearly—the weakness within themselves upon which Satan intends to prey.

A more timely, clear, comprehensive warning—a warning that satisfies the imperatives not only of justice, but of compassion—cannot be imagined. Indisputable proof that God has done at least His part, it forearms Mankind against an attack it is sufficient to withstand, but free, if it prefers, to succumb to. What Mankind will do remains to be seen. What God has done, before the fact, to protect Mankind, from dangers both within and without, is testament, as His actions throughout have been, to His incomprehensible compassion and Grace.

That Adam and Eve need help is evident from the turmoil produced in Eve by her ambiguous dream, and by Adam's failure to understand it. The dream was conjured in her by Satan, who did, it turns out, understand from spying upon the couple the essential inferiority of Eve to her husband. Into her ear, rather than into his, the toad whispers. And his blandishments prove seductive indeed. The appeal to her beauty (5.44–47), and the enticing arguments for heightened knowledge (5.50–81), induce her without much trouble or delay to taste the fruit of the Tree of Knowledge, and in consequence to soar "wond'ring" (5.89) above the earth in "high exaltation" (5.90). In sleep at least, she is attracted deeply to disobedience, and in fact transgresses God's prohibition, seduced by flattery and by the specious arguments of the unnamed, angelic seducer. And Adam is not alarmed by the dream. Reason stilled, he informs his wife, and Fancy active during sleep, fantastical shapes—even "Evil" (5.117)—may disrupt dreams. As these, however, "leave No spot or blame behind" (5.118–119), they pose no danger, and therefore may be safely disregarded.

Adam's complaisance is understandable, but in the circumstances profoundly dangerous. Though Adam does not "like This uncouth dream, of evil sprung, I fear" (5.97–98), because he knows nothing about Satan, his obvious question—"Yet evil whence?" (5.99)—remains rhetorical, and with his wife he begins the day "cheered" (5.129), convinced that, as "all was clear'd" (5.136) in their minds, all is in fact clear.

That they deserve to be disabused of this conviction is evident both from Eve's dream, and from the orison with which, their discussion ended, she and Adam begin the day. Though enticed by the angelic seducer, Eve is also aghast at the crime he leads her, though only in imagination, to commit. She sleeps "With tresses discompos'd, and glowing Cheek, as through unquiet rest" (5.10–11), and is aware, when she awakes, that she has dreamt, for the first time, of "offense and trouble" (5.34). The angel's proposal horrifies her: "mee damp horror chill'd At such bold words voucht with a deed so bold" (5.65–66). And she awakes "O how glad... To find this but a dream!" (5.92–93). Her conscience, in short, is at least as active as is her fascination with the Tree of Knowledge, and bespeaks, as does the exquisite prayer she offers with her husband (5.136–210), the depth of her desire, as of his, to serve God completely, in innocence and love.

Convinced that their intentions are pure, and their need great, God at once orders the warning. Because of the danger, external and internal, pressing upon them, and because of their innocent devotion to Him, "therefore" (5.229), God informs Raphael, he must descend to Adam at once, to "warn him" (5.237) that

> He swerve not too secure: tell him withal
> His danger, and from whom, what enemy
> Late fall'n himself from Heaven, is plotting now
> The fall of others from like state of bliss;
> By violence, no, for that shall be withstood,
> But by deceit and lies; this let him know,
> Lest wilfully transgressing he pretend
> Surprisal, unadmonisht, unforewarn'd.
> (5.238–245)

This warning—this massive admonition, directly to Adam, and indirectly (though she hears most of it, and understands all she does hear) to Eve—fulfills "all justice."

The admonition is contained in three narratives by Raphael intended to strengthen Adam for his impending encounter with Satan; an encounter destined to determine all of subsequent history: the first, a narrative of the war in Heaven, that underscores the evil Adam is about to encounter; the second, a narrative of the exquisite gift he will earn for himself, for his wife, and for all of his progeny if he vanquishes that evil; and third, a narrative about the indispensable necessity to his felicity of always subordinating the lesser of his attributes to the supremacy of reason; a narrative necessitated by a troubling narrative presented by Adam that follows Raphael's second narrative.

The first of Raphael's narratives, by dramatizing with horrific clarity rather than by discussing absolute evil precludes any argument later, by husband or wife, that either was surprised, not admonished, not forewarned by its onslaught.

The profile of Satan is hideous, and is relieved only by the reappearance of the ironic laughter that once again undercuts him. By focusing upon his rebellion against God, the narrative explores in detail the motives to Satan's willful disobedience, and the grisly emotions the disobedience unleashes. The total profile is—as it should be, to rivet its audience in Eden—horrific. And the horror is mitigated only by the mocking laughter directed at Satan (laughter that Adam seems not to hear).

The initial cause of the disobedience is jealousy. The day God announces the birth of His Son, Satan's rebellion begins. The Son, God decrees to the angelic host, "your Head I . . . appoint" (5.606), and requires that "to him shall bow All knees in Heav'n, and shall confess him Lord" (5.607–608); failure to comply to be punished by banishment "Into utter darkness . . . without redemption, without end" (5.614–615). The decree fires the destructiveness in Satan. Burning "With envy against the Son of God" (5.662), unable to bear "Through pride" (5.665) the sight of Father or Son, and "Deep malice thence conceiving and disdain" (5.666), he proceeds at once to his nefarious plot, his primary weapons specious argumentation and guile.

The first of these weapons he uses twice against his only victims in the celestial war, "the third part of Heav'n's Host" (5.710), doomed to suffer for his "Affecting all equality with God" (5.763). Anxious to mold them quickly into an army, he seduces them with a series of nonsensically rhetorical questions about God's right to require obedience (5.772–802). And, after they have been battered, on the first day of battle, by "fear . . . and . . . pain" (6.6.394), he rallies them with a tortured explanation of the benefits of their ignominious defeat (6.418–495).

His weapon of choice Satan uses more extensively. From the beginning, his plot depends upon guile. God's decree issued, "All seem'd well pleas'd, all seem'd, but were not all" (5.617). Satan awakens a subordinate "at midnight" (5.667), and poisons with conspiracy his "unwary breast" (5.695). He gathers his minions "Pretending so commanded to consult About the great reception of thir King" (5.768–769), and holds their attention "with calumnious Art Of counterfeited truth" (5.770–771). During the night after the first day of the battle, he directs preparations for the surprise attack of the second day. And on the morning of the second day he positions his troops so as "To hide the fraud" (6.555)—the unexpected artillery—through which he expects to conquer Heaven.

That the battle in Heaven occurs at all must be astounding to Adam, who cannot quite believe, before it begins, that rebellion against God—and in Heaven!—is possible (5.544-556). And witnessing it, in imagination, must unsettle him deeply. The battle itself, the realization that Satan perverts, for despicable ends, the capacity for intellectual discourse that Adam reveres as the instrument of truth, and the related realization that guile, the instrument of perverted intellect, is the weapon to which, force stymied, Satan almost instinctively turns, must alert Adam to the possibility, long before the possibility is presented to him explicitly as fact, that the adversary of God may soon prove his adversary as well, and a profoundly dangerous one.

Against this danger, two considerations are reassuring: that, despite his weaponry, Satan is soundly defeated by God, and that, throughout the narrative, he is mocked for his failure to realize that no assault upon God can succeed. Neither his specious argumentation nor his guile serves him effectively in the war in Heaven. It may therefore be legitimate to hope that they will not serve him in a war against human prey. And his essential foolishness may be a comfort. He begins to plot completely unaware that to "the unsleeping eyes of God" (5.646) all of his thoughts and actions are manifest; that his pompous speech to his minions is overheard by God, "smiling" (5.718) in "derision" (5.736) at his "vain designs and tumults vain" (5.737). He advances to battle ridiculously unaware that the army of God is "Invincible... irresistible... Indissolubly firm" (6.47,63,69); simply and laughably a "fool, not to think how vain Against th' Omnipotent to rise in arms" (6.135-136). He contends in battle drolly ignorant that God "From his stronghold of Heav'n high over-rul'd And limited [the] might" (6.228-229) of both armies at will. To his minions after the first day's defeat he asserts with ineffable stupidity that, as their wounds heal quickly, they need not fear lasting defeat (6.436). Even after the second's day's battle, he remains laughably blind to the fact that God, "secure" (6.672) on His throne, is manipulating every aspect of the war, "That his great purpose he might so fulfil" (6.675) of honoring His Son, and confounding in defeat the rebellious upstart (6.669-678). And when the Son Himself enters the battlefield, sweeping all obstacles without effort aside, like his minions Satan remains, almost inconceivably, confident of victory, and thus the butt of the rhetorical question, "In heav'nly Spirits could such perverseness dwell?" (6.788)

Whether Adam is struck more forcefully by the hideousness of Satan, or by his foolishness, cannot be determined. Whether, confronted starkly by the hideousness, he even notices Satan's foolishness, cannot be determined. But that the perverseness, in the most direct of its meanings—the turning aside—the turning askew—of Satan from God—has been presented to Adam—clearly, dramatically, in great detail—cannot be denied. Nor does Adam care to deny either that he has absorbed the profile of Satan, or that he understands why it was presented to him. As Raphael stresses, his first narrative done, he recounted vividly the war in Heaven "that thou mayst beware" (6.894) of a fell adversary not before known. And Adam acknowledges that he has succeeded. Having, together with his his wife, "The story heard attentive" (7.51), he confirms that Raphael was "by favor sent Down from the Empyrean to forewarn Us timely" (7.72–74) that somewhere, seething, intent on destruction, Satan lurks.

That his particular prey is Adam and Eve, that he has targeted them because he "envies now thy state" (6.900), and that destroying that state "would be all his solace and revenge" (6.605) against God, Raphael simply asserts, as an addendum. As has been shown, that addendum has already been rendered dramatically, in Satan's bitterness on first encountering the Garden of Eden, and Mankind (4.131–535). But it has not yet been rendered dramatically to Adam; nor can it be, directly, because Adam cannot spy upon Satan spying upon him.

It can, however, be rendered indirectly, through Raphael's second narrative, the narrative of Creation, that underscores to Adam the splendor of his state, and thus deepens both his astonishment, expressed in the orison, at the authority—the dominion over the new world—he has been granted, and, it may be fairly assumed, his understanding of the envy and malice consuming Satan as he confronts the unbearable fact of that authority, and the knowledge that it was granted to console the universe for his confounded rebellion. The narrative of the war in Heaven was beyond question presented for Mankind's "good . . . dispens't" (5.570–571). The narrative of Creation, Adam suggests, but only uncertainly, "may no less perhaps avail us known" (7.85). The uncertainty is unwarranted. Raphael's second narrative is as essential to his wellbeing as was the first. Both teach him who his adversary is, and thus warn him, in advance of his decisive assault, to beware.

Lest Adam think that the Creation is described merely to satisfy his intellectual curiosity, he is informed at the outset of Raphael's second narrative that the object of Creation was himself and his wife, conceived as replacements for Satan and his cohort, lost to Heaven as a consequence of their rebellion. To "repair That detriment" (7.152–153), God has created

> Another World, out of one man a Race
> Of men innumerable, there to dwell,
> Not here, till by degrees of merit rais'd
> They open to themselves at length the way
> Up hither, under long obedience tri'd,
> And Earth be chang'd to Heav'n, and Heav'n to Earth,
> One Kingdom, Joy and Union without end.
> (7.155–161)

This astonishing fact, reiterated, as the narrative unfolds, inevitably colors Adam's understanding of Raphael's second narrative. He is informed, as it begins, that God created the heavens and the earth "instead Of Spirits malign a better Race to bring Into their vacant room" (7.188–190). The first five days of Creation described, Adam is told "There wanted yet the Master work, the end Of all yet done; a Creature who . . . endu'd With Sanctity of Reason might . . . Govern the rest . . . chief Of all his works" (7.505–516); a creature, alone among the others, made "in the Image of God Express" (7.527–528); a creature known as Man. And, the Creation ended, the heavenly choir itself adores Adam himself and his descendants,

> Thrice happy men,
> And sons of men, whom God hath thus advanc't,
> Created in his Image, there to dwell
> And worship him, and in reward to rule
> Over his Works, on Earth, in Sea, or Air,
> And multiply a Race of Worshippers
> Holy and Just: thrice happy if they know
> Thir happiness, and persevere upright.
> (7.625–632)

Raphael's second narrative ended, Adam's astonishment at the lavishness of God's bounty is expressed both in his initial silence, and then in his assertion that the narrative has solved an old puzzle. For "a while" (8.2) after Raphael ends, Adam "Thought him still speaking, still stood fixt to hear" (8.3). Then, he explains, his confused suspicion that God created "with superfluous hand" (8.27) far more heavenly bodies than essential has at last been allayed (8.15–38). Like everything else, those bodies, it turns out, were created for him, and for his progeny, God's solace for the defection and loss of Satan.

That the second narrative has heightened not only Adam's awe at God's world, but also his understanding of Satan's envy of that world, and of its Master work, must for the moment be presumed. Soon, however, that understanding will be explicitly expressed. But that the presumption is fair may be argued from the juxtaposition of Raphael's two narratives. Adam absorbs the story of Satan, and immediately afterwards the story of a world created to replace him. A creature god-like in intellectual capacity, would he fail to grasp at once, even if he had not been explicitly told, what the reaction of the protagonist of the first to the second would be?

Raphael's two narratives concluded, God's admonition to Adam and Eve seems complete. It requires, however, a cautionary commentary by Raphael upon a narrative unexpectedly delivered by Adam regarding his response to his first encounter with Eve (8.452–559).

That encounter (8.452–559) stuns and puzzles him, because she is

> so lovely fair
> That what seem'd fair in all the World, seem'd now
> Mean, or in her summ'd up, in her contain'd
> And in her looks.
> (8.471–474)

Everything else, he informs, Raphael, "us'd or not, works in the mind no change" (8.524–525). To Eve, however, his response is very different.

> Far otherwise, transported I behold,
> Transported touch; here passion first I felt,
> Commotion strange, in all enjoyments else
> Superior and unmov'd, here only weak
> Against the charm of Beauty's powerful glance.
> (8.529–533)

And understanding "in the prime end Of Nature her th' inferior, in the mind And inward Faculties, which most excel" (8.540–542) does not diminish her allure; "so absolute she seems And in herself complete" (8.547–548) that "All higher knowledge in her presence falls Degraded" (8.551–552), and "Wisdom . . . Authority and Reason" (8.852–854) lose their force in the "awe About her" (8.558–559) created by her loveliness.

Adam's narrative troubles Raphael deeply. (8.566-653). Worried by his immoderate valuation of Eve, the propensity of her presence to degrade in him wisdom, authority and, perhaps most dangerous, reason, Raphael admonishes him, "Accuse not Nature, she hath done her part; Do thou but thine" (8.561-562), and "with contracted brow" (8.560) underscores the imperative of rational control. Adam responds, unfortunately only "half abash't" (8.595), with assurances strikingly at odds with his encomium (8.595-613), and shifts the subject away from Eve (8.614-629). A moment later, a final warning about the imperative of reasoned control issued, the angel is gone, and Adam is left, his departing words still in his ears: "to stand or fall Free in thine own Arbitrement it lies" (8.640-645).

He has been more than sufficiently warned. A pellucid profile of his adversary has been drawn. His motives and his mode of attack have been described in detail. The only weapon sufficient against him has been described. Adam understands the profile, the motives, the mode of attack. Though puzzled by Eve, he is fully capable of using the weapon. To persevere, he need only use it. It is in his hands. The choice is his.

Tragically, he decides not to use it. Made by God "just and right, Sufficient to have stood, though free to fall" (3.3.98-99), he exercises his freedom, and falls. Completely forewarned, the weapon sufficient to his need at hand, he deliberately disregards the warning, puts the weapon aside, and succumbs.

The fault is overwhelmingly Adam's. The cause is excessive love of his wife that, gaining sway over his judgment, prompts two catastrophic decisions: to allow Eve to work alone, and to die with her. Satan attacks because, obsessed with hatred and spite, he must. Eve succumbs because, vain of her beauty, and torn by a wish—that, apparently satisfied, evokes both ironic laughter and pity—to be her husband's intellectual equal, and in consequence, as she imagines fondly, to gain what she already has (his absolute love), she engages alone an adversary only her husband could hope to vanquish. But Satan's attack would never have succeeded—it would, in all likelihood, never have occurred—if Adam had kept his wife where she belonged, and where his intellect instructed him to keep her: safely at his side. And, her destruction sealed, he would himself have escaped death, had he not doubted the capacity of God to assure his happiness after his wife's death. He allows his wife to depart from his side, and resolves to die with her afterwards because, in both instances, the "Commotion strange" she has always roused in him overcomes "All higher Knowledge," that "in her presence," as usual, "falls Degraded." Though he "well" understands "her th' inferior," because essentially inferior in intellect, disarmed by his devotion to her, and therefore by a sudden, willful impulse, he allows her to lead both of them, and their race, to destruction. Primarily because of his uxorious dotage, Mankind falls.

The terrifying force of Satan's obsession is underscored by the suspension of irony in parts of the soliloquy he delivers as he positions himself for his decisive assault. Only once before has the mocking laughter at his expense been suspended. As noted, in his soliloquy on first seeing the Garden of Eden and its inhabitants, and in his subsequent assault upon them (4.1.809), Satan could not, for the first time, be laughed at, because he understood himself and his situation, and because the danger he posed was too pressing. Almost the same reasons obtain as Satan prepares for his decisive assault. He understands at least some of his motives. And the assault itself is infinitely more dangerous than the earlier assault.

To the degree that he is still self-deluded, Satan is still diminished through mockery. He looks forward hilariously to the glory he will achieve "in one day to have marr'd What he Almighty styl'd, six Nights and Days Continu'd making" (9.136–138). He exaggerates ridiculously the number of angels he seduced to rebellion (9.141), and insists with ludicrously complete conviction that through him they were "freed From servitude inglorious" (9.140–141). He assumes that God created Mankind "to be aveng'd" (9.143) upon himself, suspects that human beings were created perhaps because "such virtue spent of old now fail'd More Angels to Create" (9. 145–146), and concludes, in his profound wisdom, that, as they were created to spite him, "spite . . . with spite is best repaid" (9.178).

The Prince of Foolishness is by no means absent from Satan's soliloquy. But neither is the honest self-confrontation of the earlier soliloquy. He is not driven, as there, by conscience. But, in his more lucid moments at least, he understands clearly that, though his assault may deepen his own pain immensely, it must proceed nonetheless. Intent upon "Man's destruction, maugre what might hap Of heavier on himself" (9.55–57), he expects not

> to be myself less miserable
> By what I seek, but others to make such
> As I, though thereby worse to me redound.
> (9.126–128)

Revenge, he knows, "ere long back on itself recoils" (9.172). His terrifying resolve to pursue it nonetheless cannot be mocked, because he understands its nature and consequence. "Let it; I reck not" (9.173), he asserts clearly, focused, for the moment without self-delusion, upon his obsession.

That the danger it poses is unprecedentedly clear and present is evident from his insistence throughout the soliloquy that he must destroy Eden and its inhabitants because they are surpassingly lovely. Satan's hymn to earth, though heartfelt (9.99–118), produces only "Torment" within him, "as from the hateful siege Of contraries" (9.121–122). Unappeasably envious of what he has lost, and of Mankind, created to replace him, he can find ease "only in destroying" (9.129) from his "relentless thoughts" (9.130). Therefore, consumed with "Ambition and Revenge" (9.168), he lies in the serpent, poised to attack.

The "bursting passion" (9.98) that pollutes his soliloquy, and the occasional suspension, as it unfolds, of irony, notwithstanding, Satan is not yet overwhelmingly fearsome. The passion is awful, the suspension ominous. But against a sufficiently vigilant prey he can, in the end, accomplish nothing. If Adam and Eve stand fast—if Adam in particular stands fast—Satan, not Mankind, is lost.

That Adam decides not to stand fast is evident, tragically, from his first encounter of the day with Eve. That Eve's plan is profoundly dangerous, and that she must not be permitted to effect it, are equally evident. (Precisely why she wants to effect it will be underscored soon.) Thus, Adam's duty is clear: to restrain his wife. He understands clearly that that is so. He fails to restrain her because her pretty wiles as a woman hurt disarm him of rational self-control. Apparently a good, loving husband, he cannot stand to see her hurt. Therefore, setting reason, despite himself, aside, he reluctantly indulges her headstrong whim. And the world is destroyed.

Although he dismissed her dream too lightly, having heard it, Adam should at least suspect that Eve's wish to work alone—a wish she never before expressed—is connected to a desire for heightened knowledge. The dream struck Eve with horror. But she did eat of the Tree of Knowledge, and did, in consequence, soar above the clouds. That heightened knowledge is, for whatever reason, attractive to her, and that, left alone, she might seek it at the Tree of Knowledge, should therefore strike Adam as at least a possibility.

It does not. But he is aware of a more general possibility, that he describes to his wife in a kind and carefully structured address in four parts

(9.226–269). First, he assures her, beginning with a compliment, and referring only to her general intention, "Well hast thou motioned" (9.229). "Yet" (9.235), he continues, explaining gently that her specific intention is not at all well motioned, there is no reason to work apart. "But" (9.247) he could consent nonetheless to her specific motion—or, more correctly, might have consented, "But" (9.251) that, as "thou know'st" (9.252), a "malicious Foe . . . seeks to work our woe and shame By sly assault" (9.253–256). Where such a foe lurks, and in consequence "danger or dishonor" (9.267) threatens, a wife "Safest and seemliest by her Husband stays, Who guards her, or with her the worst endures" (9.268–269).

In structure and in substance, Adam's opening speech is intellectually impeccable. Unfortunately, Eve responds to it "As one who loves, and some unkindness meets" (9.271). Precisely the response that Adam cannot deal with, it undermines his reasoned self-command. He is plainly afraid, Eve contends, that Satan can trick her; a fear that implies he loves her less than she has thought (9.270–289). That inference, and "the sweet, austere composure" (9.272) with which she speaks, reduce Adam, anxious to speak only "healing words" (9.290), to a rejoinder consisting of a silly argument (9.292–305), a brief reiteration of the danger of an adversary subtle enough to seduce angels (9.306–308), and a flustered attempt to replace the assertion that she needs him with the assertion that they need one another. This rejoinder, delivered by "domestic Adam in his care And Matrimonial Love" (9.318–319), proves worse than useless, because Eve, convinced "Less attributed to her faith sincere" (9.320) than deserved, picks it easily to pieces. Still speaking "with accent sweet" (9.321), she brushes aside the shift in assertion (9.322–326), easily demolishes the silly argument (9.327–336), and carefully skirts the reiteration. Obviously frazzled, speaking for the first time "fervently" (9.342), and addressing his wife, for the first time, without compliment, bluntly, as "O Woman" (9.343), Adam explains how to deal with a sly adversary (9.348–263), adjures Eve once again to "Seek not temptation" (9.364), but to remain at home, but then, though reluctantly, consents to her departure, "for thy stay, not free, absents thee more" (9.372).

She is doomed. And the fault is essentially her husband's. By nature superior to her in intellect, and therefore legitimately, as she has conceded, her "Guide And Head" (4.442–443), he is responsible for her spiritual well being, and therefore he is answerable, far more than she is, if she persists in conduct he suspects may be destructive. The authority and the power to restrain her are his. If he abrogates either, in great part responsibility for whatever damage ensues will also be his. As he knows, he should simply have instructed her to remain at his side. Deflected uxoriously from self-command, he allows her instead to confront alone an adversary he knows she cannot withstand. For that blunder—for that horrific miscalculation—he, far more than she, must account.

The adversary attacks her at once, delighted to find her apart from "Her husband . . . Whose higher intellectual more I shun" (9.482–483), and confident that, by appealing in turn to her vanity and to her longing for heightened knowledge, he can destroy her almost without effort. This confidence is, unfortunately, well founded. The appeal to her vanity gains her trust, convincing her that Satan is a reliable informant. And in consequence she is easily led, through a maze of arguments she does not quite follow, to an act of disobedience that—for a reason as deserving of pity as the act is of mockery—she desires ardently, overwhelmingly, to commit.

That the appeal to her vanity is likely to succeed is indicated by the delight she felt, when first created, at her own beauty. Waking, she proceeded at once to her mirror, that roused the self-love that would forever have sufficed, had Adam not been presented to her. That she was reluctant to follow even him, because she thought him "less fair, Less winning soft, less amiably mild, Than that smooth wat'ry image" (4.478–480), and therefore "back I turn'd" (4.480) to the enchanting mirror—underscores the depth of her instinctive love of her own beauty.

With that love Satan begins; and before long convinces Eve he is a trustworthy serpent indeed. He approaches "Fawning, and lick'd the ground whereon she trod" (9.526), a votary humbly convinced that "all things living" on earth "thy Celestial Beauty adore With ravishment beheld" (9.539–541); and properly so, because she deserves to be seen "A Goddess among Gods, ador'd and serv'd By Angels numberless, thy daily Train" (9.547–548). The effect of Satan's flattery is immediate. "Into the heart of Eve his words made way" (9.550). Her trust thus, in part at least, gained, he launches into the tale of his encounter with a wondrous Tree, framing it carefully with paeans to her beauty. He will tell her, he says, in response to her question, how he attained to reason and to speech, because her beauty demands that she be obeyed (9.567–570). And, the tale completed, he asserts that the profound knowledge he has gained from the Tree is summed up and embodied in her incomparable, celestial beauty (9.606–612).

No assertion could inspire trust more completely in Eve. As no valuation of her beauty so wise could be suspect, no hesitation in following the serpent to the Tree is warranted. And not even his arguments for partaking of its fruit, when it turns out to be the Tree of Knowledge, need be lightly dismissed. God has interdicted the fruit. The serpent, however, who worships her beauty, declares it permissible. She is not long in deciding whose word is her law.

The rapidity with which she accepts Satan's arguments at the Tree, by underscoring her intellectual limitation, as measured by her incredulity, and by uncovering the motive of her disastrous need for heightened knowledge, mitigates Eve's offense, and affords her a measure of pity as, having destroyed herself, she endures, for the first and last time, the humiliation of ironic laughter.

All of Satan's arguments at the Tree (9.664–732) are rooted in a single assumption: that God's reasons for interdicting its fruit are ugly. Eve's failure to discredit that assumption is an accurate measure not only of the weakness of her mind, but also of a need to find the arguments alluring. Though advanced rapidly and with some cunning, they are far from opaque. No great effort of mind, for example, should be required to object when God is called "the Threat'ner" (9.687), when His interdiction is referred to as "a petty Trespass" (9.693) intended "to keep ye low and ignorant" (9.704), when "God" suddenly gives way to "Gods" (9.716), or when the interdiction is said to be rooted in "envy . . . In heav'nly breasts" (9.729–730). That Eve does not object to such assertions, or to other fairly obvious vilifications of God, demonstrates a limitation of intellect upon which Satan's "persuasive words, impregn'd With Reason, to her seeming, and with Truth" (9.737–738) all too easily prey.

It demonstrates also the depth of her longing for heightened knowledge. She overlooks Satan's assumptions about God not only because her mind does not grasp them, but also because she desires so ardently what the serpent offers that she cannot attend to argumentation. As noted, in her dream she eats the fruit, and soars above her usual condition. And, throughout their encounter, the serpent is aided by an obvious suspension of disbelief for which Eve's intellectual limitation may well not fully account. Especially because her dream is fresh in her mind, her failure to connect it to the serpent's tale seems almost disingenuous, as does her question, the tale ended, "[W]here grows the Tree, from hence how far?" (9.617) Her insistence, confronted with the Tree, that "we might have spar'd our coming hither" (9.647) seems less than convincing, as the expression either of complete surprise, or of unshakable moral resolve. And that she never asks for proof that the serpent did in fact eat from the Tree is suspect, as is her silence during the serpent's two long set speeches. Beyond question, Eve is "credulous" (9.644); but perhaps because of depth of desire as well as limitation of mind. From the moment the prospect of heightened knowledge is spread, as even a poison of little potency, through Eve's dream by the toad, she desires it with an intensity still not fully or explicitly explained; an intensity that may, as much as the restrictions in her capacity for reason, account for her fall.

The explanation is provided a moment after she eats of the Tree of Knowledge, during the soliloquy that subjects her to withering irony, yet shields her with a measure of pity. The irony is unavoidable, because, utterly unaware that she has just finished "eating Death" (9.792), filled with "delight" (9.787) at the "expectation high Of knowledge, nor was God-head far from her thought" (9.789–790), she launches, "jocund and boon" (9.793), into a drunken paean to the Tree (9.795–833), to whose indwelling spirit she then with "low Reverence" (9.835) bows.

The self-deluded spectacle is blackly hilarious. But the mockery Eve cannot evade is mitigated by pity as the full explanation is explicitly presented of why she has destroyed herself. It is almost an endearing explanation. She has coveted knowledge (though only since the night of her disturbing dream), not for its own sake, but because, she has hoped, it would bind her husband more closely to her. She has coveted knowledge, in short, for love's sake. She will, perhaps, not share the fruit with Adam, "But keep the odds of Knowledge in my power" (9.820), thereby

> to add what wants
> In Female Sex, the more to draw his Love,
> and render me more equal, and perhaps,
> A thing not undesirable, sometime
> Superior: for inferior who is free?
> (9.821–825)

In knowledge for its own sake Eve never shows the slightest interest. When she is born, she repairs at once to her mirror, and is coaxed from it only by Adam's ardent assertion that he loves and needs her (4.481–488). As noted, she listens to his lectures dutifully, but shifts their conversations, as soon as she can, to matters of love. Unlike Adam, she asks Raphael to explain nothing about the workings of the world, and, having listened without comment to his narratives, slips off, preferring to hear the rest of his discourse summarized by her husband, who "would intermix Grateful digressions, and solve high dispute With conjugal Caresses" (8.54–56). Nor, until the dream occurs, is she troubled by her preference for love over reason. As noted, she refers to Adam's essential superiority with unruffled complacency, perfectly content to have him rule, if he loves her completely. It is only as a result of the dream that she begins to desire heightened knowledge. The poison in the dream is Satan's insinuation that, as long as she remains his intellectual inferior, Adam cannot love her completely. That insinuation she cannot bear, because nothing (not even her beauty) concerns her as deeply as does her husband's love. The toad must whisper, however tentatively, into her soul that, given what wants in female sex, her husband cannot love her completely, that that want can be supplied with knowledge, and that knowledge alone will enable her the more to draw his love. Eve destroys herself, in short, because, suddenly convinced her husband does not love her deeply enough, she finds, as she imagines, in the interdicted fruit the aphrodisiac that will bind him utterly to her.

Having partaken of it, she returns to Adam, who proceeds at once to the second of his catastrophic decisions. Certain that she has been destroyed, he resolves to be destroyed with her. Convinced, in his dotage, that God cannot make good her loss, he sees no reason to remain alive. Therefore, condemning his race as well as himself, he willfully joins his wife in death.

His awareness that Eve is "Defac't, deflow'r'd, and now to Death devote" (9.901) is instantaneous. And so is "my resolution ... to die" (9.907), because, he asserts, her loss would reduce him to a desolation not even God could mitigate.

> Should God create another Eve, and I
> Another Rib afford, yet loss of thee
> Would never from my heart.
> (9.911–913)

The certainty that not even God would be able to lessen the ache in his heart, and the unwillingness to live with an aching heart, are decisive for Adam. In effect declaring to his wife that love for her is more important than obedience to their Creator, he joins her consciously, deliberately, in death. With her, he asserts, he has "fixt my lot, Certain to undergo like doom" (9.952–953). And, encouraged by her tears of joy that "he his Love Had so ennobl'd, as of choice to incur Divine displeasure for her sake, or

Death" (9.991–993), by her embraces, by her joy—by her fatal indifference to the will of God—thus, as she thinks, ennobled, taking the fruit from her loving hand into his equally loving hand,

> he scrupl'd not to eat,
> Against his better knowledge, not deceiv'd,
> But fondly overcome with Female charm.
> (9.997–999)

The irony in Eve's expression of joy is withering. For her love, her husband has indeed incurred divine displeasure, perhaps even death. But the delusion that, in so doing, he has in any way ennobled himself merits irrepressible laughter; and would rouse it, were such laughter possible at the moment Adam is completing the destruction of himself, his wife, and the human race.

His work done, its essential consequence in the mental life appears at once, with sickening force. Reason abandoned, passion at once usurps its place, and self-government gives way to destructive self indulgence; first, in the appearance of lust, and then in the expense of spirit that attends it (9.1011–1189). From the lust, "of thir mutual guilt the Seal" (9.1043), they awaken "As from unrest" (9.1052), shattered by guilt, self-concern, self-disgust, their relation poisoned by recrimination; as Adam, "distemper'd" (9.1131), bitterly says, pointing the finger of blame at his wife, "despoil'd Of all our good, sham'd, naked, miserable" (9.1138–1139).

The finger should be pointed at himself. Eve, willful, but driven by motives deserving of pity, by nature credulous, and intellectually insufficient to her foe, stumbles, and falls. But she would not have done so—she would not have been in a position to fall—had she been afforded by her husband the protection that she needed and deserved, and that he was obliged, and free, to afford. Because, prompted by excessive love, he chooses freely not to afford it, and because, for the same degenerate reason, he chooses to join his wife in death, he awaits with her the punishment immanent in their fall subject to the more stern indictment. Because his capacities, and therefore his responsibility, exceeded hers, he must answer to more. And, like her, and their foe, he must answer soon. The Judge whose incomparable gifts have been despised, and from whom nothing can be hidden, is at hand.

Because He is loving beyond comprehension, the punishment He imposes upon Mankind is tempered with mercy. It is, nonetheless, a horrible punishment, to endure as long as time endures. And the operation, as opposed to the pronouncement, of the mercy is contingent upon a process of self-reformation enormously difficult for Adam and Eve, in their straitened circumstances, even to attempt. Having fallen, they deserve to die, and at once. Because, however, God loves them far more deeply than they deserve to be loved, His justice, He announces, will be softened by mercy. But the suffering it will inflict upon them, and upon their progeny, is stark. A portion of it will not be mitigated until time ends. And the rest will be mitigated only if they, and later their progeny, fulfill a difficult precondition: accept responsibility for their derelictions, regret profoundly having committed them, implore God's forgiveness, and return, appropriately chastened, to Him.

This precondition gradually fulfilled, Adam and Eve are elevated by mercy from despair to joy. They are not, in consequence, relieved of the unmitigated hardships they and their progeny will be forced, as a result of their fall, to endure. They are, however, strengthened sufficiently to depart from Eden, and to begin their new, diminished lives, with the assurance that, provided they persevere in His service, ultimately, time having stopped, they will dwell through eternity in a world beyond comprehension more dear than even the world they have lost.

That they deserve to be punished, at once, and by death, is asserted by God, who asks rhetorically, "now What rests, but that the mortal sentence pass On his transgression" (10.47–49). That, despite the Fall, He intends "Mercy colleague with Justice" (10.59) is manifest in His decision to have the Son, "Both Ransom and Redeemer voluntary" (10.61), judge them. But that His mercy remains, for the moment at least, and to some extent even lastingly in time, circumscribed and contingent, is demonstrated both by the brevity and almost perfunctory nature of the Son's interview with Adam and Eve (10.92–228), and by the juxtaposition to that interview of five scenes (10.229–1104) in which the evil unleashed by their crime is dramatized in sickening detail.

That the Son comes as "mild Judge and Intercessor both" (10.96) is asserted, but not unequivocally shown. He addresses both sinners as "gracious Judge without revile" (10.118), deflects "th' instant stroke of Death denounc't that day" (10.210), covers their outward nakedness "with Skins of Beasts" (10.217), and their "inward nakedness, much more Opprobrious, with his Robe of Righteousness" (10.221–222). But he addresses Adam very sternly (10.144 -156), announces briskly the punishments decreed upon the serpent, Satan, Eve, and Adam, and is gone. Though referred to as "both

Judge and Savior" (10.209), almost no evidence is presented that he functions as savior. He rescues both Adam and Eve from immediate death. But to their obvious need to be rescued from far more than that he does not attend. The decrees pronounced, he simply leaves them to a world suddenly and hideously warped by dangers, and by a sudden degeneration in Nature, that they can neither yet comprehend nor withstand.

In the five scenes juxtaposed to his departure, reassurance and a sense of horror coexist, the horror predominant. That the dangers will ultimately engulf Mankind is precluded by the assurance, offered several times earlier, and twice repeated, once before the scenes begin (10.1–7), and again during the third scene, that God governs all of reality, and by the ironic laughter to which the forces of evil are intermittently exposed. The reassurance, however, is far less than completely soothing, because the dangers, and the degeneration in Nature, will be overcome only ultimately. For the moment, at least—and in fact throughout time—throughout human history—they will predominate. The sense of doom they produce is awful. And, until the end of the fifth scene, when at last the precondition begins to be effected by Adam and Eve, no impulse of reconstruction sufficient to mitigate them even stirs.

The Son gone, Death, Sin, and Satan appear, to announce dramatically, in the first of the five scenes (10.229–414), their expanded dominion. All three are ironically mocked; but only in passing. And the irony is far less pronounced than is the sense of heightened danger.

To the realization that his punishment will be "Not instant, but of future time" Satan responds, almost incredibly, with "joy" (10.345). And Sin, "his fair Enchanting Daughter" (10.352–353), her earlier warning obviously forgotten, that God "laughs the while At thee ordain'd his drudge" (2.731–732), and in "His wrath . . . one day will destroy ye" (2.734), asserts ludicrously that Satan will "Monarch reign" (10.375) on earth, God having perforce decided to share sovereignty with him (10.375–382). But the ironies are of slight effect, because the power of darkness has suddenly been extended. The "stupendous Bridge" (10.351) linking earth and Hell exists. Sin has correctly sensed that "Hell could no longer hold us in her bounds" (10.365). She and Death are no longer "confin'd Within Hell Gates" (10.368–369). Satan has "made one Realm Hell and this World" (10.391–392). And, as he informs them, on their "joint vigor now My hold on this new Kingdom all depends" (10.405–406). Ultimately, they will have accomplished nothing. But, for the moment at least, they have accomplished altogether too much, and have muted even the mockery they deserve.

In the second of the scenes (10.414–584) the mockery is massive, but once again undermined by hideous fact. Satan's conviction that he has returned to Pandemonium "Successful beyond hope" (10.463) and is about to lead his cohort "forth Triumphant" (10.463–464) to earth, his idiotic glee at having outwitted God, his preening delight at having "with an Apple . . . worth your laughter" (10.487–488) destroyed Mankind, his addled certainty that his punishment will entail only Adam's progeny bruising his head (10.496–501)—the abject stupidity everywhere manifest in his speech to his minions justifies the laughter roused by his punishment. The serpent, one moment "expecting Thir universal shout and high applause" (10.504–505), and the next writhing before a cohort of serpents, has earned the mockery heaped upon him. It is muted, however, by the news he has brought, that, though ultimately false, is, for the moment at least, horrific. In the end, his machinations will come to nothing, and, with Death and Sin, he will be destroyed. But the end is a very long way off. And, his temporary humiliation complete (10.572–574), he will resume his power and his shape, and return, his malice undiminished, to his new kingdom, and to his prey.

In the third of the scenes (10.585–648), though the gloating delight of Sin and Death as they prepare to devastate earth and Mankind is mocked by their own blindness, and by God, even He admits their depredations, about to begin, will scourge the world until time ends. Sin addresses her son ridiculously as "all conquering Death" (10.591), and they hurry off convinced they can "destroy or unimmortal make All kinds" (10.611–612). Watching them, in command of their every motion, God derides their ludicrous delusion that "as if transported with some fit Of Passion, I to them had quitted all" (10.626–627), and their laughable blindness to the essential fact: "that I call'd and drew them thither My Hell-hounds" (10.629–630), to be used and then, when time ends, destroyed (10.630–637). Even God admits, however, that, until time ends, they will be "cramm'd and gorg'd, nigh burst" (10.632) with feeding on the sinfulness of Mankind, and that "Till then the Curse pronounc't on both [Heaven and Earth] precedes" (10.640). They are foolish. They are blind. Ultimately, they will have accomplished nothing. But they have hurried off to feed on Mankind, ravenously, and for a very long time.

In the fourth scene (10.649–715), Nature is blighted, by the completion of a process begun at the Fall. Eve having eaten, "Earth felt the wound, and Nature from her seat Sighing through all her Works gave signs of woe" (9.782–783). Adam having joined her, "Earth trembl'd from her entrails, as again In pangs, and Nature gave a second groan" (9.1000–1001). And, Sin and Death having departed for Earth, the heavenly constellations and the winds turn noxious, producing "Like change on Sea and Land" (10.693), and discord first appears "among th' irrational, Death introduc'd through fierce antipathy" (10.708–709) among fowl, fish, and beasts.

Like the dangers to which the Fall has exposed Mankind, the degeneration in Nature is permanent. It will persist through time, as will the dangers. Frost, heat, natural calamities, the enmity of wild animals, will hound Mankind, as will Satan, Sin, and Death. The instruments of God's justice, they are not subject to essential mitigation. They must simply be faced, in their horror, and endured.

The last of His instruments, by contrast, need not be. To it a human response may be made that almost at once reconstructs at least inner reality, and prompts God further to reconstruct it, so that horror is displaced first with hope, and then with joy. Unlike the others, which inflict "from without . . . growing miseries" (10.714–715), this instrument—the scourge that lashes the human soul stricken by sin—works from "within" (10.717), and, by effecting gradually the precondition to God's mercy, transmutes the chaos within the heart into radiant order, assuring Adam (who will later assure Eve) that, however hideous their disobedience, its consequences are ultimately salvational.

The scourge begins its work with the Fall, and effects the requisite reconstruction during the fifth, and last, of the scene juxtaposed to the departure of the Son (10.715–1104). Husband and wife having eaten of the forbidden fruit, the chaos of ungoverned passion instantly begins polluting their relation. The pollution is cleansed as, during the fifth scene, each works, gradually and painfully, back towards the other. And, that process complete, God, in His mercy, strengthens them with a lavish reward, sending them forth into a diminished, dangerous world profoundly chastened, yet almost serene.

The chaos produced by the Fall is inevitable, because, for the first time, as a consequence of Adam and Eve's disobedience,

> Understanding rul'd not, and the Will
> Heard not her lore, both in subjection now

> To sensual Appetite, who from beneath
> Usurping over sovran Reason claim'd
> Superior sway.
> (9.1127–1131)

The consequences of this subversion of reason are as destructive as was the unleashing of Satan and his progeny upon the world. Adam and Eve having awakened, their lust indulged, the first ugly fight of their lives erupts, "neither self-condemning" (9.1188), each blaming the other for the Fall, "And of their vain contest appear'd no end" (9.1189). The toll exacted by the contest is disastrous. They confront the Son

> Love . . . not in thir looks, either to God
> Or to each other, but apparent guilt,
> And shame, and perturbation, and despair,
> Anger, and obstinacy, and hate, and guile.
> (10.111–114)

Adam's degeneration is especially marked, as the first three of his mental efforts after the Fall show: his attempt (brushed sternly aside by the Son) to blame Eve for the Fall (10.124-156); his whining attempt, in monologue, to blame God (10.720-844); and a vicious, unbalanced tirade against Eve (10.866-908).

"To sorrow abandon'd . . . And in a troubl'd Sea of passion tost" (10.717-718), driven by "Conscience" (10.842) into an "Abyss of fears And horrors" (10.842-843), almost unhinged by "his fierce passion" (10.865), Adam seems incapable of beginning the task of reconciliation with Eve, the task which must be completed if God, in His mercy, is to mitigate part of the their suffering.

Fortunately, the task is undertaken by Eve, who desires, beyond anything, her husband's love—who seems to desire, as has been shown, nothing else. Terrified by his tirade against her, which seems to argue that love is lost, she throws herself, weeping, at his feet, and begs him to

> bereave me not,
> Whereon I live, thy gentle looks, thy aid,
> Thy counsel in this uttermost distress.
> (10.918–920)

"Between us two let there be peace" (10.924), she implores, and proposes to importune God to punish her alone for the Fall (10.930-936). Roused from the abyss by her heart-broken pleas, Adam begins the indispensable movement back towards his wife. His corrosive passions notwithstanding, "soon his heart relented Towards her" (10.940-941), and, "his anger all . . . lost" (10.945), he agrees that they must "no more contend . . . but strive In offices of Love, how we may lighten Each other's burden in our share of woe" (10.958-961). Almost despite himself, he returns to the woman who treasures his love as "the sole contentment of my heart, Living or dying" (10.973-974).

That return achieved, the precondition for God's intervention is almost fulfilled. Adam's mind, never fully overwhelmed, steadied by love balances itself sufficiently to assert that repentance is the imperative of the moment, and to instruct Eve, still in despair, in the process and consequences of repentance. That done, God, in His mercy, prepares to mitigate far more of their suffering than in justice He should.

The sight of Eve weeping at his feet, "Immovable till peace obtain'd from fault Acknowledg'd and deplor'd" (10.938-939), by rousing "Commiseration" (10.940) in Adam helps decisively to clear his mind, which, even in his worst moments, sustains him in part. Rebuked by the Son for his effort to blame Eve for the Fall, he is sensible enough not to respond. To each of the arguments in his monologue blaming God he himself offers the convincing counter-argument; and finally he concludes, "Him after all Disputes Forc't I absolve" (10.828-829). And his vicious tirade against his wife is displaced almost at once with compassion. Not even his most ungoverned passion, raging at its utmost intensity, obscures for long the conclusion of his intellect that "all my evasions vain And reasonings, though through Mazes, lead me still But to my own conviction" (10.829-831). Reason struggling to regain its ascendancy, he confesses to himself. Softened by compassion, "as one disarm'd" (10.945) he accepts his wife's confession. And, reason once again sovereign in him, he addresses sensibly her "vehement despair" (10.1007), explaining patiently, kindly, and coherently why her two suggestions—suicide and barrenness—are unacceptable, and why they must instead "confess Humbly our faults, and pardon beg . . . with tears . . . sent from hearts contrite, in sign Of sorrow unfeign'd, and humiliation meek" (10.1088-1092).

That option accepted by both, and the precondition for God's intervention thus completely fulfilled, God's mercy, being urgent, descends at once upon Adam and Eve, mitigating, as they prepare to leave Eden (11.1–12.649), more of their suffering than should be mitigated, and sending them forth into a diminished but still promising world sufficiently strengthened by knowledge and by joy to endure the suffering justice demands they must endure for their lifetimes, and as their progeny must until the end of time.

The mercy descends upon Adam (who will share it with Eve) in a complex narrative, itself a test of his intellect, courage, and faith in God; a test that he passes, though only with enormous difficulty, and whose reward is the strength to depart from Paradise with dignity, honor, and the assurance of the ultimate triumph of the good.

A final precondition precedes the test. To qualify for it, he and his wife must obey the order of expulsion from Paradise imposed suddenly and unexpectedly by God. That, having repented, they will obey is a foregone conclusion. The act of obedience is nonetheless impressive dramatically. Their joint prayer of repentance done, both find "Strength added from above, new hope to spring Out of despair, joy, but with fear yet link'd" (11.138–139). Adam finds "peace return'd Home to my Breast" (11.153–154), and Eve that "infinite in pardon was my Judge" (11.167). The sudden disruption of their renewed tranquility is so shattering that Adam "at the news Heart-strook with chilling gripe of sorrow stood" (11.263–264), and Eve cries out, "O unexpected stroke, worse than of Death!" (11.269) Nonetheless, they obey, completely and at once, Adam asserting on behalf of both, "to his great bidding I submit" (11.314).

This assertion permits the test to begin. The narrative—Michael's review of the history of the world, from the beginning to the end of time—is the means by which God's mercy comforts Mankind as it departs from Eden. "If patiently thy bidding they obey" (11.112), God informs Michael, referring to His order of expulsion, "Dismiss them not disconsolate; reveal To Adam what shall come in future days . . . So send them forth, though sorrowing, yet in peace" (11.113–117). They have obeyed. And so the narrative of consolation begins.

For a long time it does not console; in fact, it almost unhinges Adam. The spectacle of almost unrelieved evil he is forced to witness—all of it the consequence of his own disobedience—is almost unbearable. He endures it—though barely—perhaps because Michael assures him at the outset that it will teach him "'True patience, and to temper joy with fear And pious sorrow" (11.361–362), and certainly because, trusting "to the hand of Heav'n" (11.372), he undertakes to confront "the evil . . . arming to overcome By suffering, and earn rest from labor won" (11.373-375). The evil is horrific. The suffering is intense. And from the labor of enduring it he earns, for himself and for his wife, more than rest.

The opening scenes of the narrative are sickening; especially to Adam, compelled by Michael to acknowledge "Th' effects which thy original crime hath wrought In some to spring from thee, who never . . . sinn'd thy sin, yet from thy sin derive Corruption to bring forth more violent deeds" (11.423-428). In quick succession, "His eyes . . . op'n'd" (11.429), he is forced to behold Cain killing Abel (11.429-465), a "Lazar-house" of men struck with the loathsome diseases contracted though "th' inabstinence of Eve" (11.476), the sons of Seth lured into gross, destructive immorality by the daughters of Cain (11.556-636), the "violence . . . Oppression, and Sword-Law" (11.671-672) unleashed by the children born of that immorality, the huge destruction wrought by the Flood (11.712-762).

It is almost unendurable; and Adam, still far from strong, slips back almost to rebellious thought. At the murder of Abel, he is "in his heart Dismay'd" (11.448-449). Horrified by the lazar-house, he wonders aloud, "Why is life . . . obtruded on us thus?" (11.502-504) Repulsed by the lascivious daughters of Cain, he insists that "still . . . the tenor of Man's woe Holds on the same, from Woman to begin" (11.632-633). The world flooded, "How didst thou grieve . . . to behold The end of all thy Offspring . . . comfortless, as when a Father mourns His Children" (11.754-761). His response, in fact, to all he has seen is almost bitter, almost touched with despair: "O Visions ill foreseen!" (11.763) he cries, full of degeneracy "Which neither [a man's] foreknowing can prevent, And hee the future evil shall no less In apprehension than in substance feel Grievous to bear" (11.773-776).

He does, however, bear the visions, in part because he accepts Michael's corrective glosses on his anguished ejaculations, in part because glimmers of goodness appear in the general gloom of evil, and in part because he is, as he predicted he would be, strong enough "to overcome By suffering" what he must see. To Michael's comment that the lazar-house is the inevitable outcome of "ungovern'd appetite" (11.517) he responds, "I yield it just . . . and submit" (11.526). Michael's response to his execration—that man's woe proceeds, not from woman, but "From Man's effeminate slackness" (11.634)—he accepts in silence. The existence of Seth, and his transfiguration (11.604-710), demonstrate that it is possible to be "righteous in a World perverse" (11.701). And the history of Noah, a "Son of

Light" (11.808), testifies that "The paths of righteousness . . . full of peace" (11.814–815) may be trod.

The history of Noah is the crucial turning point in Michael's narrative, because, with Adam's response to it, consolation at last materializes. The visions endured, he has proven his worthiness to be consoled. And therefore, for the first time during the narrative, he feels a lasting impulse of joy. At the sight of Noah descending from the ark, "the heart of Adam erst so sad Greatly rejoic'd" (11.868–869), wonderfully buoyed that "Far less I now lament for one whole world Of wicked Sons destroyed, than I rejoice" (11.874–875) at the worthiness of Noah to be saved.

This rejoicing will sustain him through the rest of the narrative. The means of God's mercy, it will grow exponentially as the good news—the news sufficient to send Mankind forth from Eden "though sorrowing, yet in peace"—unfolds gradually to Adam's increasingly ravished understanding: that history, despite its awful darkness, is ultimately the record of the triumph of God over that darkness, over every obstacle, human and satanic, to everlasting peace, to eternal salvation.

Though in Michael's narrative of the "world restor'd" (12.3) after the Flood the darkness persists, a light begins to glow in it; a light that gradually grows in intensity as the narrative proceeds from the Flood through the Incarnation to the end of time, by exponential degrees irradiating Adam, and sending him forth from Paradise strengthened by enduring joy.

The darkness is evident in the histories of Nimrod, the Tower of Babel, and Noah's son Ham (12.24–104), and in God's decision, "Wearied with [Mankind's] iniquities . . . To leave them to thir own polluted ways" (12.107–110). The light, however, begins to shine in His decision "one peculiar Nation to select From all the rest" (12.111–112), through whom "all Nations of the earth Shall . . . be blessed" (12.147–148), in the short term because that nation will, its stiff-necked tendencies notwithstanding, bear witness to Him in a world "stupid grown" (12.116), and in the long term because from its seed will emerge "thy great deliverer" (12.149). The father of this nation, the first Jew, Abraham, "straight obeys" (12.126) all of God's commands. And his descendants, led by their great leader, Moses, out of Egypt and through the wilderness, adhere faithfully to the Law he reveals, a "Law . . . imperfet, and but giv'n With purpose to resign them in full time Up to a better Cov'nant" (12.300–302). Their adherence will be far from complete; "sin Will reign among them, as of thee begot" (12.285–286),

Adam is compelled to hear. Nonetheless, they will merit a transcendent honor: that from the seed of their most illustrious king

> shall rise
> A Son, the Woman's seed to thee foretold,
> Foretold to Abraham, as in whom all shall trust,
> All Nations, and to Kings foretold, of Kings
> The last, for of his Reign shall be no end.
> (12.326-330)

This Son will suffer for Mankind's sake "a reproachful life and cursed death" (12.406). But "Death over him no power Shall long usurp" (12.420-421). And the Passion he endures will transfigure history. It will, Michael informs Adam, annul "thy doom, the death thou shouldst have di'd, In sin for ever lost from life" (12.428-429), defeat Satan by crushing "his strength" (12.430), in the process "Defeating Sin and Death" (12.431), and convert even Mankind's temporal death into "A gentle wafting to immortal life" (12.435). His task accomplished, the Son "to the Heav'n of Heav'ns... shall ascend With victory" (12.451-452), there to remain "at God's right hand, exalted high Above all names in Heav'n" (12.457-458), until "this world's dissolution... ripe" (12.459), he descends once again,

> To judge th' unfaithful dead, but to reward
> His faithful, and receive them into bliss,
> Whether in Heav'n or Earth, for then the Earth
> Shall all be Paradise, far happier place
> Than this of Eden, and far happier days.
> (12.461-465).

As the light in Michael's narrative intensifies, the joy it suffuses through Adam deepens, deepening the consolation that strengthens him to accept with dignity and with hope the consequences of his own, and his wife's, Fall. With the realization that the Patriarchs and Moses are "types And shadows, of that destin'd Seed to bruise The Serpent, by what means he shall achieve Mankind's deliverance" (12.322-325), Adam finds "Mine eyes true op'ning, and my heart much eas'd" (12.274). The birth of "the true Anointed King Messiah" briefly described, and the relation between Eve and Mary in consequence suddenly clear to him, Adam rhapsodizes on the Virgin Mother (12.379-382), "with such joy Surcharg'd, as had like grief been dew'd in tears" (12.372-373). And, told what this world's dissolution will yield, "Replete with joy and wonder" (12.468), he marvels at the "goodness infinite, goodness immense" (12.469) that has so miraculously turned evil into good that

> full of doubt I stand,
> Whether I should repent me now of sin
> By mee done and occasion'd, or rejoice
> Much more, that much more good thereof shall spring,
> To God more glory, more good will to Men
> From God, and over wrath grace shall abound.
> (12.473–478)

From this elevation of wonder and joy Adam descends to a confident tranquility, the culmination of God's mercy to him in closing. The narrative ended, he informs Michael that he will depart from Eden "Greatly in peace of thought" (12.557–558). He deserves to. He has sinned horribly. Confronted with good and evil, empowered by an exhaustive examination of the evil to choose the good, by endowment free to choose it, he knowingly, deliberately, chooses the evil, preferring uxorious passion to God. In just consequence doomed to death, through a painful process of self-reconstruction he restores, to the extent possible in his diminished state, his mental and spiritual equilibrium, thereby gaining access to God's mercy, that gradually strengthens him for the difficult task of exiting Paradise with dignity and a measure of joy. Although he has sinned, he has returned to God. And, God having therefore returned to him, he leaves Eden hand in hand with his wife (who has also returned), "Some natural tears ... dropp'd" (12.645) by both, but "The World ... all before them ... and Providence thir guide" (12.646–647), leading them lovingly and mercifully towards life, and afterwards towards eternal life.

Chapter Five

The Scarlet Letter

WHEN HESTER ASCENDS THE scaffold, her infant daughter Pearl in her arms, she is likened to "the image of Divine Maternity . . . but only by contrast of that sacred image of sinless motherhood, whose infant was to redeem the world," because in Hester "there was the taint of deepest sin in the most sacred quality of human life, working such effect, that the world was only the darker for this woman's beauty, and the more lost for the infant she had borne" (58).[1] The infant is incontestably "sin-born" (64), its mother's heart incontestably "erring" (65), filled with "pollution" (67). A "poor, sinful woman" (85), she is whispered to insidiously by "the bad angel" (86), who has gained at least partial dominion in her soul as a result of her sin. And in her giving birth to Pearl, "an imp of evil, emblem and product of sin" (92), "a great law had been broken" (89).

Beyond question, she has sinned horribly.

She is nonetheless impressive, though not morally, because she endures, with a kind of natural dignity, inappropriate torture, as opposed to fit punishment, at the hands of townspeople and authorities avowedly, but only misshapenly, Christian, and because her relation to Christianity is carefully, though not always completely, hidden, from her community, and from herself.

On the scaffold, Hester endures, entirely alone, a horror almost beyond endurance, to "her impulsive and passionate nature" (58) in general, and in particular to "the desperate recklessness of her mood" (55) as she is subjected first to "the very ideal of ignominy" (57) by the Puritan community, and afterwards to the torture of suddenly acknowledging, and then confronting, her husband. She suffers "an agony from every footstep" (57)

---

1. Nathaniel Hawthorne, *The Scarlet Letter* (Boston: Houghton Mifflin, 1961).

of the people thronging to see her, and feels that "under the leaden affliction which it was her doom to endure . . . she must needs shriek out with the full power of her lungs, and cast herself from the scaffold down upon the ground, or else go mad at once" (59). And the affliction visited upon her by the Puritans pales beside the sudden shock of acknowledging Chillingworth. "Dreadful as it was, she was conscious of a shelter in the presence of these thousand witnesses. It was better to stand thus, with so many betwixt him and her, than to greet him face to face, they two alone. She fled for refuge, as it were, to the public exposure, and dreaded the moment when its protection should be withdrawn from her" (64). At merely the anticipation of that moment "she pressed her infant to her bosom, with so convulsive a force that the poor babe uttered another cry of pain" (61). Having borne "that morning, all that nature could endure" (69–70), Hester is returned to the prison, to face her interview with Chillingworth, "in no reasonable state of mind" (73), and therefore in need of "constant watchfulness, lest she should perpetrate violence on herself, or do some half-frenzied mischief to the poor babe" (71).

The day on the scaffold endured, Hester's suffering worsens horribly.

> Then, she was supported by an unnatural tension of the nerves, and by all the combative energy of her character, which enabled her to convert the scene into a kind of lurid triumph. It was, moreover, a separate and insulated event, to occur but once in her lifetime, and to meet which, therefore, reckless of economy, she might call up the vital strength that would have sufficed for many quiet years. The very law that condemned her—a giant of stern features, but with vigor to support, as well as well as to annihilate, in his iron arm—had held her up, through the terrible ordeal of her ignominy. But now, with this unattended walk from the prison-door, began the daily custom, and she must either sustain and carry it forward by the ordinary resources of her nature, or sink beneath it.
>
> (78)

Thus, the day of her release, "the accumulating days, and added years . . . would pile up their misery upon the heap of shame" (79), inflicting upon Hester a deeper torture than did the day on the scaffold. "Shut out from the sphere of human charities," she is left utterly alone, "without a friend on earth who dared to show himself" (81), to endure the burden of a "sick and morbid heart" (78), the hovering presence of Chillingworth, the tribulation of a difficult, ostracized child, the venom poured unremittingly into her soul by the Puritan community, and—perhaps worst of all—the effort by Governor Bellingham, and others "of the leading inhabitants, cherishing the more rigid order of principles in religion and government, to deprive her of her child" (99)—an effort that leaves "her fate hanging in the balance" (111), and "provoked her to little less than madness" (112).

The "dreadful agony" that Hester suffers, with increasing intensity, almost unremittingly, grows "with daily torture" (85). And yet she endures it, basically because of a "natural dignity and force of character" (54), "a certain state and dignity" (55), and a certain "native energy of character" (83). These traits—an intensity of life-force of its nature, in some ways at least, impressive—in great part sustain her through everything: through the hours on the scaffold, the encounter with Chillingworth, and three subsequent years of agony, marked in particular by the threat to deprive her of Pearl; a threat that, though almost maddening, she confronts "with almost a fierce expression," the visible sign of a fierce sense of her "indefeasible rights" as a mother "against the world," rights that she is "ready to defend . . . to the death," and in whose behalf, as she clearly informs Dimmesdale, "raising her voice almost to a shriek" (112), she is prepared to betray even him.

Though never defined as a moral impulse, Hester's life-force rouses a carefully modulated degree of sympathy, because her struggle to endure is a struggle against a perversion of Christian punishment, because consciously she shuns evil, and because though she does serve it, she does so only in thought, in only one recorded moment, and in an artfully self-evasive manner.

That, having committed a horrible evil, Hester deserves to be punished, is indisputable. But, in a Christian universe, only Christian punishment is fit—punishment tempered by mercy and love. The opposite of that is inflicted upon her, both by the townspeople, and by the authorities. And so, whatever the totality of her motive in resisting, her resolve to endure against her tormentors rouses sympathy.

To one side of the prison door through which Hester exits to the scaffold, "a wild rose-bush" blossoms, its "delicate gems" offering, to the prisoner going in and out, "their fragrance and fragile beauty . . . in token that the deep heart of Nature could pity and be kind to him" (50). A similar offering of pity and kindness is incumbent upon Hester's fellow Christians. Unfortunately, it is almost non-existent. One young mother, awaiting Hester's appearance from the prison, pities her deeply (53, 56). The others in the crowd, deformed by "the early severity of the Puritan character" (51), without exception have gathered "as to a festival" (64) grimly to witness Hester crushed by "the whole dismal severity of the Puritanic code of law" (54). And so, "meagre, indeed, and cold, was the sympathy that a transgressor might look for" (52) from the townspeople, as their conversation and behavior throughout the scene at the scaffold confirm. The women in particular are "pitiless" as "self-constituted judges" (53). And one of the townsmen can affirm, without a trace of irony, that in condemning Hester "to stand only a space of three hours on the platform of the pillory, and then and thereafter, for the remainder of her natural life, to wear a mark of shame upon her bosom" the Puritan authorities have exhibited "their great mercy and tenderness of heart" (64).

In the three years following the scaffold scene, the townspeople persist, with "ever relentless vigor" (83), in enforcing "the undying, the everactive sentence of the Puritan tribunal" against "the poor, sinful woman" (85), the dismal proof of their untempered obedience to their own "hard law" (87). Everyone seems to delight in the torture, from "dames of rank ... accustomed to distil drops of bitterness into [Hester's] heart" (84), to "wretches less miserable than herself... who not infrequently insulted the hand that fed them" (83), to clergymen who "paused in the street to address words of exhortation, that brought a crowd, with its mingled grin and frown" (85). From every quarter, agony is distilled into "the sufferer's defenceless breast" (84).

The Puritan magistrates are no more impressive. "They were, doubtless, good men, just and sage." Nonetheless, they are utterly unqualified to judge Hester, because "out of the whole human family, it would not have been easy to select the same number of wise and virtuous persons, who should be less capable of sitting in judgment on an erring woman's heart, and disentangling its mesh of good and evil, than the sages of rigid aspect" towards whom, standing on the scaffold, Hester turns her face. Even the heart of the pitiless multitude seems to her "larger and warmer" (65). John Wilson, the clergyman who addresses Hester first, is a man "of kind and genial spirit." Unfortunately, however, "this last attribute ... had been less carefully developed than his intellectual gifts, and was, in truth, rather a matter of shame than self-congratulation with him." He has no right to "meddle with a question of human guilt, passion, and anguish" (66). Neither do the other magistrates, either during the scaffold scene, or during the three years subsequent to it; especially, they have no business meddling with the question of Hester's custody of Pearl. Their persistence in meddling, far more than the hard-heartedness of the townspeople, dooms Hester to the torture, not the fit punishment, of the "devilish . . . ugly engine" (57) of the pillory, and thereafter, for three years, to the obscenity of a banishment from humanity so complete that "every gesture, every word, and even the silence of those with whom she came in contact, implied, and often expressed" her enforced alienation from all nurturing "mortal interests" (84); an obscenity that culminates in the magistrates' resolve that Hester surrender custody of Pearl, against which she must struggle, utterly powerless and almost mad, to assert, very nearly without success, nothing more than "a mother's rights" (112).

The torture inflicted upon Hester at the scaffold and unremittingly for three years afterwards does not weaken Hester's bond to Christianity; because that bond, it turns out, is a fiction that hides from her a terrifying truth that she may one day embrace with ecstasy: that her soul belongs not to Christianity, but to a godless romanticism.

During her interview with Chillingworth, when Hester suspects that the cup of medicine Chillingworth offers her may contain poison, she refers to her spiritual unworthiness as a Christian, the direct and inevitable consequence of her sin. She admits that she has thought of death—"have wished for it,—would even have prayed for it, were it fit such as I should pray for any thing" (73–74).

When, profoundly puzzled by Pearl, she speculates that "God, as a direct consequence of the sin which man thus punished, had given her a lovely child, whose place was on that same dishonored bosom, to connect her parent forever with the race and descent of mortals, and to be finally a blessed soul in heaven" (88). But even that thought fills her "less with hope than apprehension," because it is undermined by her awareness of her spiritual pollution. "She knew that her deed had been evil; she could have no faith, therefore, that its result would be for good." She is convinced that "In giving [Pearl] existence, a great law had been broken" (89).

In her interview with Governor Billingham she begs that Pearl not be taken from her because "God gave me the child . . . See you not, she is the scarlet letter, only capable of being loved, and so endowed with a million-fold the power of retribution for my sin?" (112)

Walking home after successfully defending her right to keep Pearl, Hester affirms completely without reservation her conviction that her struggle is essentially spiritual, a struggle against theological darkness.

Refusing the invitation of Mistress Hibbins to join her satanic revels in the forest, Hester asserts that, had the authorities taken Pearl from her, "I would willingly have gone with thee into the forest, and signed my name in the Black Man's book too, and that with mine own blood!" (116).

The evidence of Hester's apparent bond to Christianity noted assures a degree of sympathy for her, because it demonstrates Hester's apparent concern that the Black Man not take utter possession of her soul, or gain access to Pearl's. She seems concerned, that is, if not to bridge the distance between herself and God, at least to assure that it does not widen. And thus the "triumphant smile" (116) with which she dismisses Mistress Hibbins seems to reflect a hard-earned victory in an ongoing battle that Hester wages against herself and a force of darkness inherent in the universe.

Unfortunately, the sympathy noted is not warranted, because her standing as a Christian is suspect, for three reasons. First, the battle is waged only intermittently. Second, it is waged powerfully only when Hester is threatened with the loss of her daughter—a threat she may conceive of, at bottom, as an attack not upon her Christian soul, but upon her maternal impulse. Third—and by far most important—though she struggles incessantly to evade the knowledge (thus preserving for herself some measure of sympathy), Hester is not merely, at bottom, uninterested in Christianity, but actively and adamantly antagonistic to it.

Thus, far from wishing to protect herself from the Black Man, Hester ardently desires his company; or, at the least, is in the process of coming ardently to desire it. But to admit this to herself would be unbearable. So the self-deception about her wish to flee the Black Man is necessary to the economy of her mental life. Beneath that wish is hidden, usually from herself as well as from others, the still terrifying truth. When she thinks in Christian terms, Hester supposes she is struggling against the darkness; a supposition that shields her from the truth that she does not yet want to acknowledge: that, in the bottom of her soul, she desires, more than anything, the darkness.

That desire is dramatized with perfect confidence only when she must oppose it to the irreconcilable truth at the bottom of Dimmesdale's soul. It is, however, foreshadowed timorously when she wonders why, despite the public degradation on the scaffold, and the daily torture inflicted upon her, she chooses to remain among the Puritans. The superficial reason is that she cannot escape to Europe because "her sin" (79) roots her to the soil of the Puritan community. By far the most important reason is hidden within a complex secret:

> It might be, too,—doubtless it was so, although she hid the secret from herself, and grew pale whenever it struggled out of her heart, like a serpent hole,—it might be that another feeling kept her within the scene and pathway that had been so fatal. There dwelt, there trod the feet of one with whom she deemed herself connected in a union that, unrecognized on earth, would bring them together before the bar of final judgment, and make that their marriage-altar, for a joint futurity of endless retribution. Over and over again, the tempter of souls had thrust this idea upon Hester's contemplation, and laughed at the passionate and desperate joy with which she seized, and then strove to cast it from her. She barely looked the idea in the face, and hastened to bar it in its dungeon. What she compelled herself to believe,—what finally, she reasoned upon, as her motive for continuing a resident of New England,—was half a truth, and half a self-delusion. Here, she said to herself, had been the scene of her guilt, and here should be the scene of her earthly punishment; and so, perchance the torture of her daily shame would at length purge her soul, and work out another purity than that which she had lost; more saint-like, because the result of martyrdom.
>
> (80)

Against all of the satanic temptations thus far noted Hester struggles, or at least seems to struggle, if only intermittently, at least for the most part without obvious ambiguity; anxious, it seems, to avoid further involvement with the Black Man. To the temptation above—the one that moves her most profoundly by far—she responds with an ambiguity that terrifies her. This temptation is her overwhelming desire to be reunited with Dimmesdale; the desire that exists at the center of her being—the desire that almost *is* her being. She wants Dimmesdale. She wants to be with him. She wants to be with him forever. And she is entitled to be, because they are, in her opinion, in irrefutable spiritual fact, married. They—and they only—are husband and wife. And therefore no adultery exists, and no sin exists. She is exclusively his, and she wants him back. But that total truth—that statement of what, almost alone, she wants from life—is, for the time at least, unbearable to her. And so she escapes from it, in two ways. As often as possible, "she hid the secret from herself." And whenever, despite her best efforts at repression, it manages to struggle out of her heart, suddenly a Christian she defines it as evil, and embodies it in the distancing language of retribution and martyrdom. When it slithers up at her "like a serpent from its hole" she grows pale, and insists that she desires reunion only at "the bar of final judgment," and to go from there, their "marriage-altar," to an eternity—but to an eternity together—of "endless retribution." But even that is insupportable. It is "the tempter of souls" who "had thrust this idea upon Hester's contemplation"—who forces it upon her unwilling consciousness. Always she "strove . . . to cast it from her . . . to bar it in its dungeon." And finally, in her desperate effort to keep it there, she "compelled" herself to believe she remains in New England to "purge her soul," through daily torture, of the serpent itself; and through the martyrdom of so doing to become virtually a saint.

Unfortunately, however, for her peace of mind, the self-deception works only now and then. The serpent struggles "over and over again" from its hole. And whenever it does, she seizes "with passionate and desperate joy" at its idea. And though she "barely looked the idea in the face," over and over again she does in fact look. And therefore what she finally compels herself to believe is "half a self-delusion." It is true that the scene of her guilt should be the scene of her earthly punishment. That she wishes to be punished—that she wishes the serpent purged from her soul—is the self-delusion. What she truly wishes, in the depths of her soul, is to embrace the serpent—passionately, and forever.

Fortunately for her stature as a participant in the dramatically inevitable debate between her soul and Dimmesdale's, except when her repressive defenses weaken, Hester is unaware—because she forces herself to remain unaware—of her deepest wish. Therefore, and because, as noted, she is tortured, rather than punished in an appropriately Christian fashion, and because she seems to flee, though only intermittently, yet for the most part consciously at least in good faith, from the darkness—Hester, though indisputably sinful, is afforded her carefully measured sympathy until her torturers begin to think kindly of her, and therefore to desist from the torture, and as she herself becomes, to the extent that she can, aware of her own deepest desire, ceases to fear it, justifies and prepares to embrace it.

Her portrait established, Hester recedes, as the portrait of her polar opposite in commitment is drawn: an unshakable Christian of impressive endowment, his soul torn almost completely apart by two related moral defects, and by a principle of evil in the universe itself functioning through a decent human being transformed by an obsession into a fiend. The portrait of Dimmesdale defines the imperatives of Christianity, dramatizes the consequences to Dimmesdale of sinning against them, and by dramatic juxtaposition underscores Hester's indifference to them.

A man of remarkable spiritual gifts—gifts perhaps unique in his society—Dimmesdale nonetheless suffers, through seven horribly destructive years, exclusively from the unbearable awareness that he has offended God, by committing adultery, and—subsequently—and more profoundly—by surrendering to a combination of cowardice and hypocrisy that prevents him from returning, through repentance, to God. This awareness unhinges his soul, and allows the Devil, operating through Chillingworth, access to it; so that his conscience, morbidly inflamed by himself and by the Devil, drags him inexorably down from being to non-being, and almost to madness; a descent for which he alone is fully responsible, and during which he therefore is more often mocked than pitied, because though, unlike Hester, he sees the better, he follows the worse.

By endowment Dimmesdale is not only religious, but a Christian blessed with the rarest of gifts. He is "a true priest, a true religionist, with the reverential sentiment largely developed, and an order of mind that impelled itself powerfully along the track of a creed, and wore its passage continually deeper with the passage of time . . . It would always be essential to his peace to feel the pressure of a faith about him, supporting, while it confined him within its iron framework." (122) And for the faith he has chosen he has many "precious" qualifications: "high aspirations for the welfare of his race, warm love of souls, pure sentiments," and a "natural piety" not only "strengthened by thought and study" but—astonishingly—"illuminated by revelation" (129). By virtue of this illumination in particular Dimmesdale is by nature superior even to the vast majority of his fellow-clergy. Some of them are "more profoundly versed" in theological scholarship than he is. Others have "a far sturdier texture of mind than his." Still others, "true saintly fathers," have been "etherealized . . . by spiritual communications with the better world" while still in this inferior world. "Not improbably, it was to this latter class of men," whose voices "came down, afar and indistinctly, from the upper heights where they habitually dwelt," that Dimmesdale, "the man of ethereal attributes," by virtue of "many of his traits of character, naturally belonged." And, but for his fall, his achievements would have rivaled theirs. "To their mountain-peaks of faith and sanctity he would have climbed" (141). In fact, he is by nature superior even to "these fathers, otherwise so apostolic," and might even have exceeded them.

They lack "Heaven's last and rarest attestation of their office, the Tongue of Flame" (140), the ability to express "the highest truths through the humblest medium of familiar words and images." This ability Dimmesdale does have. And therefore "angels might ... have listened to and answered" (141) perhaps his voice alone among the spiritually gifted clergy in New England.

It is a remarkable—perhaps, for his community, a singular—endowment. Unfortunately, through seven years Dimmesdale squanders it; not so much by the sin of adultery, probably committed, as even his tormentor imagines, without premeditation, "in the hot passion of his heart" (136), as by the deeper, because fully conscious and considered, sin of declining, through the years after the adultery, to do what, as a Christian, he knows he must do: cleanse his soul by confessing publicly, enduring humiliation, and accepting a punishment as dire as his partner's.

On one occasion, Dimmesdale offers a feeble rationalization for persisting in sin. "It may be," he says to Chillingworth of men who refuse to confess their dark secrets, that "guilty as they may be, retaining, nonetheless, a zeal for God's glory and man's welfare, they shrink from displaying themselves black and filthy in the view of men; because, thenceforward, no good can be achieved by them; no evil of the past be redeemed by better service." But Chillingworth's theological response to this position unmasks it as nonsense. "These men deceive themselves . . . Their love for man, their zeal for God's service,—these holy impulses may or may not coexist in their hearts with the evil inmates to which their guilt has unbarred the door . . . But, if they seek to glorify God, let them not lift heavenward their unclean hands! If they would serve their fellow-men, let them do it by making manifest the power and reality of conscience, in constraining them to penitential self-abasement!" (132) Everything in this response is correct, except Chillingworth's contention that Dimmesdale deceives himself. He, of all people, must understand a tenet of theology so rudimentary. And that he does understand it he indicates by exercising "his ready faculty ... of escaping from any topic that agitated his too sensitive and nervous temperament" (132), by simply waving the discussion away.

But he cannot wave it away from himself. Dimmesdale avoids penitential self-abasement for two reasons he understands completely: that he is a coward, morally crippled by "the dread of public exposure, that had long been the anguish of his life" (152), and a hypocrite. He has known this from the outset. Years earlier, addressing Hester as she stood on the scaffold, he begged her to identify her partner in public, lest her silence "tempt him—yea, compel him, as it were—to add hypocrisy to sin," because "perchance he hath not the courage to grasp . . . for himself . . . the bitter, but wholesome cup" (68) forced to her lips. Both the hypocrisy and the cowardice have, from the outset, defined his behavior, reducing him to charades of penance he himself bitterly mocks, undermining his essential being, and exposing him to assaults by the Devil; and—the total consequence—very nearly uprooting his sanity.

The charades take two forms: a regimen of morally inappropriate penances, and a series of crafty mock-confessions. The penances consist of "practices, more in accordance with the old, corrupted faith of Rome, than with the better light" of his own church. Dimmesdale flagellates himself physically with a "bloody scourge." He fasts—"not, however, in order to purify the body and render it the fitter medium of celestial illumination,—but rigorously . . . as an act of penance." And, in conditions certain to undermine his balance, he keeps morbid vigils, "night after night," with which, as with the other penances, "he tortured, but could not purify, himself" (143). The mock-confessions are more subtle, and therefore perhaps spiritually more debilitating. "More than once—nay, more than a hundred times," Dimmesdale enters the pulpit "with a purpose" to inform his congregants that "I, your pastor, whom you reverence and trust, am utterly a pollution and a lie!" And he does speak, calling himself "altogether vile . . . the worst of sinners . . . an abomination" (142), and so on. But he knows "the light in which his vague confession would be viewed." He is completely aware, "subtle, but remorseful hypocrite that he was!" that with every such sermon he has striven "to put a cheat upon himself by making the avowal of a guilty conscience," but has gained "only one other sin, and a self-acknowledged shame, without the momentary relief of being self-deceived" (143).

Dimmesdale's midnight vigil upon the scaffold is, like the sermons, a "mockery of penitence . . . in which his soul trifled with itself." He is driven to the scaffold by the "Remorse which dogged him everywhere" to torture himself with "the agony of heaven-defying guilt and vain repentance." (147) As he knows, "there was no peril of discovery" (146). And so when, after shrieking aloud, he mutters "It is done!" he is merely posturing theatrically, and must know it. Soon afterwards, when Mr. Wilson passes within inches of him in the darkness, creating the occasion of real confession, Dimmesdale remains silent, uttering the invitation to "the good old minister" to join him only in his imagination. And when Pearl and Hester do join him, and the child, holding his hand on the scaffold, seeks his promise to do what alone, he knows, will redeem him—"to take my hand, and mother's hand, to-morrow noontide"—he declines, until "the great judgment day" (152).

For the cowardice, rooted in the dread of exposure, "which invariably drew him back" whenever, during seven debilitating years, "Remorse ... hurried him to the verge of a disclosure" (147)—for the hypocrisy that compounds his original sin—for the charades the hypocrisy and cowardice empower—for the totality of his moral weakness Dimmesdale pays an extraordinarily high price, in mockery, in a massive self-contempt that almost entirely deprives him of being, and in the access to his soul afforded by his weakness to the Devil. He is deservedly ridiculed with sarcastic asides; for example, that he might stand at his vigil upon the scaffold "if it pleased him, until morning should redden in the east, without other risk than that the dank and chill night-air would creep into his frame, and stiffen his joints with rheumatism, and clog his throat with catarrh and cough; thereby defrauding the expectant audience of to-morrow's prayer and service" (146). His daughter mocks him, by pretending to reveal Chillingworth's identity to him, but instead whispering gibberish into his ear, and by laughing directly into his face and asserting, "Thou wast not bold!—thou wast not true!" (155) He mocks himself, continually and deeply. Especially because "it was his genuine impulse to adore the truth, and to reckon all things shadow-like, and utterly devoid of weight and value, that had not its divine essence as the life within their life," the self-imposed necessity to live a lie fills him with self-loathing. The veneration of his congregants in particular tortures him with "inconceivable ... agony" (141), because he knows that to them he has spoken "the very truth, and transformed it into the veriest falsehood"—and not once, but more than a hundred times. And "therefore, above all things else, he loathed his miserable self!" (143) And therefore, as well, he is very nearly deprived of his being, because "it is the unspeakable misery of a life so false as his, that it steals the pith and substance out of whatever realities there are around us ... To the untrue man, the whole universe is false,—it is impalpable,—it shrinks to nothing within his grasp. And he himself, in so far as he shows himself in a false light, becomes a shadow, or, indeed, ceases to exist." In consequence, Dimmesdale continues to exist at all solely because of "the only truth" still in him, "the anguish in his inmost soul" (144).

Upon this anguish the emissary of the Devil works. Originally a decent human being, "calm in temperament, kindly, though not of warm affections, but ever, and in all his relations with the world, a pure and upright man" (129), Roger Chillingworth is gradually and inexorably converted by Hester's adultery into a fiend obsessed with destroying Dimmesdale's soul. Even before he chances upon irrefutable evidence of Dimmesdale's guilt, the "uninstructed multitude," whose intuitions are "often so profound and so unerring, as to possess the character of truths supernaturally revealed" (126), notices "something ugly and evil in his face," and begins strongly to suspect that he is "Satan's emissary" (127). The "ominous ... gleams of ghastly fire" (128) that sometimes erupt from his eyes support this suspicion. And when he does chance upon the secret covered by Dimmesdale's vestment, he wheels about in a "ghastly rapture" which mimics exactly "how Satan comports himself, when a precious human soul is lost to heaven, and won into his kingdom" (137). Thereafter, he is wholly "the Pitiless ... the Unforgiving," obsessed with "his black devices" (138), the arch-fiend's factotum—perhaps, in fact, "the arch-fiend" (155) himself.

And all of his energy, his "remarkable intelligence" (61), all of his "strange, penetrating power ... to read the human soul" (60), and—more horribly—to torture the human soul vulnerable because poisoned by unconfessed sin—all of Chillingworth's satanic being is focused upon Dimmesdale. The result is catastrophic:

> Would he rouse him with a throb of agony? The victim was forever on the rack; it needed only to know the spring that controlled the engine;—and the physician knew it well! Would he startle him with sudden fear? As at the waving of a magician's wand, uprose a grisly phantom,—uprose a thousand phantoms,—in many shapes, of death, or more awful shame, all flocking round about the clergyman, and pointing with their fingers at his breast!
>
> (139)

Chillingworth proceeds "with a subtlety so perfect," and self-torture, that the assassin's machinations are unimpeded even by his victim's "dim perception of some evil influence watching over him." Everything about his physician gradually becomes "odious in the clergyman's sight." Conscious, however, "that the poison of one morbid spot was infecting his heart's entire substance" (139) and that in consequence he is prone to unfounded suspicions, unfortunately for his own immediate ease he dismisses the dim perception, and thus abandons his last defense against the deepening assaults of "his deadliest enemy" (140).

The total effect upon Dimmesdale of his own moral defects and his satanic enemy is the undermining and near destruction of his sanity. His two profound sins—the adultery, and—worse—the refusal, rooted in cowardice and hypocrisy, to confess—expose him to the self-inflicted torture of debilitating charades and self-disgust, and the torture, inflicted by Chillingworth, of devilishly exacerbated conscience and fear. Those tortures, inflicted over seven years, understandably erode Dimmesdale's balance; so thoroughly that during his midnight vigil he wonders "if he were going mad" (149). At the minimum, he is "in a highly disordered mental state" (154). And in fact, as Hester will soon note, "he stood on the verge of lunacy, if he had not already stepped across it" (165).

His portrait completed, that Dimmesdale is in no condition to engage in a debate is certain. But, through him, the position that Hester will soon oppose has been clearly defined, and so, by dramatic juxtaposition, has been her absolute distance from it. Whatever his weaknesses, Dimmesdale is unshakably a Christian, and through him the imperatives of a Christian life are defined. He lives in hell for seven years, consumed by agony and self-disgust, exclusively because he has lapsed from God, and is unworthy, because weakened by sin, to re-establish contact with God. What he must do is perfectly clear: repent, confess, and—in public, before his entire community—accept his punishment, however severe. For the reasons noted, he cannot yet do that. Without God's grace, he will never muster the strength to do it. But in no other way can he hope for peace. In no other way can he hope to be saved.

In no other way can Hester be saved. But salvation is essentially of no interest to her, as the juxtaposition of her portrait and Dimmingdale's underscores. The appeal that she repent and confess, that consumes Dimmesdale, interests Hester not at all. The appeal originates in Dimmesdale from within, and he aspires therefore to a full consent. The appeal to Hester comes entirely from without, and therefore inevitably falls upon deaf ears. Dimmesdale yearns, with all his soul, to embrace God again. Hester yearns, with all her soul, to embrace Dimmesdale again. Given a choice between Hester and God, Dimmesdale would not hesitate. Hester would not hesitate either. But their choices would be irreconcilably different, because their views of reality are irreconcilably different.

The positions to be debated established, in two intricately constructed scenes the debate itself occurs. In the first, the meeting between Hester and Dimmesdale in the forest, romanticism triumphs. In the second, the day of Dimmesdale's Election Sermon, that triumph is overturned, and Christianity prevails. The consequences of the first clash are catastrophic;

immediately for Dimmesdale, and potentially for Hester (and for Pearl). The consequences of the second are salvational; immediately for Dimmesdale (and for Pearl), and potentially for Hester (though, because she does not desire salvation, Hester ends, in her opinion, with nothing more than a broken heart).

Throughout the debate, Hester remains to some significant degree unaware, sometimes of what her position is, and almost always of its spiritual consequences. As a result, a degree of sympathy, carefully modulated, is maintained for her (though none is afforded to her position). Basically because she is a woman, and love in her has been suppressed, she does not see clearly enough—nor does she care to see—what her deepest longing would lead to. Therefore she is, in some appropriate measure, pitied, and excused. No such concession is granted to Dimmesdale. Because the essential issues in debate are perfectly clear to him, and because he knows precisely what the collapse of his position would entail, he is scorned and condemned relentlessly until, through the sudden intervention of grace, he is granted the strength at last to affirm the glory of God.

Before Hester can debate her position, she must become, if not entirely conscious of it, as least more conscious than during the three years after the day at the scaffold. And, to the extent that her consciousness can expand, during the four years before the debate occurs, it does expand; though in a manner easily misunderstood, and potentially catastrophic to herself, to the only two human beings she loves, and to the Puritan community.

The community misunderstands the change completely. To the townspeople Hester seems to grow, with the years, more Christian. She submits "uncomplainingly" to their "worst usage," demands nothing of them, lives in "blameless purity" (159), and is somehow converted into "a well-spring of human tenderness" to the sick and dying, "unfailing to every real demand, and inexhaustible by the largest . . . a Sister of Mercy" (160). As a result, the initial "hatred" of the townspeople is "by a gradual and quiet process . . . transformed to love" (159). Many of them refuse eventually "to interpret the scarlet A by its original significance. They said it meant Able; so strong was Hester Prynne, with a woman's strength" (160). And many see "a kind of sacredness" (161) in her. Even the authorities, though slower to react, because bound by "an iron framework of reasoning," nonetheless find "their sour and rigid wrinkles . . . relaxing into something which, in the due course of years, might grow into an expression of almost benevolence" (161).

Unfortunately, the shift in attitude of the community is undeserved. The townspeople, and no doubt the authorities as well, assume that, because she has "no hope, and seemingly no wish," to profit from her behavior, "it could only be a genuine regard for virtue that had brought back the poor wanderer" (159) to the path of God's truth.

They are completely wrong. In fact, Hester has been wandering for years down a path that would have horrified the Puritans; accompanied by "shadowy guests that would have been as perilous as demons" to Hester had they been seen with her, and enjoying "a freedom of speculation " (163) for which, had she been discovered, "she might, and not improbably would, have suffered death from the stern tribunals of the period, for attempting to undermine the foundations of the Puritan establishment" (163–164). Over the years, her life "had turned, in a great measure, from passion and feeling, to thought." And, as "the links that united her to the rest of human kind . . . had all been broken" (158), she "cast away the fragments of a broken chain"—of "the world's law"—of the Puritans' law—and imbibed the spirit of "an age in which the human intellect, newly emancipated, had taken a more active and a wider range than for many centuries before"—which had in fact overthrown not only "the whole system of ancient prejudice," but with it also "much of ancient principle" (163). Over the years, she has, in short, been imbibing modernity, and its irreconcilable challenge to the Christianity never rooted in her soul to begin with. Years earlier, she had been terrified of that modernity, and had clung, with shifting degrees of conscious sincerity, at least to the language of ancient principle. She no longer does. She no longer sees why she needs to, or should. The new philosophy, which puts all in doubt, encourages Hester to assert the value—perhaps even the sacredness—of her own deepest needs. And, finally, she seems prepared to do so.

In consequence, she needs to be shielded, because, in proportion as she is not, sympathy for her will not be sustained. And she is shielded, to the extent possible, in a number of ways, as the debate approaches.

Before the meeting in the forest occurs, her incapacity to deal with modernity in general is stressed, as is her ignorance of why she wants to meet with Dimmesdale. Moreover, the evil she is about to stumble into is extenuated by dramatic juxtaposition to a far deeper evil consciously perpetrated. During the meeting itself, once she has made her proposal to Dimmesdale not much can be said in her behalf; therefore she is more powerfully censured than ever before. However, until she utters the proposal, she is shielded by continued ignorance of her own intention, by the shift in dramatic focus to Dimmesdale, and by the agony she endures in losing him permanently.

Hester is unable to deal with modernity basically because she has lost her intuitive being as a woman. Women can deal with seminal problems only instinctively, through recourse to their "ethereal essence" (164), their emotional vibrancy. But Hester's essence is dead, or entombed. The tenderness of her being—all that would inspire "Love . . . Passion . . . Affection"—has been either "crushed out of her, or . . . crushed so deeply into her heart" that, whether only for the moment or permanently, she has "ceased to be . . . a woman" (162). And so she cannot grasp the problems of modernity. "A woman never overcomes these problems by any exercise of thought. They are not to be solved, or only in one way. If her heart chance to come uppermost, they vanish. Thus, Hester Prynne, whose heart had lost its regular and healthy throb, wandered without a clew in the dark labyrinth of mind . . . There was wild and ghastly scenery all around her, and a home and comfort nowhere." (164–165)

In the labyrinth of Dimmesdale, she is similarly lost. In her opinion, she must meet him in the forest because during the midnight vigil "he had appealed to her . . . for support against his instinctively discovered enemy," and because "he had a right to her utmost aid" (158). Her motive seems to her completely altruistic. She is going to the forest to reveal to Dimmesdale the identity of Chillingworth—and for no other reason. She is not aware of any other reason. Certainly she goes as an act of love. But the obvious possibility—that she may be going to offer love—never occurs to her.

It does not occur to her either at any point during her interview with Chillingworth. Before she turns at last to the forest, Hester resolves to meet with Chillingworth, to do "what might be in her power for the rescue of the victim on whom he had so evidently set his gripe" (166). And so, sending her daughter off to play, she confronts the old man. It is not in her interest to succeed in her appeal, because if she does, there will be no need—no occasion—to meet with Dimmesdale. But she does not know that, and so when she pleads with Chillingworth to stop torturing Dimmesdale she is, to her knowledge, completely sincere. Moreover, when Chillingworth refuses to stop, she says, referring to everyone involved, that she sees "no path to guide us out of this dismal maze" (172). Once again, she speaks with complete sincerity, apparently unaware of the offer she will make—but does not yet consciously intend to make—to Dimmesdale in the forest.

Because Hester is wandering without a clue in the labyrinths both of modernity and personal love, in significant measure she is forgiven and pitied, for in significant measure she knows not what she does.

By contrast, Chillingworth knows exactly what he is doing, and why. For seven years he has knowingly devoted himself "to the constant analysis of a heart full of torture, and deriving his enjoyment thence, and adding fuel to those fiery tortures which he analyzed and gloated over" (169). In consequence, he has become, as he says, "a fiend" (171), unwilling and, he insists, unable, because driven by "fate" (173), to leave the Devil's service.

The stark contrast between Chillingworth's premeditated, conscious malice unrelentingly inflicted through seven years with satanic joy, and Hester's agonized, self-ignorant stumbling through an almost impenetrable maze, underscored by dramatic juxtaposition the moment before Hester begins her assault upon God, preserves a measure of sympathy for her when she needs it most. In a moment, she will assert, upon spiritual grounds, the superiority of passion to Christian truth. When she does so, no defense will be possible for her. And therefore, more than ever, she needs the extenuation provided, not only by the man she has profoundly wronged, who pities her "for the good that has been wasted in thy nature" (172), but by the dramatic context as well.

The interview with Chillingworth ended, Hester proceeds towards the debate itself. And the closer she draws to it, the less that can be said for her, as the last two events before she enters the forest show. The first, her inappropriately bitter meditation upon Chillingworth, demonstrates that in seven years Hester has made no spiritual progress. And the second, a conversation with her daughter, demonstrates that, in fact, she seems to have regressed.

As Chillingworth walks off, for two related and entirely indefensible reasons, Hester gazes after him "bitterly," full of "hate." First, she argues, he caused her to commit "her crime most to be repented of, that she had ever endured, and reciprocated, the lukewarm grasp of his hand, and suffered the smile of her lips and her eyes to mingle and melt into his own." And second, she argues, she is far more deeply sinned against than sinning. "It seemed a fouler offense committed by Roger Chillingworth, than any which had since been done him, that, in the time when her heart knew no better, he had persuaded her to fancy herself happy by his side" (175). In other words, the "crime" of marrying an older man she did not love warrants repentance more than does the sin of adultery. And the desire of Chillingworth, at the time of their marriage a "kindly . . . pure, and upright man" (128), to attain "the simple bliss" of harmonious marriage, and to warm his wife "by the warmth which [her] presence made" (75) in his heart, was a more foul offense than her subsequent infidelity. Therefore Hester is entitled to hate him, because "He betrayed me! He has done me worse wrong than I did him!" (175). To Romantics—among whom Hester has now, for the first time openly and clearly, taken her stand—such arguments may well make excellent sense. To the Christian they are degenerate nonsense, deserving only the condemnation they at once receive. At the most, she suffered only an injustice. And she "ought long ago to have done with this injustice. What did it betoken? Had seven long years, under the torture of the scarlet letter, inflicted so much of misery, and wrought out no repentance?" (175–176) The questions are rhetorical. Hester's emotions, as the stooping figure of Chillingworth recedes, throw "a dark light on Hester's state of mind" (176) that reveals the temporal passions, all of them swirling about thwarted love, where Christianity, and repentance in particular, should be.

And the imperatives of that love are surfacing inexorably. Chillingworth gone, Pearl is summoned back from her play. Walking homeward with her mother, she asks, for the thousandth time, what the letter on her mother's breast means. For a moment, to some degree still self-deceived, Hester wonders whether speaking openly to Pearl "might help her to overcome the passion, once so wild, and even yet neither dead nor asleep, but only imprisoned within the same tomb-like heart." But she rejects that option almost at once, because she does not want the passion overcome. For the first time "in all the seven bygone years" she betrays the symbol she wears, by lying to Pearl. The consequence is instantaneous and dire. "A stern and severe, but yet a guardian spirit" who had hovered about her through all those years "now forsook her; as recognizing that, in spite of his strict watch over her heart, some new evil had crept into it, or some old one had never been expelled" (180). The spirit departs. Against the old evil he has accomplished nothing. And a new evil has perhaps crept past him, into Hester's soul. She moves towards the forest completely alone, abandoned by God, as she wishes to be.

Some extenuation can still be offered. In the several days before the forest walk, Hester herself remains aware only of her "resolve to make known to Mr. Dimmesdale . . . the true character of the man who had crept into his intimacy" (181). Of her bottommost yearning, to regain Dimmesdale's love, she seems still completely unaware. And the forest, when she enters it, seems to her to reflect "the moral wilderness in which she had so long been wandering" (182), the labyrinth through which she has been confusedly stumbling. But the extenuation is slight, and is carefully offset, even before Dimmesdale appears. To her daughter Hester admits that her adultery was, at least in the opinion of the Puritan community, the work of the Devil; and thus she shows herself aware that, in that opinion at least, if no longer in her own, to offer love to Dimmesdale again is once again to respond to the Devil's prompting. "Once in my life I met the Black man!" she says, in reply to Pearl's insistent questioning. "The scarlet letter is his mark!" (184) Thus, if she is planning another meeting, she knows with whom, in one opinion at least, it will be.

And nature itself knows, either that a second meeting is imminent, or what the first one made of Hester; and that, in either case, she deserves to be shunned. The beam of sunshine that follows Pearl flees from her mother, as though knowingly. As Pearl says, "It runs away and hides itself, because it is afraid of something on your bosom." (182). Similarly, the little stream "would not be comforted, and still kept telling its unintelligible secret of some very mournful mystery that had happened—or making a prophetic lamentation about something that was yet to happen—within the verge of the dismal forest" (186). In fact, the stream is doing both: recounting Hester's mournful past sin, and lamenting beforehand the dismal transgression about to occur.

With the appearance of Dimmesdale, that transgression begins.

To forestall it—though perhaps still entirely unaware of its onset—Dimmesdale presents the argument from Christianity, asserting that he has found, through "a seven years' cheat" (191), only "despair" (189), the inevitable consequence of living in utter "falsehood . . . emptiness . . . death" (191). Hester's effort to undermine this argument from within Christianity merely strengthens it. Her insistence that Dimmesdale has ministered effectively to his congregants he brushes aside by repeating Chillingworth's earlier rejoinder (131–132). And to her insistence that, because he has "deeply and sorely repented," his "sin is left behind . . . in the days long past," he replies correctly, of Hester as well as of himself, "Of penance I have had enough! Of penitence there has been none!" (190).

The argument from Christianity cannot be undermined from within. And so Hester, perhaps realizing that, turns to an argument rooted in a different view of reality altogether; a view whose overriding imperative is passionate, indestructible love, self-sanctifying love. By virtue of it she

Dimmesdale are married. "Since the night of the vigil, all her sympathies towards him had been softened and invigorated." He is her husband. He is being destroyed. And no one but she can rescue or comfort him, "the man once,—nay . . . still so passionately loved" (192). She is fully aware of that now—at last. And she cannot bear to be deprived of him. Therefore when he threatens never to forgive her for keeping Chillingworth's identity secret, and by implication to abandon her, she throws herself at him. And, his head pressed against her bosom, and the charge of her passion flowing through him, she proceeds on her own terms; correctly confident that the "enthusiasm" (197), the "magnetic power" of her appeal as a woman—her erotic appeal—will overwhelm the objections he continues, as a Christian, though feebly, to voice. "The judgment of God" is upon him, he insists, "too mighty" (195) for him to struggle against. And therefore he is "powerless to go . . . lost as my own soul is" (196). Hester pretends to argue as a Christian. "Heaven would show mercy," she insists, "hadst thou but the strength to take advantage of it" (195). And he could still "Preach! Write! Act!" (197) But these arguments are nonsense, as she must know, having a moment before heard Dimmesdale's unanswerable responses to them. But, his head on her bosom, he himself has forgotten those responses. And to her they are meaningless. Her essential argument is that the Christians are wrong; or that their imperatives must defer to more profoundly impressive imperatives. "What we did had a consecration of its own. We felt it so. Hast thou forgotten it?" Of course, he has not. "I have not forgotten" (194). And that consecration now demands that he throw off the yoke not only of Chillingworth, but of all "these iron men, and their opinions," who have "kept thy better part in bondage too long already" (196), and choose instead to be "happy" and "free" (196). The consecration, of course, was of erotic love. The better part is erotic energy; his, and her own. And happiness and freedom will be attained by running off from the community of Christians. And not alone. "Thou shalt not go alone!" (197) she assures him emphatically. Her bosom, her strength—her love—will sustain him.

A moment before Hester at last reveals herself openly, her position is condemned, by a solemn old tree in the forest, groaning to another as if retelling the lovers' history, "or constrained to forebode evil to come" (194). And after she reveals herself, she is condemned massively, by Pearl, and by a sudden, hideous change in Dimmesdale, the direct and inevitable consequence of Hester's victory thus far in their debate.

The first boon to Hester of that victory seems ineffably lovely. She casts the scarlet letter away, removes the cap that has for years confined her luxuriant hair, and smiles, with a radiance and tenderness "that seemed gushing from the very heart of womanhood . . . Her sex, her youth, and the whole richness of her beauty, came back from what men call the irrevocable past," and bestow upon her "a happiness before unknown" (201). Nature itself rejoices, filling the forest suddenly with light, as it almost must, because "love, whether newly born, or roused from a death-like slumber, must always create a sunshine, filling the heart so full of radiance, that it overflows upon the outward world." But the nature that responds is "that wild, heathen Nature of the forest, never subjugated by human law, nor illumined by higher truth" (202). And it reflects precisely the heathen, wild spirit of Hester, no longer subject to human law, or enlightened by the higher truth of God. For Hester, "the whole seven years of outlaw and ignominy had been little other than a preparation for this very hour" (199). And her preparation has been little more an evolving apprenticeship to a destructive falsehood misperceived as truth. For seven years "she had wandered, without rule or guidance, in a moral wilderness; as vast, as intricate and shadowy, as the untamed forest . . . The tendency of her fate and fortunes had been to set her free . . . Shame, Despair, Solitude. These had been her teachers,—stern and wild ones,—and they had made her strong, but taught her much amiss" (198). She has wandered, without a clue, and stumbled horribly. The freedom she has attained is bondage. Her teachers have been among the worst imaginable. And though they have taught her to persevere against indefensible oppression, they have hardened in her catastrophic convictions. She has learned a great deal; but not the truth.

Her daughter at once reminds her of that, decisively, furiously, utterly without quarter. Her victory, in her confident opinion, sealed, Hester calls Pearl back to her. But the child refuses adamantly to come. Seeing Dimmesdale with her mother, she stops at the brook-side, refusing to step over. Her behavior can be explained psychologically, but only in part. With the advent of Dimmesdale, suddenly "another inmate had been admitted within the circle of the mother's feelings, and so modified the aspect of them all, that Pearl, the returning wanderer, could not find her wonted place, and hardly knew where she was" (207). But from birth Pearl has been not only, or even perhaps primarily, a child realistically drawn, but also "a symbol" (153), "the scarlet letter . . . endowed with life" (101), and "appointed" the "mission" (179) of monitoring, as her conscience, her mother's behavior.

And this symbolic function Pearl fulfills perhaps most clearly standing at the brook-side and refusing to sanction Hester's degeneracy; for the moment, in fact, voiding it. With a single hostile glance at Dimmesdale she reduces him to guilty fluttering. "As Arthur Dimmesdale felt the child's eyes upon himself, his hand—with that gesture so habitual as to have become involuntary—stole over his heart" (208). Hester proves a more difficult—but only a somewhat more difficult—challenge. When a finger pointed "with a singular air of authority" at the spot where the scarlet letter should be produces no effect on Hester, Pearl "stamped her foot with a yet more imperious look and gesture," and then, at a rebuke from her mother, "suddenly burst into a fit of passion, gesticulating wildly," throwing herself into "contortions," and uttering "piercing shrieks" (208). That is enough; Hester is restored to the consequences of her sin. "A deadly pallor" (209) upon her face, she retrieves and refastens the scarlet letter, confines her hair once again beneath her cap; and, for the moment, reverts to what she has been. "As if there were a withering spell in the sad letter, her beauty, the warmth and richness of her womanhood departed like a fading sunshine, and a gray shadow seemed to fall across her." This reversion mollifies Pearl, as she shows by kissing her mother, "in a mood of tenderness that was not usual with her." But she is far from being completely satisfied, for immediately afterward, with evident mockery, she "kissed the scarlet letter too!" (210) And to Hester's insistence that Dimmesdale loves both herself and Pearl she responds with evident disbelief, "Doth he love us? . . . Will he go back with us, hand in hand, we three together, into the town?" (211)

As she knows, Dimmesdale will do nothing of the kind; and for a reason far worse than compelled him to decline the same invitation during the midnight vigil. There, he had declined as a Christian, through cowardice. Here, he would decline for a reason vastly more hideous and reprehensible: that, in the encounter with Hester, he has consciously—with full knowledge—sold his soul to the Devil.

That, given his weakness, and Hester's strength, he should have done so is understandable; but it is almost completely indefensible. Through seven years, Dimmesdale has been torn, and has torn himself, almost to shreds. When he encounters Hester, his strength is gone (158), and he is slipping towards, if he has not already slipped into, insanity (165). And Hester is bursting with erotic energy, finally unshackled. Therefore it is not surprising that Dimmesdale walks through the forest "death . . . too definite an object to be wished for, or avoided" (187), that he begs Hester to decide his fate—"Think for me, Hester! Thou art Strong. Resolve for me!" (195)—that she so overwhelms his mind, "darkened and confused" by remorse, that his conscience cannot strike a balance between "fleeing as an avowed criminal, and remaining as a hypocrite," that it is "human" to avoid "death and infamy," and that "a glimpse of human affection and sympathy" is overpoweringly attractive to "the faint, sick, miserable" sinner. But that is all that can be said in his behalf; and, in the circumstance, it is far from enough. "Were such a man once more to fall, what plea could be urged in extenuation of his crime? None" (199), unfortunately, but the extenuation above. And, in the face of the evil that instantaneously erupts from his soul, it is insignificant at best.

He is censured at once for is failure to recall

> that the breach which guilt has once made into the human soul is never, in this mortal state, repaired. It may be watched and guarded; so that the enemy shall not force his way again into the citadel, and might even, in his subsequent assaults, select some other avenue, in preference to that where he had formerly succeeded. But there is still the ruined wall, and, near it, the stealthy tread of the foe that would win over again his unforgotten triumph.
>
> (199–200)

Dimmesdale, of all people—the pastor, the intellectual, the student of divine doctrine –should know that eternal vigilance against the Devil, eternally prowling, is the irreducibleprice of Christian liberty. And he does know it. But he no longer cares, because he has opened the citadel himself to his foe. When Hester asserts he will not leave alone, he looks at her with "a kind of horror at her boldness, who had spoken what he vaguely hinted at, but dared not speak." So he has participated in the formulation of her offer; they have colluded in plotting the escape. And though he looks at Hester with "fear," nonetheless "hope and joy" (199) shine out of his face. He is prepared to go. Despite his fear, he is more than prepared. "The decision once made, a glow of strange enjoyment threw its flickering brightness over the trouble of his breast." His spirit rises, "as it were, with a bound" (200).

Unfortunately for his spiritual wellbeing, it is a joy that wells up from the darkest, the ugliest, depth of his soul. As Chillingworth has noticed, Dimmesdale has "a strong animal nature" (129), that caused him "to do a wild thing . . . in the hot passion of his heart" (136). That passion, expressed as anger, shatters Hester when she reveals to Dimmesdale the identity of Chillingworth. "Never was there a blacker or a fiercer frown" than

Dimmesdale turns upon Hester. The frown reflects "a dark transfiguration" (193), as does every expression of Dimmesdale's wild passion, because "that violence of passion . . . was, in fact, the portion of him which the Devil claimed" (192–193). And it is precisely that portion that causes the sudden rush of "strange enjoyment" in Dimmesdale; "the exhilarating effect . . . of breathing the wild, free atmosphere of an unredeemed, unchristianized, lawless region" (200).

And, having resolved to breathe deeply indeed, he is, unless God rescues him, lost. What Hester has called his "better part" is, he agrees, no longer in bondage. It is, in fact, mirrored in her erotic energy. And therefore he cries out in joy, "O Hester, thou art my better angel!" (200) and hurries home, that angel within him, completely on the loose.

It is a sickening sight. He is, indeed, an utterly changed man. But "the excitement of Mr. Dimmesdale's feelings," which "lent him unaccustomed physical energy, and . . . an unweariable activity that astonished him" (215), have not the value he thinks they have. The town he enters is the same one he left; "but the same minister returned not from the forest." His "inner man" has undergone "a revolution in the sphere of thought and feeling . . . nothing short of a total change of dynasty and moral code." And the change is infernal. The revolution has enthroned the Devil. "At every step" Dimmesdale feels "incited to do some strange, wild, wicked thing or other" (216). And, on his encounters along the way home, over and again, he almost does. To one of his own deacons he almost utters "certain blasphemous suggestions that rose into his mind" (217). To a pious old woman he is almost driven to present "a brief, pithy, and, as it then appeared to him, unanswerable argument" (217–218), certain to destroy her, against the immortality of the human soul. Into the bosom of a worshipful young virgin he is tempted to drop "a germ of evil that would be sure to blossom darkly soon, and bear black fruit betimes" (218). To a group of children he is tempted to teach "some very wicked words," and with a drunken sailor to share "a few improper jests . . . and heaven-defying oaths" (219). In every instance he is driven to depravity by "the great enemy of souls" (217), "Satan . . . the arch-fiend" (218), to whose service he is now completely devoted. He strongly suspects that is so. "Have I then sold myself to the fiend," he thinks, rather than asks himself, after encountering "the old witch-lady" (220), Mistress Hibbins, "whom, if men say true, this yellow-starched and velveted old hag has chosen for her prince and master!" (220–221) That is precisely what he has done:

> The wretched minister! He had made a bargain very like it. Tempted by a dream of happiness, he had yielded himself, with deliberate choice, as he had never done before, to what he knew was deadliest sin. And the infectious poison of that sin had been thus rapidly diffused throughout his moral system. It had stupefied all blessed impulses, and awakened into vivid life the whole brotherhood of bad ones. Scorn, bitterness, unprovoked malignity, gratuitous desire of ill, ridicule of whatever was good and holy, all awoke, to tempt, even while they frightened him. And his encounter with old Mistress Hibbins, if it were a real incident, did but show his sympathy and fellowship with wicked mortals and the world of perverted spirits.
>
> (221)

At this moment, Hester has triumphed. The debate with Christianity appears at an end. Dimmesdale, its advocate, has abandoned its defense. And nothing, therefore, appears to oppose the consummation of Hester's romantic yearning. But the condemnation of her has been withering, and entirely justified. Through the explosion of her wild, unlawful energy, Hester has rendered herself at last in great measure culpable, having become at last as conscious as she can be of what she is doing, and why; Dimmesdale has been shattered—"lost" (218), deprived, in all likelihood for eternity, of God, and doomed to the fellowship of wicked mortals and perverted spirits; Pearl has been doomed, in all probability, by the total suppression of conscience in her parents, to a life of unrelieved irritation and rage; Chillingworth remains completely unchecked in his diabolical master's service; and Hester herself, for many years attracted ardently to "the insidious whispers of the bad angel," yet still "a struggling woman . . . only half his victim" (86), has at last consigned herself entirely to him. The triumph of Romanticism, and thus of evil, appears complete.

Only an act of God—an act of His grace—can reverse that triumph. And, astonishingly, such an act intervenes, with salvational results. Dimmesdale is restored to spiritual health. Pearl is released from her symbolic task, and freed to develop into a loving woman. Chillingworth is neutralized. And Hester, though left (as she wishes to be) in spiritual limbo, is precluded from unleashing further chaos. The debate between the human actors having ended catastrophically, through the intervention of their Master it ends as it should.

To his astonishment, Dimmesdale is aware of this intervention as it occurs. He sits down to finish the Election Sermon his "former self . . . gone"

(221–222). Miraculously, however, he begins suddenly to write "with such an impulsive flow of thought and emotion, that he fancied himself inspired; and only wondered that Heaven should see fit to transmit the grand and solemn music of its oracles through so foul an organ-pipe as he" (223–224). On reasonable grounds Dimmesdale is justified in wondering that heaven should play its music through so unredeemed a sinner as himself. As a theologian, however, he should know that grace is, by definition, the free gift of God's love to the undeserving; a mystery that must "solve itself, or go unsolved forever" (224). And this gift, mysteriously transfiguring his tormented soul, assures the triumph of his last day on earth.

That Dimmesdale is in fact, rather than that he merely fancies himself, inspired is not established beyond dispute until after he has delivered the Election Sermon. Until then, it is not clear if the voice in his own voice, or that of his Creator. So it still not clear whether God has suddenly appropriated Dimmesdale's being.

That Dimmesdale works through the night on the Election Sermon "with earnest haste and ecstasy" implies strongly that the message he is writing is sacred, as does the "golden beam" that in the morning "laid itself across the minister's bedazzled eyes" (224).

His spiritual condition as he walks in the procession later in the morning is somewhat less certain. "Never, since Mr. Dimmesdale had first set foot on the New England shore, had he exhibited such energy . . . [such] strength . . . not of the body." (237) This strength "might be spiritual, and imparted by angelic ministrations." Or it may be only the effect of "earnest and long-continued thought," or even of the "loud and piercing music" of the procession. Beyond question his mind is "far and deep in its own region, busying itself, with preternatural activity," with the Election Sermon. And beyond question his "spiritual element" has taken up his body, "converting it to spirit like itself" (238). But that the spiritual element is utterly in command of his being, and that the intellectual element is merely serving it, cannot yet be established beyond dispute.

Even during the Sermon itself, it is not certain whose being prompts "the complaint of a human heart, sorrow-laden, perchance guilty, telling its secret, whether of guilt or sorrow" (242). If his Master is speaking through him, Dimmesdale's complaint is completely sincere, and inevitably the prelude to public confession, and thus salvation. If, however, he is speaking in his own voice, he may once again be playing his old trick of hypocritically pretending, in the pulpit, to confess (142–143). And the voice still cannot be indisputably defined.

Only as the sermon ends, and even then only gradually, is the controlling presence of divine intervention, predominant since the previous night, affirmed beyond dispute. As Dimmesdale draws towards the close of the sermon, "a spirit of prophecy had come upon him, constraining him to its purpose as mightily as the old prophets of Israel were constrained," and producing "the effect . . . as if an angel, in his passage to the skies, had shaken his bright wings over the people for an instant . . . and had shed down a shower of golden truths upon them" (247). But this dazzling pronouncement is at once in part undercut by a comment that seems, but in fact is not, entirely ironic. Back in the procession, in the open air, Dimmesdale is assaulted rhetorically with the following questions:

> How fared it with him then? Were there not the brilliant particles of a halo in the air above his head? So etherealized by spirit as he was, and so apotheosized by worshipping admirers, did his footsteps in the procession really tread upon the dust of earth?
>
> (248)

The ridicule of Dimmesdale is staggering. But it is justified only if the sermon was presented in his own voice, or if, the sermon done, God's voice will abandon him, and leave him once again to his hypocrisy and cowardice. But the sermon was presented in God's voice. At least at its close, Dimmesdale spoke as a prophet; by definition, the words were God's, not his own. And the likelihood that, having experienced the immediate presence of God, Dimmesdale will revert to his old, insufficient self is very slight. And thus the ridicule is anticipatory, directed only at the very slight likelihood, and is therefore more apparent than real. The halo above Dimmesdale's head is real. His spirit has been etherealized. And his footsteps barely do tread upon the dust of earth. "The energy—or say, rather, the inspiration which had held him up, until he should have delivered the sacred message that brought its own strength along with it from heaven—was withdrawn, now that it had so faithfully performed its office" (249). But this energy is withdrawn only now. From the moment it appeared the previous night, perceived by Dimmesdale—correctly, it turns out—as inspiration, to the close of the Election Sermon, it has sustained him utterly, as the presence of God inevitably does.

And even after it has been withdrawn, its trace in his soul assures the triumph of his last moments on earth. Dimmesdale falters only twice: when the procession passes Hester and Pearl at the scaffold, he hesitates before stretching his arms out to them; and on the scaffold he hesitates before revealing publicly the whole of his guilt. But these hesitations last only a moment. He does call his daughter and her mother, finally, to their rightful place by his side. And he fights back successfully "the bodily weakness,—and, still more, the faintness of heart,—that was striving for the mastery of him" (253). Finally, he repents—completely, openly, to salvational effect. His look, as he invites Hester and Pearl to the scaffold, is "triumphant" (250). Having torn the garments from around his breast, he stands, revealed to all the world, with a flush of "triumph" and "victory" (253). And his death he defines in his dying words as "triumphant ignominy" (254).

He is completely correct. The open confession restores his soul. It restores him to God. He understands at last that he has been impelled by "grace" (251)—by the free, undeserved gift of God's love—"to put in his plea of guilty at the bar of Eternal Justice" (252). He hastens to do so, secure in God's mercy (252, 254). And as he asks, finally, for his abandoned daughter's forgiveness and love, "a sweet and gentle smile" spreads over his face, "as of a spirit sinking into deep repose"—the repose of a soul returning in lasting peace to its Maker, and praise therefore—"Praised be his name! His will be done!" (254)—in its departing breath.

At the last moment, Dimmesdale has saved himself. And his salvation has repaired a part of the world beyond himself. Most importantly perhaps, he has given his daughter access to a balanced and vibrant life. He has sapped the satanic life from his tormenter. And he has tried—though entirely without success—to restore the soul of the woman who has loved him, and will continue to love him, not wisely, but too well. At the outset of the climactic Election Day, Pearl's fate is still undecided. She is still "a bright and sunny apparition" (226) whose "singular inquietude and excitement" (227) reflect precisely the nihilistic resolve of her mother. She is capable still of nasty mockery. Had she been sure it was Dimmesdale who had passed in the procession, she informs her mother, "I would have run to him, and bid him kiss me now, before all the people; even as he did yonder among the dark old trees" (239). She asks old Mistress Hibbins "eagerly" what Dimmesdale's hand upon his heart is hiding. The old woman's invitation to the reputed "lineage of the Prince of the Air" to ride with her "some fine night, to see thy father" (241) still does not seem quite completely outlandish. And neither does Pearl's flirtation with the "wildest," most dissolute, presence on Election Day, the mariners who "transgressed, without fear or scruple," all of the Puritans' "rules of behavior" (231), and whose depredations at sea "would have periled all their necks in a modern court of justice" (232). These mariners—these pirates—gaze "wonderingly and admiringly at Pearl," conscious, as the "wild Indian" is, "of a nature wilder than his own" (243). And their captain, "smitten" (243) with the elusive "witch-baby" (244), tosses to her the gift of a gold chain, and enlists her as his messenger to her mother. His apparent sense that she is a kindred spirit does not seem misguided; especially when she taunts him "with a naughty smile," and threatens to have her reputed father, "the Prince of the Air . . . chase thy ship with a tempest" (244). The wildness, the recalcitrance, the unpredictable perversity, are still deeply rooted in Pearl.

And they might have remained there, but for her father's triumph, that, in a few redemptive moments, uproots them. The instant Dimmesdale calls out, for the first time, as a father to his daughter—"Come, my little Pearl!"—stretching forth his arms in love to her, "the child, with the bird-like motion which was one of her characteristics, flew to him, and clasped her arms about his knees" (250). During his salvational ordeal on the scaffold, "the little hand of the sin-born child" remains "clasped in his" (251), each hand drawing strength from the other. And when at last, dying, and "almost . . . sportive with the child," he asks for the kiss she has always withheld, she grants it, and achieves redemption:

> Pearl kissed his lips. A spell was broken. The great scene of grief, in which the wild infant bore a part, had developed all her sympathies; and as her tears fell upon her father's cheek, they were the pledge that she would grow up amid human joy and sorrow, nor forever do battle with the world, but be a woman in it. Towards her mother, too, Pearl's errand as a messenger of anguish was all fulfilled.
>
> (254)

Thus, in redeeming himself, Dimmesdale redeems his daughter also. He cannot do as much for Chillingworth or Hester, because neither of them would consent to be redeemed. But his triumph at least debars both from further evil.

To Hester's insistence, before the forest scene, that he can desist from torturing Dimmesdale further—"Thou . . . hast it at thy will to pardon"— Chillingworth replies, "I have no such power as thou tellest me of . . . By thy first step awry, thou didst plant the germ of evil; but, since that moment, it has all been a dark necessity . . . It is our fate" (173). Such a man, who denies both grace and the freedom of the soul to choose the good, cannot be redeemed. But he can be neutralized. And he is, by Dimmesdale's repentance upon the scaffold. The instant Hester draws near to Dimmesdale, Chillingworth, sensing the danger to his satanic obsession, thrusts himself forward "to snatch back his victim." But it is too late, as both he and Dimmesdale know. "Ha, tempter! Methinks thou art too late!" Dimmesdale tells him. "Thy power is not what it was! With God's help, I shall escape thee now!" (250) Chillingworth acknowledges he has been defeated. "Hadst thou sought the whole earth over," he says, bitterly disappointed, "there was no place so secret,—no high place, nor lowly place, where thou couldst have escaped me,—save on this very scaffold" (251). And with this acknowledgement, Chillingworth ceases, in effect, to exist. As Dimmesdale, his open confession done, sinks down upon the scaffold, "Old Roger Chillingworth knelt down beside him, with a blank, dull countenance, out of which the life seemed to have departed," repeating "Thou hast escaped me!" (253) His physical death within the year (259) is almost a redundancy. He is, in effect, destroyed, as he should have been, by the victorious liberation of goodness in his victim.

The same can almost be said for Hester. She is, of course, not physically destroyed. Nor, if she had died, would she have been consigned with Chillingworth to the nether regions, where his "Master would find him tasks enough, and pay him his wages duly" (258). Unlike him, she has never "made the very principle of . . . life to consist in the pursuit and systematic exercise of revenge" (258). But, like him, she has been devoted to evil. Like him, she refuses to be redeemed. And therefore, like him, she must be neutralized. And she is—from her perspective, ironically, by Dimmesdale.

Throughout the climactic Election Day scene, Hester's commitment to her Romanticism is unwavering. Throughout, she wants, as she has always wanted, only one thing: to be restored, in love, to Dimmesdale. Nothing could convince her to give him up. Therefore, for her own good, he must be placed beyond her reach. And he is, through his own triumphant exertions. As a consequence, Hester is devastated, for good. But she needs to be, and deserves to be, devastated.

As the day unfolds, Hester's soul is gradually drawn from triumph to despair as her excited conviction that Dimmesdale is hers gradually dissolves into the realization that she has lost him forever. As the people gather to watch the procession, she is aware that, even in respect of wearing the scarlet letter in public, she is about to "convert what had so long been agony into a kind of triumph," because, unbeknownst to them, she is "about to win her freedom" from the pain they have for years inflicted upon her. This specific prospect, and the prospect of general triumph and freedom—of being free at last "to drink the wine of life " (226)—excite her wildly. "The singular inquietude and excitement" in Pearl's mood reflect precisely "the emotions which none could detect in the marble passiveness of Hester's brow" (227). The moment of her liberation is at hand; created by her unaided strength. It is intoxicating.

Unfortunately, however, it is poisonous as well, as her conversation with Mistress Hibbins underscores. The old "witch-lady" (116) knows, she whispers to Hester, who has been in the forest, and with whom, and whose souls have been consigned to "the Evil one" (240). And thus, though Mistress Hibbins—and Hester—might protest, it is known whose souls must, if possible, be rescued.

Dimmesdale's attempt to rescue Hester's has already begun. And so has her protest. Just before she speaks with Mistress Hibbins, the procession passes by, leaving in Hester the first hint of defeat. Remembering "how deeply" she and Dimmesdale "had known each other" in the forest, she is certain "one glance of recognition . . . must needs pass between them." But none does, because, she realizes, Dimmesdale is suddenly and unexpectedly "so remote from her own sphere, and utterly beyond her reach . . . unattainable . . . in that far vista of his unsympathizing thoughts." In consequence, "a dreary influence came over her . . . Her spirit sank" (238). And, being a woman, she censures him bitterly. "Thus much of woman was there in Hester, that she could scarcely forgive him . . . for being able so completely to withdraw himself from their mutual world; while she groped darkly, and stretched forth her cold hands, and found him not" (239). He is everything to her. She needs him. And he is gone.

Whether or not he is gone forever she still cannot know. But she is comforted neither by a remark of Mistress Hibbins nor by the Election Sermon itself. Mistress Hibbins assures her that "when the Black Man sees one of his own servants, signed and sealed, so shy of owning to the bond as is the Reverend Mr. Dimmesdale, he hath a way of ordering matters so that the mark shall be disclosed in open daylight to the eyes of all the world!" (241) As she must know, if Dimmesdale is unmasked before all the world, she will lose him forever. And with that profoundly unsettling prospect perhaps still in mind she stands outside the meeting-house, at the foot of the scaffold, and as the sermon unfolds feels "a sense within her,—too ill-defined to be made a thought, but weighing heavily on her mind,—that her whole orb of life, both before and after, was connected with this spot, as with the one point that gave it unity" (242–243). Something, she senses, is about to happen at the scaffold; something momentous, something that weighs heavily on her, something inimical to her heart's desire.

Her sense is correct. The catastrophe, as she understands it, strikes. And though she struggles with all her strength against it, it prevails nonetheless, defeating her for good. Moments after the sermon ends, Dimmesdale is before her, insistent that she mount the scaffold with him. She complies, "but slowly, as if compelled by inevitable fate, and against her strongest will" (250), her deepest being protesting against the surrender of her love. When Dimmesdale asks her rhetorically, "Is this not better . . . than what we dreamed of in the forest?" she answers, first, "I know not! I know not!" But then, remembering another possibility, already dear to her many years earlier (80), she agrees it is better, but on a single condition only. "Yea, so we may both die, and little Pearl die with us!" (252) The possibility is her last, forlorn hope: that she may spend eternity with the man she loves. "Shall we not meet again?" she asks, as he lies dying. "Shall we not spend our immortal life together? Surely, surely, we have ransomed one another, with all this woe!" Where, or when, she is with him is immaterial. That she should be with him is all that matters. It is all that has ever mattered to her. It is all that Hester has ever wanted, or ever will want.

And, in all likelihood, she is not to have it, even hereafter. "Thou lookest far into eternity," she says, "with those bright dying eyes! Then tell me what thou seest." Dimmesdale is not entirely certain. "God knows; and He is merciful!" But she ought not to have asked—at least, not him; his dying words strike down her last hope. "I fear! I fear! It may be that, when we forgot our God,—when we violated our reverence each for the other's soul,—it was thenceforth vain to hope that we could meet hereafter, in an everlasting and pure reunion."

She would have accepted reunion on any terms—in purity, impurity—anywhere, any time. But her soul would have been the darker for it, and the souls of others, and the world itself. And so she is denied it. The debate ends, at last, against her. The God of the Bible is more important than romantic love. Its imperatives must yield before His. As Dimmesdale says with his dying breath, whatever the cost to lovers, to love, "His will be done!" (254)

Precisely why Hester returns, after a long absence, to New England, and spends the rest of her life there, is never quite explicitly explained. The conjecture, however, that she does so to be near Dimmesdale—near his grave, and in the place she knew him—is supported by every relevant statement and event in the drama, and by the assertion that "there was more real life for Hester Prynne here, in New England," than anywhere else. Moreover, she seems to return to consider, for the first time, as a Christian, repentance for her sin. "Here had been her sin; here her sorrow; and here was yet to be her penitence." (260)

Given Hester's history, it may be that in her penitence some ulterior motive exists; perhaps the touching wish to be reconciled, through service to God's suffering children, with God himself, and perhaps thereby with His redeemed servant, her still beloved husband.

During the seven years of her torment, Hester gained the increasingly high regard of the Puritans by living in "blameless purity" for apparently selfless reasons. In their opinion, "with nothing to lose, in the sight of mankind, and with no hope, and seemingly no wish, of gaining anything, it could only be a genuine regard for virtue that had brought back the poor wanderer to its paths" (159). They were, of course, wrong. Hester had only "seemingly" no hope of gain. The scarlet letter still "had not done its office" (165). And therefore "society was inclined to show its former victim a more benign countenance . . . perchance, than she deserved" (161). By contrast, through "the toilsome, thoughtful, and self-devoted years" of Hester's life after her return, she has in fact "no selfish ends, nor lived in any measure for her own profit and enjoyment." Perhaps the scarlet letter was at last doing its office; some part of it at least; and in a very specific fashion. People burdened with "sorrows and perplexities" came to Hester for consolation and comfort. "Women, more especially," came to her cabin; more especially still, women weighed down by "the continually recurring trials of wounded, wasted, wronged, misplaced, or erring and sinful passion,—or with the dreary burden of a heart unyielded, because unvalued and unsought." Perhaps Hester became, in short, a counselor to women disappointed in the most profound of their needs: to be loved.

To all of them she said essentially the same thing: that eventually God, in His mercy, would rescue them; that He assure that all would be fulfilled. "She assured them . . . of her firm belief, that, at some brighter period, when the world should have grown ripe for it, in Heaven's own time, a new truth would be revealed, in order to establish the whole relation between man and woman on a surer ground of mutual happiness" (261). Earlier, confused by modernity, she argued that the task of changing the situation of women was, and would continue to be, "hopeless," because, to achieve the surer ground, it would be necessary to have "society . . . torn down, and built up anew . . . the very nature of the opposite sex, or its long hereditary habit, which has become like nature . . . essentially modified," and woman undergo "a still mightier change; in which, perhaps, her ethereal essence, wherein she has her truest life, will be found to have evaporated" (164). It was too much, then, to hope that human beings could effect such changes. But it was not too much, now, in Hester's opinion, to hope—to assure others, and no doubt herself—that God could effect them, and that a "divine and mysterious" new truth will appear, a "revelation" announced by an "an angel and apostle"—a "prophetess . . . a woman . . . lofty, pure, and beautiful; and wise . . . [through] the ethereal medium of joy." And thus, through God, the surer ground would be established, and the love between women and men rendered "sacred" (261).

It was Hester's consummation most devoutly to be wished; for all of the world's women disappointed in love, and, unto her dying breath, for herself. And it lay perhaps—the old serpent—coiled in her soul around even her repentance: the simple longing to be reunited—by God—by anyone—anywhere—anyhow—with the man she loved—dead, as alive—passionately, and forever.

Whether this longing was fulfilled is not known. After "many, many years," Hester was buried "near" Dimmesdale's "old and sunken grave, yet with a space between, as if the dust of the two sleepers had no right to mingle." On the other hand, "one tombstone served for both" (262). What was granted them thereafter is not known.

Chapter Six

Crime and Punishment

During most of the month that ends with him engulfed in evil, Rashkolnikov is "carried away by his dreams" (21)[1] of committing murder that he tries, with diminishing effect, not to take them seriously. At the beginning of the month

> he had put no great trust in those dreams of his; he merely excited himself by their hideous but fascinating audacity. But now, a month later, he began to regard them in a different light and, in spite of all those bitter monologues about his own impotence and indecision, he had unconsciously got accustomed to looking on his 'hideous' dream as a practical proposition, though he still did not believe that he would ever carry it out. He was even now going for a 'rehearsal' of his plan, and with every step he took, his excitement grew stronger and stronger.
>
> (21–22)

Though only as the month unfolds, the possibility of murder gradually becomes "a practical proposition." His initial excitement at the "fascinating audacity" of the dream persists. And the rehearsal itself implies intent. But Rashkolnikov is still very far from resolved. He has only begun to regard his dreams "in a different light." Their audacity still seems "hideous." He is not yet conscious that the proposition is practical. And "he still did not believe that he would ever carry it out." Moreover, the rehearsal itself seems to restrain him. Walking towards the moneylender's house, Rashkolnikov insists his intent is absurd. "Am I really capable of doing that? Is that serious? Not a bit of it! It isn't serious at all" (20). In the old woman's apartment

---

1. Fyodor Dostoyevsky, *Crime and Punishment*, translated by David Magarshack (Baltimore: Penguin, 1972).

he thinks, "Good Lord, how beastly it all is!" (25) Back on the street, the rehearsal over, disgust, "which had begun to oppress and disturb his mind while he was on his way to the old woman" (26), overwhelms him, apparently expelling the dream from his heart; so that, on entering a restaurant and settling down with a drink, "he felt better immediately and his mind became clear. 'The whole thing's silly!' he said to himself hopefully . . . In spite of his annoyance with himself he was already looking very cheerful, as though he had suddenly got rid of some terrible burden" (26).

The burden, however, still oppresses him. Conscience has apparently triumphed. But the rehearsal scene itself records ominous incitements to aggression. And in the three related episodes that follow, conscience is swamped, and the resolution to murder quickly achieved. Information scattered through the scene is unsettling. "For some time past" Rashkolnikov has been "in an irritable and overstrung state." He has been "crushed by poverty" (19). His nerves are "overwrought" (20). And "much bitter contempt" (21) has accumulated in his heart. He is not therefore doomed to murder. But the strain of his condition may have weakened his resistance to morbid suggestion. The "bitter contempt" seems especially ominous, because it is directed at least in part inwardly, at Rashkolnikov's own "impotence and indecision." The revulsion at these supposed vices being intense, only a slight impetus may be required to overcome them. And the three linked episodes that follow the rehearsal—a meeting with Marmeladov, a letter from home, and an encounter with a young girl apparently just raped—supply a massive impetus.

The deepest effect upon Rashkolnikov of the meeting with Marmeladov—his decision, made at once, to confess to Sonia after committing the murders—will not be revealed until a very late conversation with Sonia (345). Nor will its immediate effect be evident until Rashkolnikov has responded to the letter from home. But something of his reaction, and perhaps of its consequence, may be surmised from the nature of Marmeladov's story, and from Rashkolnikov's reaction on leaving Marmeladov's room. Both the story and the reaction may heighten dangerously Rashkolnikov's disgust at a number of evils, both social and individual, to which violence may soon seem not only a fit, but an imperative, response.

By his own admission, Marmeladov is responsible for a great deal of his trouble. He is, he says, "a dirty swine" (31) and a "born blackguard" (32), and his drinking has helped ruin himself and his family. But he is also in part a victim of society, as Rashkolnikov himself, "crushed by poverty," does not, perhaps, fail to notice. "Chronic destitution," Marmeladov says, is regarded as "a crime," and the destitute man is "swept out with a broom from the society of decent men in the most humiliating way possible" (29). Marmeladov is probably not doomed by society to self-degradation. But destitution probably was inevitable; or so at least a bitter on-looker unable even to pay his rent, and therefore himself either anticipating or suffering humiliation, might conclude. Rashkolnikov may see Marmeladov and himself as in part at least victims of social injustice.

He unquestionably sees helpless, suffering innocence in that light. Though in the restaurant he feels "a sudden desire for company," he reverts, even before Marmeladov joins him, to the "all-too-familiar unpleasant and irritating feeling of aversion for any stranger who tried to encroach on his privacy" (29). And this, or some related feeling, seems to persist through Marmeladov's story; except when Marmeladov is discussing Sonia. By the time Marmeladov asks to be taken home, Rashkolnikov has "been wanting to go for some time" (41), in part at least because the second portion of Marmeladov's story—the story of his drunken spree, and his fervent credo—has not absorbed him. But to the first portion, that focused upon Sonia's introduction to prostitution, "Rashkolnikov listened attentively" (37). Anyone even residually decent would pity Sonia's terrible self-sacrifice, and perhaps admire her. Rashkolnikov does both. Having delivered Marmeladov to his wife and young children, he exits, leaving behind, unobserved, some coins. This humane gesture seems, however, decisively undermined by disgust. "Sonia must have her make-up," he thinks. "Dear Sonia! What a girl! What a gold mine they have found!" (44) The sarcasm is only partly genuine. It does not obscure his sympathy and admiration for her, his pity for Mrs. Marmeladov and the children, or even his solicitude for Mr. Marmeladov, whom he has carefully borne home. But compassion for the consequences of social injustice and inborn human degeneracy seems far less important than his revulsion at the evils themselves, and his preoccupation with other, degenerative ideas.

As though ashamed of his humanity, he covers it with contempt. He regrets at once having left the coins. Thinking of Sonia's profession, he smiles "sardonically" (44). And he reviles her family for making "jolly good use" of their gold mine. "Took it for granted. Wept bitter tears and got used to it. Man gets used to everything—the beast!" (44) He admits that "he would not have taken the [money] back even if he could," and that "man in general" (44) may not be a beast. But as he leaves the Marmeladovs, dark rather than charitable thoughts seem to control him. And he is no better disposed the next morning. "He woke up late . . . after a disturbed night. His sleep had not refreshed him. He woke up feeling ill-humored, irritable, and cross, and he looked around his little room with hatred" (45). The underlying cause of his black disposition is the brooding of the past month, that has exasperated him horribly; a reaction common to "a certain type of monomaniac who dwells too much on one single idea" (45). But its immediate cause must be in part at least the encounter with Marmeladov. And the relation of that encounter to the "single idea" is at once clarified by Rashkolnikov's reaction to the letter from home, whose contents he instantly links to the events of the day past, to fatal effect.

Everything in and about the letter argues Rashkolnikov's profound love for his mother and sister, and his unendurable rage at the trouble they confront, their proposed response to it, and his utter incapacity to alter that response by lawful means. He demands the letter "in great excitement," refuses to open it while the maid is present, preferring "to be left alone" with it, and when the maid does leave "quickly raised the letter to his lips and kissed it" (47). The love is unmistakably reciprocated. "You are all we have in the world, Dunya and I" (48), his mother writes, and "if only you are happy, we shall be happy" (57). To assure his happiness, both women have slaved to support him, and would sell themselves; as indeed, Rashkolnikov concludes at once, Dunya has done. His proud sister, who would "rather live on bread and water than sell her own soul," who would "certainly not exchange her moral freedom for a life of comfort . . . would sell herself for someone she loved, someone she worshipped" (61)—in fact, has already contracted to do so—and to Luzhin, a creature twice her age for whom she feels no love, and who is so detestable that had Rashkolnikov met him then "he would most probably have killed him" (59). Moreover, the parallel between his family's situation and that of the Marmeladovs is crushingly obvious. For "Darling Roddy" the sacrifice the women propose is "nothing! In such an emergency [they] would not even mind going the way of Sonia! Dear little Sonia, Sonia Marmeladov, the eternal Sonia while the world lasts! . . . Do you, dear Dunya, realize that little Sonia's fate is in no way more degrading than yours with Luzhin?" And Rashkolnikov himself is no better able to protect her from Luzhin than Marmeladov has been able to protect Sonia. Dunya's sacrifice must not occur. "I won't have it!" But the obvious question intrudes at once. "And what can you do to prevent it? Will you forbid it? What right have you to do that? What can you promise them in return, to lay claim to such a right?" (62)

He can promise them nothing, and therefore he can forbid nothing; unless he resorts to extraordinary means, at once. And the means are at hand. Fears that his family may be ruined by their circumstances have long tormented him, "and at last they had rent his heart," leaving him in "utter desolation and despair." From these emotions "a fearful, wild and fantastic question" has emerged, that has "exhausted his mind and heart, clamoring for an immediate solution." And now, his mother's letter having "burst upon him like a bombshell" (63), the question—not yet explicitly phrased—is suddenly resolved. He must "do something at once and quickly, too" (63). And, unsurprised, he acknowledges what that something is:

> Suddenly he gave a start: a thought flashed through his mind, a thought that had also occurred to him the day before. And he did not start because the thought had flashed through his mind. He knew, he felt that it would most certainly cross his mind and was already waiting for it. And, besides, it was not only yesterday that the thought had occurred to him. But the difference was that a month ago—and even yesterday, for that matter—it was only a dream, whereas now—now it came to him no longer as a dream, but in a sort of new, terrifying, and unfamiliar guise, and he himself suddenly realized it.
>
> (63–64)

The resolve has appeared. Forced past Rashkolnikov's fantasizing by the specific events that confirm the fears upon which he has long been brooding, the commitment to murder presses openly into his consciousness as a practical proposition he may indeed carry out. And that he should carry it out is stressed at once by his encounter with a young girl, that for a few minutes "absorbed all his attention" (64).

He meets her as he is walking the streets distractedly, digesting the letter from home, his thoughts "whirling through his brain like a blizzard" (59), at precisely the moment when horrible parallels will strike him most vividly. And the parallel between the girl and his sister is all too obvious. The "gentleman" might almost be stalking Dunya. Rashkolnikov, furious, rushes at him, "lips foaming with rage" (65), fists clenched. But though he is able to intervene successfully, he knows he is impotent. Even the kindhearted policeman who appears must, Rashkolnikov thinks, be struck by the oddity of a man "dressed in such rags and giving away money!" (67)—by the absurdity of a pauper offering protection. This absurdity crushes Rashkolnikov. He shouts at the policeman to abandon the girl, and walks off, bitterly reviling himself. "And what the hell made me interfere? Who am I to help her? Have I the right to help anyone?" (68) Lacking the necessary power, he has no right. Despite him, the evil will persist, and in all likelihood engulf his sister. "A young lady of a good family, by the look of her," says the policeman. "Her parents must be poor, I suppose. There are hundreds like her about, sir. Looks like a decently brought up girl, a well-bred young lady" (67). She could be Dunya, as Rashkolnikov has been aware from the outset. And if she does not succumb, it will be merely through accident. "That's how it should be, they say. It's essential, they say, that such a percentage should every year go—that way—to the devil . . . And what if Dunya should somehow or other find herself among the percentage?" (69) She must not, of course. But she very well may, unless her brother's resolution remains firm.

It does, despite a final, massive challenge. Leaving the young girl, Rashkolnikov walks towards Razumikhin's room, but decides not to enter. "I shall call on Razumikhin, of course; but not now—I shall call on him another time, on the day after I've done it, after that has been settled, and when everything is different." (71) The struggle within him is far closer to completion than it was a day earlier, or before he read the letter from home, or even before the encounter with the young girl. He still hesitates. The thought that resulted from his response to the letter was "terrifying." When it appeared "the blood rushed to his head and everything went black before his eyes" (64). And "when he realized what he was saying" about the visit to Razumikhin, "'After that?' he cried, jumping up from the seat. 'But is that to be? Will it really happen?'" (71) But those are relatively minor scruples, easily disposed of. The dream, however, that Rashkolnikov now endures, is not. It is "a terrible dream" (72), the last huge assault upon him of his conscience, and it very nearly aborts his resolve.

In the dream Rashkolnikov reverts to his childhood, and champions sensitivity, profound respect for life, and religious fervor against the unbearable bestiality of Russian peasants. The beloved church in the center of a cemetery, and pious memories of the place, engross him. Nearby, but spiritually a universe away, outside a pub, peasants are murdering a horse. It is unendurable; the child's soul cries out in protest. And when the horse is finally dead, the child, whose intervention has accomplished nothing, appalled that men kill, compassionately kisses the bloody carcass. As he does so, Rashkolnikov wakes up, "his soul . . . in confusion and darkness" (78). It is inconceivable that he would murder the old woman. "No, I couldn't do it! I just couldn't do it! Even if there were no mistake whatever in all my calculations . . . I just couldn't do it!" (78–79) And that conclusion drawn, an immense wave of relief sweeps over him, and evil apparently releases its hold:

> He was pale, his eyes were burning, he was utterly exhausted, but he felt suddenly that he could breathe more freely. He felt that he had already cast off the terrible burden that had so long been weighing upon him, and all of a sudden he felt greatly relieved and at peace with himself. 'O Lord,' he prayed, 'show me the way and I shall give up this—damnable dream of mine!' . . . It was as though the abscess which had been coming to a head in his heart for a whole month had suddenly burst. He was free! He was free! He was free from all those obsessions, magic spells, delusions, witchcraft!
>
> (79)

Had this fervor persisted, he would have murdered no one. But, though intense, it is surprisingly shortlived. An instant before it engulfs Rashkolnikov, he is wondering, in an unfinished sentence, if he "just couldn't do it . . . why—why am I still-" (79). And immediately after he declares his freedom, the event occurs that steels his resolve irreversibly: he overhears a conversation in which Lizaveta informs him that the moneylender will be alone at seven the next night. That event "always seemed to him afterwards a sort of predestined turning point of his fate" (79). Predestination having struck, thought and free will become equally irrelevant. He enters his room "like a man sentenced to death. He thought of nothing, and indeed he was quite incapable of thinking; but he suddenly felt with all his being that he no longer possessed any freedom of reasoning or of will, and that everything was suddenly and irrevocably settled" (81). There was in fact "nothing at all remarkable" (81) in the meeting with Lizaveta. But, unable to endure any longer the "agonizing inner struggle" (89) of the month past, and intent upon submerging conscience in action, Rashkolnikov submits himself to fate, and proceeds to the murder half-consciously, as though doomed to commit it.

Conscience barely subsists. Except by absolving himself of all responsibility, Rashkolnikov cannot approach the act. And so he resolutely refuses to think, and becomes an automaton. From the time he leaves Lizaveta, to the moment of the murders, "it was as though someone had taken him by the hand and drawn him after himself, blindly, irresistibly, with supernatural force, and without any objections on his part" (90). The conversation overheard, he returns to his room and sits motionless for an hour. "He could never remember whether he had been thinking about anything at that time" (85). That night he sleeps "unusually long"—so that his mind cannot oppress him—and "without dreams" (86)—so that his conscience cannot renew its assault. From late morning, when he awakes, until early afternoon, he lies in bed, staring at the wall, thinking nothing. Thereafter, until six o'clock, "he kept day-dreaming," about matters utterly unrelated to his intent; "mostly he imagined himself to be in Africa, in Egypt, in some sort of oasis" (87). From six to seven he is feverishly occupied with preparations. On the way to the murder "his mind was preoccupied with all sorts of thoughts that had nothing to do with his present business" (92). And as he stands in front of the old moneylender's door, ringing the bell, "his reason seemed to stop functioning altogether from time to time" (94). Thus fortified, he enters the apartment, and hatchets the two women to death.

A brief hint of why he has done that is contained in Rashkolnikov's memory of a conversation he overheard in a restaurant; a conversation that mirrored precisely "a strange idea . . . hatching in his brain . . . an idea that he was beginning to find more and more fascinating" (82). A student and a soldier were deciding in essence that if the old moneylender, a social parasite, were murdered, and her money used to finance the careers of poverty-stricken young people, no crime would have been committed. This "idle talk . . . was to exert a very great influence on Rashkolnikov as the whole thing grew and developed" (85). But precisely how it did grow and develop, and in the mind of precisely what sort of man, has not yet been explained. As has been noted, "much bitter contempt had accumulated in the young man's heart" (21). He has been engaged in "bitter monologues about his own impotence and indecision" (22). He is "exhausted after a whole month of concentrated wretchedness and excitement" (27), and has become virtually a "monomaniac" from dwelling "too much on one single idea" (45). He has decided, as he informs a horrified maid, that he wants "to get rich all at once" (47). But, though towards the end of the month "his casuistry was as sharp as a razor, and he could no longer find any conscious objections to his plans in his mind," still "at heart he never really took himself seriously, and he went on, slavishly and stubbornly, fumbling for some valid objections in all directions" (89-90). And the man performing these mental gyrations is "superciliously proud and uncommunicative," and seems to have regarded at least his fellow students as greatly his inferiors in "general development, knowledge and convictions" (69). The fragments are tantalizing. Rashkolnikov has decided that "what he intended to do 'was not a crime'" (90). But "the whole process of reasoning which had brought him to that conclusion" (90) is not clear. Thus, though poverty as a motive has been convincingly dramatized, when the murders occur the impression is deliberately enforced that they have not yet been completely explained. The vulnerability of Sonia, Dunya, and the young girl apparently raped rouses in Rashkolnikov fury and despair, as does his inability, because penniless, to help them, or his mother, or the Marmeladov family. The profound injustice empowered by poverty maddens Rashkolnikov, and draws him to the parasitic old moneylender. But some deeper force draws him there also; a force within himself not yet, except in passing hints, known.

Whatever motivated them, the murders committed, pressures at once begin tormenting Rashkolnikov so crushing that within days he resolves either to kill himself or to confess to murder; a resolve negated only unexpectedly and unknowingly by Sonia.

Self-disgust and conscience are not such pressures. An unrelenting sudden sense of unendurable isolation, and an unrelenting terror of being exposed as a murderer, are.

Both conscience and self-disgust torment Rashkolnikov briefly soon after he murders, but then for a long time disappear, until they are forced on him again; self-disgust to devastating effect, conscience to salvational effect.

Summoned to the police station, he puts on a blood-stained sock. "But no sooner did he put it on than he pulled it off again in horror and disgust" (112). He felt these emotions an instant after the murder of Lizaveta, when "sheer horror and disgust at what he had done" overwhelmed him, and he proposes "to go down on my knees" (113) at the police-office and confess. Later, on the way to Razumikhin, he admits to himself that he has committed "a horrible, mean, and dastardly crime" (128). And in a terrifying dream, Rashkolnikov cannot imagine why an assistant superintendent should be beating a landlady. "And how could he do such a thing?" he wonders, lying, eyes open, "in such an unendurable state of infinite horror as he had never experienced before" (134). Thereafter, however, conscience disappears completely until Sonia forces it to engulf him. And, that notwithstanding, during his imprisonment, in the Epilogue, Rashkolnikov insists perversely that he "did not repent of his crime," and steadfastly asserts, "My conscience is clear" (552).

Having left the police station and buried the loot, Rashkolnikov is shocked to stumble upon "a new, unexpected, and extremely simple" observation that throws him first "into utter confusion" (128) and then into a horrible rage. Ostensibly he murdered in order to gain wealth. Yet he never inspected the loot, and a moment before burying it had been on his way to dump all of it into a river. Moreover, "he had practically decided to [discard] it yesterday when he was squatting over the box and taking out the jewel-cases from it. Yes, it was so!" (128) That being the case, he had acted not "consciously" but "like a damned fool," without "a firm and definite idea." Therefore the new life postulated in his theories will not begin. And so "To hell with the new life!" he thinks suddenly, "in a fit of boundless rage" (128) at his own ineptitude. This rage he at once transfers outward, into "a sort of infinite, almost physical feeling of disgust with everything he came across—malevolent, obstinate, virulent" (129). But basically it is self-disgust And, though for a long time it too disappears, It too is forced upon him again, and devastates him.

The fear of exposure, the first of the unrelenting pressures, torments Rashkolnikov as soon as he wakes up in the morning after the murders. It tormented him during the escape the night before when, but for a set of accidents, he would have been captured. In the morning, the torment persists. Leaping from the sofa, he inspects his clothes, and temporarily hides the loot. Soon thereafter he is thunderstruck to be told of the summons to the police, who must, he assumes at once, suspect him of murder. His relief at learning the cause of the summons notwithstanding, the encounter at the station unnerves him so horribly that when he overhears the superintendent's correct explanation of how the murderer escaped, he faints. He leaves the station "seized with terror from head to foot," once again convinced that the "dirty swine . . . suspect!" (124) Fearing a search, he rushes home, empties his room of the loot, and walks about with it, "worried and anxious, for half an hour at least" (127) before finding a safe burial-ground. He then relaxes—from this particular fear—until the nightmare that closes the day, during which he assumes that the superintendent beating the landlady "surely meant they would come to him too, 'for it must be all on account of . . . what had happened yesterday.'" Once again "terror gripped his heart" (134), so that the day ends as it began, with Rashkolnikov petrified that he will soon be exposed as a murderer.

The second of the relentless pressures, the experience of solitude, appears more slowly, but to more devastating immediate effect, because, a wholly new and unexpected experience, it harrows Rashkolnikov's soul. Standing in the police station, apparently safe, he is "overwhelmed by a gloomy feeling of agonizing and infinite solitude and seclusion, of which he all of a sudden became acutely conscious." This feeling is "something utterly unfamiliar, something new and sudden, something he had never experienced before . . . And the most agonizing part of it was that it was a sensation rather than a conscious idea; a direct sensation, the most agonizing sensation he had ever known in his life" (122). Its impact stuns him so convulsively that he resolves to confess; a resolution "so strong that he even got up to carry it out" (123). Somewhat later, he rushes to Razumikhin, but retreats at once, realizing that neither Razumikhin nor anyone else can help him, because "I'm alone—by myself—and that's all!" (130) That realization is underscored soon afterwards, when, gazing at the cupola of a distant church, he senses a sudden and irrevocable detachment from all of his past. "Dreadfully unhappy . . . he felt as though he had cut himself off from everyone and everything at that moment" (133).

Unable to bear the total pressure of his first day as a murderer, Rashkolnikov collapses, and through three subsequent days of delirium and half-consciousness manages to forget completely "about that" (136). When he awakens on the fifth day, the oppressions of self-disgust and conscience have disappeared. But the two relentless pressures have not. In a long scene in Rashkolnikov's room, they at once begin a massive assault under whose impact Rashkolnikov, despite himself, buckles, overwhelmed by the need for immediate release from a total pressure he can no longer endure.

Throughout the scene, Rashkolnikov remains upon the sofa, in the morning stubbornly ignoring Razumikhin, and in the evening his back to the discussions in progress, or staring abstractedly beyond Luzhin, his spiritual detachment underscored physically. And he is silent, except under unbearable duress. His terror of exposure is more directly conveyed. In the morning Razumikhin unknowingly torments him with the news that Zamyotov, the chief police-clerk, dropped by during his delirium, as he was shouting for his socks. Indeed, "Zamyotov went hunting for your socks all over the room," Razumikhin recalls, responding to Rashkolnikov's demand for information with the merry question, "Not afraid of letting out some little secret, are you?" (144) And in the evening he launches, in conversation with Zamyotov, into a brilliant analysis of the absurdity of regarding the house-painter Nickolay as the murderer of the two women. To this analysis he appends, as Luzhin enters, an accurate description of how the murderer escaped, and soon afterwards, having shunted Luzhin's conversation aside, agrees that the murderer was one of the old woman's clients, and concludes that "he's neither clever nor experienced . . . that it's most certainly his first crime" and that "he lost his nerve" (169). Throughout this conversation Rashkolnikov struggles to restrain himself. Though "he felt his arms and legs had gone numb, as if paralyzed . . . he did not attempt to move, but gazed obstinately" (153) at a point on the wall. Two outbursts aside (157,168), he succeeds. The cost, however, of self-restraint is high. When Luzhin enters, interrupting Razumikhin, Rashkolnikov turns from the wall, his face "very pale" and bearing "an expression of great suffering, as though he had just undergone a very painful operation, or just been taken out of a torture chamber" (162). And, Luzhin having left, Rashkolnikov demands furiously that Zossimov and Razumikhin also leave, calling them "torturers!" (172)

His room at last empty, Rashkolnikov suddenly becomes "perfectly calm" (173); but not because the pressures crushing him have suddenly vanished. They have not. In fact, acting singly and collectively, they have broken him down. Acknowledging that this is so, Rashkolnikov suddenly resolves to gain relief at once. Therefore there is suddenly "no trace of his recent crazy raving or of the panic fear that had haunted him for the last few days" (173). Though still weak, he has "reached a point of complete calm that comes from a fixed idea . . . that this must be brought to an end today, once and for all, now! . . . because he did not want to go on living like that" (173–174).

As he leaves his room, quietly and unobserved, Rashkolnikov "did not know where he was going" (173). Nor has he "the faintest idea" of how to "end it" (173). But, despite his adamant refusal to think, he seems to have resolved upon suicide. "All he felt and knew was that everything had to be changed, one way or another. 'Any way!' he repeated with desperate, immovable self-confidence and determination" (174). He wanders the streets comparing himself to "a man sentenced to death . . . one hour before his execution" (177). But, quite by accident, entering a restaurant and meeting Zamyotov, an alternative to suicide—confession—appears. Thereafter, until Sonia appears, those two options contend within Rashkolnikov as the means to "end it," confession at last prevailing.

At precisely what point during the encounter with Zamyotov Rashkolnikov's resolve shifts from suicide to confession is not clear. He may resolve to confess because, suicide being imminent, there is no reason not to confirm Zamyotov's suspicions. Or he may regard confession as an alternative to suicide. But that he does move towards confession is plain, though Zamyotov, puzzled by his frenetic wit, cannot decide if he is serious. "I declare to you," says Rashkolnikov, "or rather I confess, or better still, I am making a statement and you are taking it down" (180). And thus he leads Zamyotov—and himself—on, until finally "the terrible words trembled on his lips . . . another moment and . . . he would utter it!" And he does utter it, though only as a question—"And what if it was I who murdered the old woman and Lizaveta?" (184)—before suddenly, having "recovered his senses" (185), he backs off.

Leaving the restaurant, he meets Razumikhin, from whom, after a short talk, he rushes away. In a moment, but too late to follow his friend, Razumikhin realizes that Rashkolnikov cannot "be left to himself now . . . He may drown himself" (188). He intends to do so, and, but for a coincidence, would have leapt into the river. Standing on a bridge above it, he watches a distraught young woman jump, in an unsuccessful attempt at suicide, and concludes, "No, that's horrible . . . I couldn't do it." Therefore only one option remains. And so "No use waiting. The police station . . . " (189).

As he moves towards it, in a preliminary action he confesses again—or comes so close to doing so explicitly that, as he must know, his formal confession will be a foregone, almost unnecessary conclusion. Suddenly finding himself at "the house" (190), he enters, goes upstairs, walks into the moneylender's apartment, and begins talking to the workers redecorating it. His conversation and presence are so suspicious that one of the workers asks what kind of man he is. "Come along to the police station with me," Rashkolnikov answers. "I'll tell you there" (192). He goes back down, the workers in tow, and in the street attracts a group of people, among whom a consensus quickly develops that he should indeed be taken to the police. "Come along!" (193) he responds, apparently aware that the consensus is of his own making, and anxious that an irrevocable statement be made.

A caretaker pushes Rashkolnikov into the street, dispelling the interest of the crowd (but not that of an unnamed artisan). Not deterred, Rashkolnikov moves on to the station himself, impelled most immediately by the most profound of the pressures upon him, the immersion in solitude. "The whole world was dead and indifferent . . . dead to him, and to him alone" (194). That awareness, and the total accumulated pressure, having crushed him, he is left with neither choice nor strength. Therefore he has "now definitely made up his mind to go to the police station, and he knew for certain that everything would soon be over" (194).

He is mistaken. Suddenly he encounters an accident; a horrible accident of revolutionary consequence for Rashkolnikov's soul. Suddenly, unexpectedly, it negates his resolves. As if by magic, suicide and surrender vanish, and a profound determination to persevere emerges. The accident is the fatal trampling of Marmeladov, and the cause of the revolution—incompletely explained—is his daughter Sonia.

As the accident unfolds—from the moment Rashkolnikov comes upon it, to the moment he leaves Marmeladov's room, Marmeladov having died—no hint is offered of Rashkolnikov's reaction either to events that occur or to the characters involved. In consequence, the astonishment conveyed by the reaction, when at last it does occur, is underscored. Walking down the stairs, he suddenly feels "full of a new, great and exhilarating sensation of tremendous energy and will to live which suddenly surged up within him" (206). After a short, crucial encounter with Polya, Sonia's younger sister, the new sensation wells into a storm of life:

> "Enough!" he said solemnly and resolutely. "No more delusions, no more imaginary terrors, no more phantom visions! . . . My life hasn't come to an end with the death of the old woman! . . . Now begins the reign of reason and light and—of will and strength . . . We'll try our strength now!" he added arrogantly, as though addressing some dark power and challenging it . . . " What I want is strength—strength! . . . and strength must be won by strength . . . " he added proudly and self-confidently. His pride and self-confidence increased every minute; and the next minute he was already a different man from the one he had been a minute before.
>
> (208)

The change is overwhelming, but difficult to explain. A satanic impulse—the will to prevail over the relentless pressures that torment him—has suddenly, unexpectedly possessed Rashkolnikov. "But what was it exactly that had brought about such a change in him?" He "did not know himself" (208). And not even a partial explanation is given. But, somehow or other, the cause is Sonia. When Polya appears, having rushed after him down the stairway at Sonia's behest, Rashkolnikov "laid his hands on her shoulder and looked at her with a kind of inexpressible joy" (206). In the very short interaction that follows, a profound communion, apparently of love, is suddenly established between Rashkolnikov, Polya, and the absent Sonia, as both Rashkolnikov and Polya are aware. Having answered with a heartfelt embrace Rashkolnikov's question, "And are you going to love me too?" the little girl "went away completely enraptured by him" (207). And Rashkolnikov, suddenly convinced that "life is real!" for "Haven't I lived just now?" (208) launches into his defiant outburst. A few moments later he sputters disconnectedly but happily to Razumikhin, to whose party he unexpectedly proceeds, "I've just been present at the death of someone . . . and I—I gave them all my money—and also I've been kissed by such a dear little creature, who, if I had killed anyone, would also—I mean, I saw someone else there—with a bright red feather . . . " (211). Though Razumikhin cannot know it, and though the fact seems implausible, Rashkolnikov is suddenly experiencing either love, or some emotion remarkably like it.

The need for the joy this emotion releases is great and obvious. During the harrowing days since the murders, Rashkolnikov has felt joy only, and momentarily, on kissing his mother's letter (47), on discovering, at the police station, that he is not a suspect (115,117), on burying the loot (127), and on outwitting Zamyotov (185). And in the agonizing month preceding the murders, he apparently felt nothing even pleasant. Thus, being desperate, he is more than ready to accept delight. But why Sonia, of all people, rouses it in him will not be explained for a long time. The beginning of a hint is contained in his remark to Razumikhin that, even if he were a murderer, Sonia would, as her sister does, love him. The conviction that she would must derive from his sense of her profoundly forgiving and self-sacrificing nature, drawn for him by Marmeladov in the restaurant, and confirmed by her response to the poor man as he dies. But at the moment motive has been dwarfed by fact. Therefore the question—Why Sonia?—remains unanswered.

Rashkolnikov's will to persevere—for whatever reason—secured, he embarks, with apparent self-confidence, upon "the reign of . . . will and strength." That reign is, however, at once challenged, in turn, by the arrival of Dunya and Mrs. Rashkolnikov, by Rashkolnikov's first encounter with Porfiry, and by the unexpected encounter with an unnamed artisan. The first two of these challenges Rashkolnikov withstands, though at substantial cost. The third suddenly terrifies him—so that a reign that initially leaves him "in excellent spirits" (208) ends with a nightmare.

Rashkolnikov's reaction to the arrival of Dunya and Mrs. Rashkolnikov and to the unexpected appearance, as they speak, of Sonia demonstrates his strategy against the isolation. The strategy is two-fold: the rejection of his family, and the integration into his life of Sonya. The first of these actions begins at once, because Rashkolnikov is at once overwhelmed by its necessity. His sister and mother having appeared in his room, "a sudden, unbearable realization of what he had done struck him as though by lightning" (212), and he faints. But his response to them has already been fixed. His first demand, on waking, is that they leave. Like Razumikhin and Zossimov a day earlier, they "torture" (214) him; but far more profoundly. The conversation in his room had heightened terribly his terror of exposure. The presence of his family heightens unbearably his sense of isolation. The murders committed, all of his past now lies "at the bottom of some fathomless chasm, deep, deep down" (133), and therefore he cannot, as he knows, touch anyone (except, for reasons not yet discussed, Sonia). That being the case, his beloved mother and Dunya, whom of all the world he longs to touch, threaten to tantalize him beyond endurance, and in consequence must be disposed of, permanently, and at once.

Razumikhin virtually forces them out. And when they return the next morning, Rashkolnikov has already prepared the charade through which he will rid himself of them. The change in his behavior is marked and impressive. Zossimov, who notes it, cannot help "marvelling at the way Rashkolnikov, who the day before had behaved like a monomaniac and flown into a rage at the slightest word, now managed to control himself and hide his feelings." Having determined that "for another hour or two the torture ... could no longer be avoided" (240), Rashkolnikov endures it from behind a mask, that slips only rarely, and behind which his family cannot penetrate. That it is a mask neither woman doubts. The night before, watching her son recover on the couch, Mrs. Rashkolnikov had "caught a glimpse ... of something unbending" (214). Now, as "he went on, as though repeating a lesson he had learnt by heart that morning," she notes, "He's been talking so nicely, but I'm dreadfully afraid" (242), though of precisely what she does not know. Dunya, more clearheaded, thinks he is "making his peace with us and apologizing as though he were performing some official ceremony, or as though he had learnt it all by heart" (243). Predictably, the peacemaking seems artificial, as "they were all aware" (244). Worse, in the conversation that surrounds it, Rashkolnikov occasionally gives way to surliness. When Dunya objects "firmly" to an element of a theory he advocates, he looks at her "almost with hatred" (244). Suddenly, and "as though intentionally" (246), he asks his mother why she is talking nonsense. He embarrasses Dunya and Razumikhin by joking tactlessly about their sudden love (247). He demands that she choose between Luzhin and himself. Then—in perhaps his most callous thrust—he professes complete indifference to her fate: "Marry whom you like, for all I care!" (250) And when Sonia suddenly and unexpectedly appears, he forces her acquaintance upon his mother and sister; an experience to which Dunya responds with great beauty, but which both women recall, even later that day, with embarrassment (319). Throughout the conversation, Rashkolnikov's behavior is so unsettling that, having left, Mrs. Rashkolnikov declares to Dunya—almost inconceivably, given the mother's nature—"I am glad to have come away . . . You can't imagine, darling, how relieved I am, somehow. Little did I dream on the train yesterday that I would be glad of that of all things" (257). Her relief underscores Rashkolnikov's success. The women will return, though only once more, for a final conversation. Thereafter, except for a brief leavetaking, they and Rashkolnikov will not meet. The necessity of rejection is painfully unclear to them, and Rashkolnikov's remark that "everything here seems to be happening in quite another world," and that "you, too, seem to be miles away" (248), explains nothing, because its context must be a mystery to them. They cannot understand that, precisely because they have been "so near and dear to him," they threaten to become "quite unbearable" (248), because their conversation and presence both recall "the horrible feeling he had recently experienced, that makes "his blood run cold": the awareness, received "with appalling clarity that . . . not only would he never again have a chance of talking freely as much as he liked, but that he would not be able to talk to anyone about anything" (246). Because his mother and his sister underscore that awareness, they must be disposed of.

And because Sonia is his sole defense against it, she must be incorporated into his suffering. She therefore enters as Dunya and Mrs. Rashkolnikov are preparing to exit, at Rashkolnikov's insistence mingles with them, and remains when they are gone. The first of Rashkolnikov's strategic objectives—the rejection of his family—almost accomplished, he turns to the second, devoting to Sonia the attentions of a lover. When she appears, "all at once he . . . grew confused." At the sight of her meekness, "his heart was wrung with pity" (253). To her invitation to attend the funeral he replies "in a faltering voice, and without finishing the sentence" (254). When he notices her fear of his mother and Dunya, to whom she obviously feels inferior, his "pale face flushed, he gave a violent start . . . his eyes blazed" (254), and he insists upon introducing her at once. And his innocuous question to her on departing "he asked with a sudden change of tone, as if he really wanted to say something quite different to her" (260).

The effect of these attentions is not lost upon any of the women. Sonia departs in a terrible flutter, to "reflect on every word, every detail. Never in her life had she experienced anything of the kind before! A whole new world opened up before her—dimly, incomprehensibly" (260). Dunya, appraising the relationship at once, and no doubt grateful to the woman who has touched her brother, takes leave "with an attentive, courteous bow" (256) to Sonia (thereby earning, to her intense delight, the only expression of Rashkolnikov's affection during their encounter). And Mrs. Rashkolnikov, less disposed to share her son, notes jealously, "She's got a hold over him" (258). But only Rashkolnikov understands clearly—or thinks he does—what benefits the relation with Sonia will yield. His sister having gone, he suddenly says, "looking brightly" at Sonia, "May the Lord grant peace to the dead, but the living still have to live! Isn't that so? It is, isn't it?" (257) Neither Sonia, nor Razumikhin, standing by, equally puzzled, can know that Rashkolnikov is repeating part of the satanic outburst that revolutionized his soul on the previous night. But the conviction felt then—that "my life hasn't come to an end with the death of the old woman! May she rest in peace . . . "—and the exultation—"We will try our strength now!" (208)—are present once again, and for the same reason: Sonia, who does not know it, has roused them.

Her support assured, much is possible; even combat against the fear of exposure. It is no accident that Rashkolnikov resolves to confront Porfiry while Sonia is still present, his family, who drain his strength, having left, or that he insists upon her knowing his specific plans. She is the immediate cause of them. That she does not understand she is supporting him must amuse Rashkolnikov as they part company, she proceeding home, he to Porfiry.

The process of discarding his family accomplished, and that of integrating Sonia into his life having begun, Rashkolnikov's total strategy against the isolation is succeeding. So strength exists, where it did not before, to confront the police. But—for reasons still not discussed—the alliance with Sonia exposes Rashkolnikov to what he would regard, if he saw it approaching, as overwhelming danger. And uprooting himself from his mother and Dunya has been a painful, debilitating experience. Therefore whatever victory he has attained has perhaps been purchased at too high a cost.

The victory over Porfiry is beyond question too costly. Rashkolnikov triumphs in avoiding Porfiry's specific trap, and in successfully countering the objections to an article he wrote and advocates. But, by confirming that he is under suspicion of murder, the encounter heightens Rashkolnikov's anxiety. And the specific triumphs are severely undermined by the torture Porfiry inflicts throughout, shrewdly, and to grave effect. Moreover, in part because the encounter has weakened him, Rashkolnikov cannot withstand the assault, immediately thereafter, of the unnamed artisan, that almost destroys him.

Walking with Razumikhin towards Porfiry's flat, Rashkolnikov wonders whether he is "wise or not in going there" (263). He is far from wise, as the outcome demonstrates.

Approaching Porfiry's flat, he cleverly devises a mask of lightheartedness, that he carefully manipulates as Porfiry is introduced. Somewhat later, he boldly decides "to take up the challenge" (276) of defending his article, and does so clearly, and—despite the perversity of its thesis—impressively. And, at the end of the encounter, having strained "every nerve in his body in an agonizing effort to discover what sort of trap Porfiry had set for him and how to avoid it," he suddenly feels a proud delight, for "he had seen the trap and was exulting over it" (283). But for this moment of delight, and the intellectual satisfaction of defending a thesis, he has endured a tense and painful encounter. Disregarding Rashkolnikov's lightheartedness, which he sees through at once (464), Porfiry stares fixedly at him, and soon informs him, at first subtly, but then, though not quite openly, more directly, that he is indeed under suspicion. "A queer, undisguisedly sarcastic look" and perhaps a wink—he cannot be sure—terrify Rashkolnikov. "'He knows!' it flashed through his mind like lightning." He is then informed "calmly and coldly" (268) that he has been expected for some time, and told "with a barely perceptible touch of irony" that only he has "not found it necessary" (269) to come forward. As the conversation on criminality approaches, Rashkolnikov is convinced that "they don't even disguise the fact that they're hunting me down like a pack of hounds!" (271) And during the conversation itself, Porfiry's intent to entrap Rashkolnikov by a mocking analysis of the implications of his thesis is almost undisguised. Even Razumikhin notices "Porfiry's unconcealed, insinuating, captious and discourteous sarcasm" (280). The last two of his four major questions in particular almost accuse Rashkolnikov of murder. And his closing remarks on would-be Napoleons is uttered "with terrifying familiarity. Even in the intonation of his voice there was this time something that could not possibly be mistaken" (282). Against Porfiry's total assault Rashkolnikov struggles intelligently, powerfully, and with impressive self-restraint. Conscious from the outset that his anger will betray him (269), he continually checks it, even when he is "shaking with rage" (271). Summoning his strength, he declares inwardly, "You're making a big mistake, gentlemen. You won't catch me so easily" (271). He understands at once that Porfiry's distortion of his thesis is "deliberate" (275), and responds to Porfiry's insolent questions sometimes "calmly" (281), sometimes "with defiant and scornful contempt" (282), but never either weakly or foolishly. Leaving with Razumikhin, he has some cause for self-satisfaction. Yet he feels none. As on the day before at the close of the conversation between Razumikhin and Zossimov, so now, having escaped from Porfiry, he must feel that he has once again been removed from a torture-chamber.

Abruptly interrupting his conversation with Razumikhin, Rashkolnikov rushes home "in a fit of terror and madness" (287), and searches his room, to be certain no piece of evidence remains there. Finding nothing, he goes out again, his thoughts still "in a turmoil" (288), but the exhausting episode at last over, and a moment's rest perhaps therefore possible.

He is hammered at once almost into insensibility. Suddenly, the artisan appears, walks at his side down the street, utters "Murderer!" (289) and disappears. In any circumstances, the apparition would have been unsettling. Coming after all that he has endured, and immediately after the encounter with Porfiry, it devastates Rashkolnikov. At first he cannot focus on anything. "Thoughts or scraps of thoughts passed through his mind, vague ideas without order or connection" (290). But suddenly the self-disgust earlier noted re-emerges and begins, accompanied by a mounting "delirium" (292), to tear him to pieces. "Suddenly he felt with loathing how weak he had become—how physically weak!" (290) And the physical weakness is only the symptom of a spiritual impotence insurmountable because basic to his nature. He ought never to have murdered, not because the murder (at least of the moneylender) was wrong—"The old hag is all rubbish . . . She doesn't matter!" (291)—but because he was not strong enough to murder. Suddenly, the cryptic references at the outset of the action to Rashkolnikov's "bitter monologues about his own impotence and indecision" (128–129) are clear, as for the first time the underlying emotional motive to the murders becomes clear. Rashkolnikov acted not to help his "starving mother" (291), or to further some "magnificent and praiseworthy aim" (292), but simply to "step over." But "I did not step over—I remained on this side" (291). Moreover, he knew before committing the murders that after the fact he would prove weak. And therefore he is disgusting—a "louse" (211); indeed, "perhaps worse and nastier than the louse I killed, and I knew beforehand that I would say that to myself after killing her!" (292) The truth of his incompetence is devastating. To escape it, he lapses into a deep sleep. But it persists, as nightmare. Led back by the artisan to the scene of the murders, he once again strikes the old woman with the hatchet. But she is unhurt, and rocks with silent laughter. And an enormous crowd, that suddenly appears, watches as his repeated blows achieve nothing, and as, attempting to escape, he finds that his feet refuse to move (292–294). Consciousness and dream yield the same awareness: he cannot murder, because he lacks the strength to murder, and detection is certain.

When suddenly he awakens, Rashkolnikov, prostrate, physically and mentally, must continue to persevere not only against the unendurable sense of isolation, and by the terror of being exposed as a murderer; but by profound disgust at himself.

But he does continue to persevere; by completing the accomplishment of the first half of his strategy against the isolation by announcing to Mrs. Rashkolnikov, Dunya, and Razumikhin during a joyous celebration of the banishment of Luzhin (309–321) that he will never see them again. "The heartless, bad-tempered egoist!" Dunya shouts, furious not only in her own behalf, but "burning with indignation" (328) at the effect of the sudden reversal upon her mother. Mrs. Rashkolnikov, moments before delighted, is crushed. Though the women cannot know it, Rashkolnikov's disappointment is perhaps more profound than their own. And the irony of the scene must devastate him. He is witnessing, as he knows, a perfect denouement. The villain routed, money having appeared "as though dropped from heaven" (325), his sister and friend united in love, his mother secure, a business likely to thrive projected, an enthusiastic circle of friendship closed, Rashkolnikov's world has suddenly been molded to the heart's desire. But he is excluded from it. Therefore he cannot endure the celebration. And it will probably prove vain. The artisan having exposed him, as he fears, much of the moment's delight will vanish. As the others chatter excitedly and laugh, Rashkolnikov therefore "still sat in the same place, sullen and abstracted" (324). And suddenly, to Dunya's "incredulous astonishment," he gets up to leave; not only for the moment, but for good. "Perhaps this is the last time we will ever see each other," he says. Then, "a look of harsh determination on his pale face," he announces that, though he loves his family, they must leave him alone, or "I shall begin to hate you" (328), and rushes off to Sonia.

At the moment, no other refuge exists. His family discarded, someone sympathetic must share his isolation and thus shore up his will, and only Sonia, he has concluded, can do so. The conclusion that she will share his isolation is correct. But because it is rooted in a huge and almost comical mistake, Sonia begins almost at once to undermine him, unknowingly, and despite his brutal attempt to harm her.

The attempt is prompted by his need to identify her experience with his own, and perhaps by other motives as well. And its outcome contributes eventually to his ruin. As Razumikhin has said, Rashkolnikov "dislikes showing his feelings, and he'd rather be cruel than put his real feelings into words." Moreover, "there are times . . . when he is not moody, but simply cold and inhumanly callous" (232). The ugly assault with which he greets Sonia perhaps hides Rashkolnikov's embarrassment as revealing his crucial dependence upon her. Perhaps he is being gratuitously cold, or venting the accumulated tension of the day upon a meek and therefore safe target. Or perhaps he hammers at the total vulnerability of herself and her family to convince Sonia that she should feel the self-disgust he does, because "You have betrayed and ruined yourself for nothing" (337), as he has done. (His need to establish this similarity between them is soon explained.) Whatever Rashkolnikov's total motive, the assault is more costly than he imagines at the moment. Though he reduces Sonia to horrified tears, he stumbles unexpectedly across her stronghold. And, standing within it, she attacks his will to persevere.

The stronghold is the God of Christianity. Rashkolnikov, profoundly astonished at the fact, fails—though doing so is almost impossible—to realize that Sonia cannot, in consequence, be the person he imagines, or anything but a deadly threat to his will. As he describes relentlessly the catastrophes awaiting Mrs. Marmeladov and her children, Sonia retreats meekly to her God. And Rashkolnikov, in pursuit, suddenly realizes that she has been sustained throughout her troubles only by an altruism religiously based. "It was only now," in the midst of the encounter with her, that he realizes what the family has meant to her—that "the thing that has kept her from the canal till now is the thought of sin and *them, those* . . . " (338). The realization astounds him—and leads him, in turn, to two astoundingly imperceptive conclusions. The first, drawn at once, is that Sonia is mad. "What is she waiting for? A miracle? Yes, that's it. And are not these symptoms of insanity?" Moreover, she is addled: "'Feeble-minded! Feeble-minded!' he kept repeating to himself" (339). The second conclusion, apparently drawn "long ago . . . when your father told me about you" (345), and confirmed later, in disregard of her reading from the Gospel, is more bizarre still. The reading set for a moment aside, and a long subsequent silence broken, Rashkolnikov announces that he and Sonia must remain together, because in a crucial respect they are indistinguishable spiritually. "We're both doomed, so let's go together!" She is damned because, as he asks rhetorically, "Haven't you, too, done the same thing? You, too, stepped over—you had the strength to step over—you've laid hands on yourself—destroyed a life—your own life (it's the same thing)" (334). Therefore she must adopt his principles. "We have to take the suffering upon ourselves . . . Freedom and power—power above all. Power over the trembling vermin and over all the ant-hill. That's our goal. Remember that" (345). No explanation complimentary to Rashkolnikov can account for the absurdity of that conclusion, or for his failure to comprehend its dangers. He has recognized that she possesses "holy feelings" (337), that "not a drop of real vice had penetrated into her heart" (338), and that her religious impulses "were indeed her present, and perhaps, her old secret, a secret she had probably cherished since she was a child" (341). Moreover, he notes her profound rapture as she nears a climax in her reading. She is unmistakably a Christian "who has still preserved the purity of her soul" (338). Yet he stubbornly insists that she is damned, that no difference exists between his hideously egotistical destructiveness and her Christ-like self-sacrifice, and that she, God's most meek and willing servant, would consent to pursue freedom and power, or to think the least of His creatures vermin. The most charitable explanation of this gross and absurd failure of insight is provided by Sonia, who has noticed from the outset that he is "blinded and unbelieving" (343); that his understanding is limited because he lacks faith. Perhaps, alternatively, his need for Sonia overwhelms his capacity to see her clearly. Or perhaps "his brain is in a frightful muddle just now," and in fact "never was in particularly good working order," because he possesses "a large, expansive nature without at the same time possessing a spark of genius" (503).

Whatever the cause of Rashkolnikov's error, its consequences begin to effect him at once, and he is apparently blind to the immediate or long-range dangers they pose. His susceptibility to religious pressure is real, and if not deflected threatens to drain his satanic will. In her letter, Mrs. Rashkolnikov had asked if he still said his prayers, "as you used to" (57). As noted, before the murders, and during the day immediately afterwards, his conscience troubled him. As he lay prostrate, demolished by the artisan, he recalled bitterly having troubled "all-merciful Providence, calling upon it to be a witness" (292) to the nobility of the murders. And now, apparently heedless of the danger, he abruptly demands that Sonia read of the resurrection of Lazarus. The choice of text must reflect for Rashkolnikov his own resurrection, begun in his first encounter with Sonia, that returned him to "life," and must bespeak an appeal that she continue to sustain him; if not by uncovering in him a sincere wish to be saved by God, and almost certainly not regret at having murdered the two women; some impulse, nonetheless, as yet unidentified, that may drain his satanic strength. Sonia, in contact with the word of God, hopes for far too much, too soon—that "he, he, too . . . will hear it now, and he, too, will believe—yes, yes! now, this minute!" (343) He will not believe for a long time. But even the hint of a movement towards God must weaken his resolve. And Sonia, to whom he has attached himself irrevocably, can move him only—and perhaps more powerfully than he imagines—towards God. Already he has resolved to confess to her the next day. The word "confess" does not occur to him, and indeed he insists emphatically as he exits, "I shall not come to you to ask for forgiveness" (345). But within her stands God, and therefore she must hasten what he insists is his doom.

The next morning, on his way to Porfiry, Rashkolnikov once again seems impressively strong. Despite the artisan, he has discarded his family, and—successfully, to his own mind—integrated Sonia into his life. Therefore he feels sufficiently recovered to gird "for the new battle" against the magistrate. Moreover, on reflection the artisan seems increasingly less potent as a threat. Indeed, his intrusion "the day before was nothing but a dream, exaggerated by his sick and overwrought imagination. The idea had begun to take hold of him even on the previous day, during the hours of his greatest anxiety and despair." (347) Buoyed, though apprehensive, Rashkolnikov engages Porfiry for the second time. And once again he escapes; though, despite his exultation, ravaged by torture.

In their first encounter Porfiry attacked his nerves indirectly, by assaulting his theory. Here the attack on his nerves is direct. Even at the outset, though off balance (because uncertain how best to use the artisan, overhearing the encounter behind a closed door), Porfiry manages occasionally to insert amid "the welter of empty, meaningless phrases" that reflect his uncertainty "a few enigmatic words" (352) that unsettle his opponent. His reference, for example, to the strategy of first diverting a suspect's attention and then hitting him "on the head with the back of a hatchet—ha, ha, ha!—right across the crown of the head" (352) must wrack Rashkolnikov horribly. And, his bearing reestablished, Porfiry begins the torture in earnest, at first expounding with terrifying clarity upon the murderer's chief internal weakness, and then playing upon it to such excruciating effect that Rashkolnikov almost breaks down completely. Almost from the outset, Rashkolnikov insists upon being interrogated "according to the rules" (350). Porfiry refuses, noting that when a magistrate's chief aid is a suspect's anxiety, he should not be confronted too soon, or in form. He should not, for example, be arrested too soon, "because I'd give him as it were, a definite status... satisfy him psychologically and set his mind at rest." It is far more effective to leave him at large, for "were he to know all the time, or at least suspect, that I knew everything and was keeping him under close observation day and night," he would eventually commit some decisive blunder, worn down and betrayed by the "state of continual terror and suspense in the knowledge that he was under suspicion" (354). Moreover, his anger, "a kind of inexhaustible mine" (355) for his opponent, would work against him. In the present case, the magistrate's suspicions have been roused by three events that reflect "human nature" (357): Rashkolnikov's collapse in the police station, his reckless baiting of Zamyotov in the restaurant, and his conversation with the workmen at the scene of the murders; and perhaps by a fourth event, that Porfiry, despite the obvious insincerity of his protest, "I do not suspect you" (363), is preparing to spring as his "little surprise" (364) when, suddenly and unexpectedly, Rashkolnikov is rescued.

The rescue occurs not a moment too soon, for though throughout the interview Rashkolnikov has fought with intelligence and courage, when Nikolay appears he is almost completely exhausted and unhinged. He is reckless only at the outset of the battle, when, despite his awareness that "he might in one way or another give himself away in his hatred" (347), he hurls "a sarcastic and rather incautious challenge" (349) at Porfiry, and suddenly looks at him "with undisguised hatred" (350). Thereafter he is impressively cunning; but to no effect. Porfiry is correct: the tension of incessant suspicion is unendurable. Therefore the magistrate's onslaught succeeds. Rashkolnikov realizes almost at the outset that he has "probably fallen into a trap," and that there is "some purpose behind" (350) Porfiry's chatter. A sudden outburst of good humor in Porfiry makes Rashkolnikov "start and prepare himself at once for any contingency" (353). And he sits in silence through the disquisition on manipulating a suspect, summoning "all his courage in readiness for the unknown and terrible catastrophe," sensibly resolved "not to speak, not to say a word till the right moment," because "he realized that that was his best policy in the present circumstances" (356). The resolve, however, cannot be maintained. He enters "afraid" of Porfiry, and hating him "savagely, immeasurably" (347). Almost at once he notices that "his nerves were becoming frayed and his agitation was increasing" (348). And under torture, despite the need for restraint he breaks down, suffering what Porfiry correctly calls "an attack of nerves," shouting repeatedly that he will not permit the investigating magistrate "to laugh in my face and torment me" (358). But he cannot prevent it, because, Porfiry having dissected him surgically, his defenses are gone. "You're sick to death of all this foolishness and all these suspicions. I'm right, am I not? I've guessed your state of mind, haven't I?" (359) He has not only guessed, but has gained control of, his state of mind. Therefore, proceeding methodically towards his little surprise, he is able without much additional trouble to reduce Rashkolnikov to "a real frenzy" (364), from whose consequences he is saved only by the accidental entrance of the workman.

Leaving Porfiry, Rashkolnikov returns home, and, reviewing the encounter, begins to feel the pleasure of at least temporary triumph. "A little more and he might have betrayed himself completely," he thinks. But "so far no facts had been disclosed" (370). And therefore, sensing that "at least for that day" he is safe, "his heart suddenly almost leapt with joy" (371). When the artisan appears a moment later, eliminating both himself as a threat and Porfiry's "trump card" (370) by retracting his accusation and condemning Porfiry's resort to torture, Rashkolnikov is elevated to the ecstasy he felt when Sonia first burst upon him, and, reviling proudly his weakness on first encountering the artisan, he once again resolves to persevere. He leaves his room for the funeral meal—where, not incidentally, "he would soon see Sonia" (371)—feeling "more cheerful than ever" and firmly resolved:

> "Now we carry on with the fight!" he said with a malicious grin as he went downstairs. His malice was directed against himself: he remembered his "lack of spirit" with a feeling of shame and contempt.
>
> (373)

Having totally recovered, he thinks, from the disaster into which the artisan had plunged him, and having triumphed over Porfiry, he feels totally prepared for the battles ahead. But a triumph more pyrrhic, or preparedness more fragile, would be hard to imagine. The toll exacted by Porfiry has been fearful. The discarding of his family has been terribly painful. Sonia is a hidden mine against him. And the accumulated pressure of the total scourging he is enduring continues inexorably to assault this will. Therefore, despite his heady resolve, Rashkolnikov is much closer to defeat than he thinks.

The defeat is completed in three related events: The funeral meal for Mr. Marmeladov, Rashkolnikov's second encounter with Sonia, and the death in madness of Mrs. Marmeladov. As these events unfold, Rashkolnikov's remaining strength dissipates, as Sonia completes her unintended betrayal of him. For his continued failure to grasp that that betrayal is inevitable Rashkolnikov continues to be mocked in passing. And he is mocked more extensively for failing to realize that the funeral meal and the death underscore by dramatic juxtaposition the gross ignorance of human nature and of life that refutes utterly the satanic theory that led him to murder.

Rashkolnikov enters Sonia's apartment hoping desperately to be re-energized by contact with her. Instead, without, as usual, intending to, she crushes him, by insisting that only Christ can redeem him. Against this insistence he cannot, despite himself, contend. His strength sapped by the torture inflicted on him during the days since the murders, he is guided, despite himself, away from Satan, and towards God, for a long time ludicrously blind to the nature of his guide.

The torture having almost broken him, he approaches Sonia overwhelmed by the "heavy... load of horror and suffering in his heart" and by "his own feelings, which were becoming so unbearable to him." Suddenly he "felt all his strength ebbing out of him and he was overcome by fear" (419).

His strength has not returned. In fact, what remains of it is about to be destroyed by Sonia, to whom he turns as a refuge of last resort. She, however, can shelter him only in a refuge he abhors, but nonetheless, despite himself, accepts.

On his way to her apartment Rashkolnikov "felt that all his hopes rested on [Sonia] and that everything depended on her," because through her "he thought of relieving himself of at least part of his suffering" (435). Sonia is more than willing to help. But her shelter is Christ. That shelter

Rashkolnikov still scorns. But, forced to accept it—forced to accept the love and advice of an emblematic servant of Christ—despite himself Rashkolnikov is guided towards defeat.

At the outset of their encounter, Rashkolnikov begins tormenting Sonia, by stressing, as on their previous encounter, her vulnerability. However, he soon desists, not in response to her anguished pleas, but because he lacks the strength to go on. Suddenly, "his assumed insolent and impotently defiant tone" vanishes, and he acknowledges—though not yet quite completely—the influence of her piety upon his resolve. "I told you yesterday that I wouldn't come to ask for forgiveness, and now I practically began by asking forgiveness" (422). Indeed, he has begun his "confession" (420). As it unfolds, Sonia's influence becomes increasingly strong, and at last, though only for a moment, decisive. At her cry of despair, the confession grasped, "a feeling he had not known for a long time overwhelmed him entirely, and at once softened his heart. He did not resist it: tears started in his eyes and hung on his eyelashes" (425).

He is almost completely in Sonia's power. And though he struggles to disentangle himself, the bonds tighten, and his slight remaining strength dissipates. As he speaks with Sonia about the murders "one could . . . catch a glimpse of his utter exhaustion" (430). Gradually a fever takes "complete possession of him" (431), and the prospect of redemption through confession and suffering increasingly attracts him. Though he insists that if he opts for Sonia's refuge her triumph will be "hollow" (427), he confesses that the murder was "wicked" (428), that he "did wrong in killing the old woman" (429), who "wasn't a louse" (430), that as he planned the murder he "always imagined that Satan was tempting me" (432), and that he has come to Sonia now because "the devil . . . [has] made a laughing stock of me" (433). In their first encounter, Rashkolnikov had responded scornfully to Porfiry's concern for the murderer's conscience. "Whoever has a conscience will no doubt suffer, if he realizes his mistake" (281). To Sonia's outburst—"To go about with this on your conscience! And all your life!"—he replies, "I shall get used to it." But the reply is made "sullenly and pensively," for he must know that he cannot evade Satan forever. Moreover, he must fear the implications of Sonia's horrified question: "How can you possibly live all your life without human companionship?" (434) He cannot, as the question he has already asked Sonia implies: "Well, what am I to do now? Tell me" (433). As he must know, she can offer only one answer: God. And though the answer is loathsome, he is exhausted enough virtually to provoke it, and to hear its corollary, suffering, broached. He rejects the cross that Sonia holds out; but only for the moment. He will soon, despite himself, take it up.

No other option, except perhaps self-destruction, exists. His betrayal by Sonia having drained his remaining strength, the cross is perhaps not so odd a burden. Returning to his room, he recognizes that "never, never had he felt so terribly lonely." And from this loneliness a "strange" prospect emerges: that "perhaps it really will be better in Siberia" (438). The refuge he will find there in suffering and penance will be abhorrent. But—finally—no other refuge exists.

That he has been guided towards confession, penance, and expiation by a woman he regards almost to the moment her piety defeats him as his partner in Satan is almost hilarious. His confession completed, he notes, for the first time, and apparently with surprise, that he and Sonia are "different from each other—so different" (427). His blindness, throughout their earlier encounter, and through most of the present one, to Sonia's devotion to the Gospels and to God exposes him, for the first time, to ironic laughter, muted only by pity for his confusion and suffering.

The ironic laughter at his expense is intensified by the funeral meal and by the death of Mrs. Marmeladov, that argue indisputably that Rashkolnikov is blind not only to Sonia's Christianity, but to the Christian view of human nature and of life that refutes utterly the satanic theory that prompted him to murder. The theory that he expounds to Sonia is vile. And because he fails completely to see that the life teeming about him refutes it utterly, he earns not only explicit censure, but the humiliation of ironic laughter.

The theory he explains in detail to Sonia, who presses to understand why he murdered. A number of superficial motives discarded, his true motive is finally laid bare. He murdered not to aid his family, or to further his career, but because, having decided that "he who dismisses with contempt what men regard as sacred becomes their law-giver, and that he who dares more than anyone is more right than anyone," he resolved to test his "courage to dare . . . I only wanted to dare, Sonia, that was my only motive." As Sonia realizes, "this gloomy confession of faith was his religion and law." Uttering it, he is raised to "a gloomy exultation" (431). And he struggles to remain constant to it. It would be senseless to confess, he insists, because "How am I guilty," he asks rhetorically, before other men? They are only vermin who understand nothing, and moreover "don't deserve to understand." And because he, despite his recent lapses, is perhaps greatly superior to them, he ought to persevere. "Perhaps I am a man, and not a louse. I may have been in too great a hurry to condemn myself. I'll give them a good run for their money" (434).

The explicit censure of Rashkolnikov for embracing a vile faith, religion, and law is pronounced by Sonia, who must, he insists, in their encounter after the funeral meal, accede in principle to the murder of vermin such as Luzhin. She refuses, of course, on theological grounds, because, as she says, she has no way of knowing "what God's intentions may be," and no wish to be "a judge to decide who is to live and who is not to live" (422).

The humiliation of irony laughter is inflicted upon Rashkolnikov by the scenes that frame his encounter with Sonia. Both of them feature his "ordinary" people, the "lice" and "vermin," and demonstrate irrefutably that, their deficiencies notwithstanding, most of them are more estimable and far more complex than Rashkolnikov imagines, and that, moreover, not even vermin, if any exist, may be murdered. The scenes deliberately deride Rashkolnikov's satanic theory: immediately before and immediately after Rashkolnikov expounds it, life refutes it. And because he does not realize that it does so, for the first time he is extensively mocked.

The guests, invited and not, who descend on the funeral meal do not lack moral defects. Lebezyatnikov, "a seedy, scrofulous little man" (377), and "really a bit stupid," belongs to a legion of "vulgar people... more-dead-than-alive abortions and semi-literate half-wits" (378). Mrs. Lippewechsel, an unwitting buffoon, is almost a caricature of "undisguised pride" (393). At Luzhin's heart "the black serpent of injured pride had been gnawing... all night" (374), and is preparing to strike Sonia. Mrs. Marmeladov is consumed with "pride and vanity" (392). And a more motley crew than the unnamed guests who crowd the table would be hard to imagine. Almost all of them are moved predominantly by vanity and pride. Mrs. Marmeladov most obviously, but the others as well, are obsessed with thinking well of themselves, and with impressing everyone with their worth. But, Luzhin aside, they are not therefore vermin, or even incapable of impressive behavior. Lebezyatnikov, who despite his faults is "rather soft-hearted" (378) and "good-natured" (390), admires Sonia's " wonderful nature" (383), has spent time reading and talking to her, and at the moment of crisis steps forward courageously, condemning Luzhin. Mrs. Lippewechsel has from the outset "thrown herself heart and soul into the preparations" for the meal, and through her efforts "everything had been done as well as could be" (393). When Sonia is attacked, Mrs. Marmeladov, though at least "partially deranged" (392) and almost dead, rouses herself to a moving defense (408, 410). Even the unnamed motley guests, in the midst of drunken, ugly self-indulgence, are capable of humanity. Mrs. Marmeladov's defense creates "a deep impression," moving them to "pity for the unhappy woman" (410). When the villainy is unmasked, the tone of some of their exclamations becomes "menacing" (413), and they all begin "shouting and crowding around Luzhin, uttering oaths and threats" (417). A drunken officer even hurls a glass at his head.

Mrs. Marmeladov's defects are not obscured by the fact that she is dying. But neither is her spiritual preeminence. No sooner has Rashkolnikov concluded his long exposition to Sonia than Lebezyatnikov rushes in, to announce that Mrs. Marmeladov has suddenly gone mad. Though in her death-throes, she remains profoundly impressive, struggling with her last breath to maintain her dignity, to support her family, to demand justice. The entire scene is "pitiful and horrible" (445), and the death, however awful, is meaningful.

Because, in his youthful intellectual arrogance, Rashkolnikov denies that anything about the life of Mrs. Marmeladov, or about the lives of "ordinary people" like her, deserves pity or reflects meaning, the meal and the death deservedly mock him. As Porfiry has said, being young, Rashkolnikov prizes "the human intellect . . . highly," and therefore "can't help admiring the playful keenness of wit and the abstract deductions of reason" (356). But in so doing he overlooks the crucial facts of "life and human nature" (357), and in consequence is blinded by the love of categories to the complexities of truth. Not all of the guests at the funeral meal are as impressive as Mrs. Marmeladov, whom "it was quite impossible to crush . . . morally" (392). But none of them, except possibly Luzhin, is unmixedly vile. And none deserves the abuse that Lebezyatnikov, despite his stupidity, correctly accuses Luzhin of inflicting upon Sonia, and that Rashkolnikov inflicts upon almost everyone: "aware of a fact which you mistakenly consider deserving of contempt, you at once deny a human being her right to any humane consideration" (384).

To inflict such abuse is to invite derision. Even the worst of the "vermin" are God's creatures. Only God understands their value. And the man who mocks the value God assigns to their lives—or to their death—will himself be mocked. Rashkolnikov's reactions to the guests at the funeral meal, and to Mrs. Marmeladov's death, are not explicitly recorded. But they are unmistakably implicit in the theory he expounds. The guests are vermin. Luzhin, the worst of them, deserves to be murdered. Even Mrs. Marmeladov, ordinary at best, is not among the superior few who dismiss "with contempt what men regard as sacred" (431). Therefore her death should be either desirable—Rashkolnikov has already suggested that it would be, given her circumstances (335)—or insignificant, and therefore undeserving of pity.

He is profoundly wrong, destructively wrong; about Mrs. Marmeladov, about the guests, about human nature and life in general. And ridiculously wrong. At no point does he seem to honor—or even to admit the existence of—Sonia's sanctities. Indeed, only Luzhin's villainy as the prelude to his encounter with Sonia strikes him, and from that encounter he draws exactly the wrong conclusion. His imperceptiveness is perhaps to be excused, because he is almost exhausted, in body and in mind. But the life surrounding his theory mocks it utterly. Therefore he approaches the catastrophe of surrender not only shorn of strength and will, and explicitly censured for moral turpitude, but extensively ridiculed for blindness.

Therefore only humiliation and suffering remain, the indispensable preludes to eventual Grace: that conscience, resurgent and irresistible, empower the sinner to confess before the world, and to bear, hopeful in God, his cross.

Those preludes he endures; and, though still unwillingly, accepts the punishment that must eventually redeem him.

The confession is in Sonia's words: "Go to the cross-roads, bow down to the people, kiss the earth, for you have sinned against it, and proclaim in a loud voice to the whole world: I am a murderer!" Profoundly shaken by "this new and overwhelming" (536) sensation, "everything within him grew soft all at once . . . tears gushed from his eyes," and "he knelt down in the middle of the square, bowed down to the earth, and kissed the filthy earth with joy and rapture" (537).

The ecstasy of course lasts only a moment. It, and the other cries of the heart, gain expression only because he has been "utterly crushed . . . by his feeling of hopelessness and desolation and by the great anxiety of all those days, but especially of the last few hours" (536). The Devil still governs Rashkolnikov's soul; lasting regeneration will occur only gradually, and he will "pay a great price for it" (559). But having murdered, and having, by carefully distinguished degrees, been crushed by defeat, he is prepared for the acceptance, through suffering, of Christ.

www.ingramcontent.com/pod-product-compliance
Lightning Source LLC
Chambersburg PA
CBHW060608230426

43670CB00011B/2031